THE ETHICAL STATE

AN ESSAY ON POLITICAL ETHICS

JOHN DAVID GARCIA

The Ethical State

AN ESSAY ON POLITICAL ETHICS

WEXFORD COLLEGE PRESS

Mens Sana Incorpore Sano

Published as a Wexford College Press paperback 2003
by arrangement with Watchmaker Publishing, Ltd.

ISBN 0–9721786–4–3

Wexford College Press
www.WexfordCollegePress.com
books@WexfordCollegePress.com

Printed and bound in the United States of America

0 9 8 7 6 5 4 3 2 1

Dedicated to my Good Friends,
Anthony J. Parrotto and Alicia Herrejon

TO WHOM IT MAY CONCERN:

John David Garcia was a man of towering intellect and singleness of purpose that, in many ways, defied the logic of less audacious people, myself included. If he had taken the path of monetary acquisition he would have wound up a technology billionaire. Instead he sacrificed everything for the cause of his view of a moral society, which will continue to resonate far beyond his lifetime. His generosity of spirit and inner sweetness has rarely been demonstrated by anyone who I have ever known. Besides, if it wasn't for John David, my career as a novelist may never have happened.

Kindest Regards,
Warren Adler

CONTENTS

AUTHOR'S PREFACE

The sole ultimate ethical goal in the universe that does not lead to its own contradiction is that we must always do our best to maximize creativity for everybody, without ever decreasing anyone's creativity, including our own.

A creative act is any act that increases truth for anyone without decreasing truth for anyone else, including ourselves.

Truth is information that, when we believe it, increases our ability to predict and control the total environment for ourselves, without decreasing this ability for anyone, including ourselves.

Falsehood is any information that, when we believe it, decreases anyone's ability to predict and control any part of the total environment, even if it increases this ability for someone, including ourselves.

We love persons if, and only if, we behave ethically toward them, by increasing their creativity, to the best of our ability, and never knowingly behave unethically toward them, by decreasing their creativity deliberately.

We should always do our best to love our neighbor as ourselves.

We have forgotten how to love if we do not value our own creativity and love ourselves.

Our neighbor, in this context, is any human being who shares the Evolutionary Ethic with us.

We should do our best to share the Evolutionary Ethic with everyone we meet, without being pushy and trying to impose our values on those who do not already share them; we will always fail if we do not love our neighbor, and try instead to impose our values; values must be freely chosen.

We should remain friendly, but invest the minimum of time interacting with people who seem to reject our values, always remaining open however to the possibility that they may change and become our friends in the future.

We should pursue a friendship with all those who seem to share our values and turn them into good friends.

A friend is anyone who loves us and whom we love in return.

A good friend is anyone whom we love at least as much as we love ourselves.

I would like to thank all the good friends I have had in my life. I thank all those whom I shall always regard as my good friends. I thank Kay, Marilyn J., Auda, Lloyd, Leib, Roberta, Pauline, Gloria H., Jackie, Sandra, Mary, Ralph, Marilyn K., Sydney, Victor, Leticia, Peter, Yvonne, Guillermo, Juan, Susan, Robert, Joy, Michael H., Gloria S., Amit, Maggie, Isabel, Ben, Mike A., Galia, Luna, Irwin, Eva-Cecilia, Hebe, Rosario, Romulo, Vera-Aida, Salvador, Gaby, Javier, Lorena, Juan Carlos, Karina, Monica, Russell, Kimi, Bill, Antonio, Ann-Marie, and Ron.

I would particularly like to thank my friends, Harvey, Tom, Norman, Sumner, Phyllis, Humberto, George, Arthur, Prudenzia, Blair, Leon, Kate, Teresa, Ken, Eta, and Elizabeth. Although you may no longer consider yourselves my friends, I will always remain your friend.

Special thanks go to Russell Brand, Bill Cassaday, and my editor Russell Becker for the many comments and suggestions they gave me about how to improve the early drafts of this book.

I would most of all like to thank those good friends I have had who became my complements. You know who you are. I thank you without naming you, except for my beloved wife, who became my first complement, my daughters, and one other.

A complement is a good friend of the opposite sex whom we shall always love more than we love our self. They need not love us any longer. But they loved us once, and we grew to love them more than ourselves, forever.

The person who is our complement always contributes greatly to our ethical and creative development. My beloved wife, Bernice, was the first person with whom I formed a complementary pair, but I did not realize it until late in life. I also know now that our four daughters, Miriam, Karen, Jackie, and Laura, were always complements to me, although I did not realize this until even later in my life.

I write this book for all the good friends I have had in life.

Among my best friends is the late Henri Lurié, who was the best friend I ever had, but I did not realize this until very late in life, after he died. I dedicate this book to one of the best friends I have ever had, and who still lives. I dedicate this book to my former publisher, Anthony J. Parrotto, who supported me, helped me clarify and better communicate my ideas, and published my books, even when he knew that he would almost certainly lose money on them. Tony, I dedicate this book to you, and to your lovely family. May you all continue in long life and great creativity.

Above all, I also dedicate this book, with the greatest gratitude, to my complement, Alicia Herrejon, who has been my partner and collaborator since 1997 Although poor health, family obligations, national borders, and the vagaries of life no longer allow us to work together closely, Alicia shall always be part of everything I create. I owe my life and this book to her.

John David Garcia
Eugene, Oregon
September 5, 2001

Prologue

Philosophy of Education for an Ethical State

The purpose of the Ethical State is to maximize creativity. There are many things we must do to be maximally creative, such as maintaining our health, protecting our life and property, and educating ourselves. Although education is intended to be a private undertaking within the Ethical State, an educational strategy is the best way to begin to organize such a State, until it eventually becomes sovereign, when the educational responsibilities of the citizens will be taken over by private organizations in accordance with the citizens they serve. Until that time arrives, some of the Ethical State should concentrate on an educational strategy and allow most of the other functions of the Ethical State to be taken up by the Federal, state, and local governments of the United States.

I have attempted to use the educational approach outlined here in my teaching and seminars. It has also been employed in a few schools for young children which have yet to establish themselves on an ongoing basis. It will take many years to implement the full potential of this approach, which seeks to discover what environmental factors—physical, biological, and psychosocial—will help children and adults maximize their creativity.

"Creativity," as used here, is a characteristic of any act which increases truth in any way for at least one person, including oneself, without decreasing truth for any person, including oneself.

"Truth" is any information that increases our intelligence or ethics without decreasing anyone else's intelligence or ethics.

"Intelligence" is our ability to predict and control our total environment—physical, biological, and psychosocial.

"Ethics" are the set of rules that we follow to make sure that we use our intelligence to best maximize intelligence, including our own, and not to diminish anyone's intelligence, including our own.

Creativity (**C**) is produced by an interaction of intelligence (**I**) and ethics (**E**). This interaction may intuitively be expressed in its simplest form by the equation **C=IE**.

Intuitively, "creativity" is the process by which we discover scientific laws, invent machines, produce works of art, and nurture and teach others and ourselves to do these things. The most creative thing we ever do for ourselves is to help maximize the creativity of another.

These notions of creativity lead to the following summary of what is ethical.

(1) Any act that increases anyone's creativity without decreasing anyone else's creativity is an ethical act, an example of a person behaving ethically. This is the meaning of "good."

(2) Any act that decreases any person's creativity in any way is an unethical act, an example of a person behaving unethically. This is the meaning of "evil."

These notions of creativity and ethics lead to a natural, scientific ethics that are in complete harmony with Judeo-Christian ethics in general and modern science in particular. We call this system of ethics the "Evolutionary Ethic," because it grows naturally and logically out of the scientific facts that are known about the process of evolution, about which we still have a lot to learn.

The Evolutionary Ethic

We should do our best to maximize creativity without ever decreasing anyone's creativity.

The Evolutionary Ethic can be used scientifically and rationally to optimize any social science or process. This is particularly true about how best to educate our children and ourselves.

Traditional educational systems, throughout the world, emphasize learning to regurgitate information exactly as it was given. This requires intelligence, but not ethics. These same systems seem to destroy imagination and creativity in children. Almost all children enter primary school still highly imaginative and creative, but they usually leave high school devoid of imagination and creativity. Something in the traditional educational process destroys the children's imagination and creativity.

In order to maximize overall creativity, it is more important to maximize ethics than intelligence. This is so because, although intelligence (**I**) is always positive, ethics (**E**) can be negative, thereby giving us negative creativity (**C**). Negative creativity is what we call "destructiveness." Negative creativity is intelligence used to diminish another's intelligence and/or ethics. Positive creativity always increases another's intelligence and/or ethics, without diminishing anyone's intelligence or ethics.

Traditional schools do not diminish intelligence. Rather, they diminish and eventually destroy ethics, by punishing creative behavior and rewarding repetitive, non-creative behavior. This teaches a student to value happiness more than creativity, and to believe that happiness can be maximized by conforming to authority and by never displaying any independent or imaginative thinking, since the latter usually leads to some form of punishment.

Creative persons, if they do not always treat destructive persons with love, are susceptible to the destructiveness of others. If we

17

increase the intelligence of unethical persons, we merely increase their ability to destroy. Even ethical persons, especially if they are very intelligent and not yet highly ethical, are occasionally destructive; their destructive acts may lead to imposing serious harm on others. Young children and very ethical adults are the only persons who are always more creative in their behavior than they are destructive. Creativity is best maximized with young children.

To maximize creativity, an educational system must take into account the relationship between ethics and intelligence. At the same time it must not inhibit the flow of information to ethical persons. A technique for accomplishing all these objectives is to create an educational system based on love, in which an increase in ethics is inextricably interwoven with an increase in intelligence.

Yet even if we are able to transform ourselves so that we are ethical, totally loving, devoid of fear, and totally creative in all our acts, this is still not enough to maximize creativity. We must also maximize our intelligence, because $C = IE$. We have two impediments to maximizing intelligence. The first is our own fear, which inhibits our ability to learn and forces us to specialize. The second is the negative ethics of others, and their consequent fear and destructiveness.

Education in secular schools is inevitably separated from any ethical considerations. In seeking solely to maximize intelligence, they minimize creativity. This is the result of specialization and of the destruction of ethics through conditioning by fear.

Religious schools often corrupt their ethical teachings with dogma and compulsive ritual, thereby alienating those who are scientifically and creatively oriented. As a result, religious schools tend to produce few scientists, while producing many of the least creative psychosocial specialists.

In order for an educational system to maximize creativity, as opposed to merely increasing intelligence, it must have the following characteristics.

1. It must be based entirely on the Evolutionary Ethic.

2. It must emphasize growth in ethics and love along with growth in intelligence, and give preference to the former over the latter when and if conflicts arise.

3. It must in no way use fear to condition the student.

4. It must encourage love and cooperation, rather than competitiveness, among students.

5. It must at all times provide the opportunity, not the obligation, for the student to generalize in all fields of knowledge, including the arts, rather than specializing in a single field. Conversely, a student must always be free to specialize by choice, while being told the consequences of this action.

6. It must provide objective feedback to the students about how well they are learning without in any way having this feedback serve as reward or punishment. Solely the act of learning is a reward. The sole punishment is not learning. Objective results are necessary to avoid self-delusion. The students should learn to find at least as much joy in discovering their mistakes as in discovering their successes.

7. Creative independence of students should be encouraged and never criticized before the fact, even when it seems obvious that a student's ideas will be wrong. We learn by our mistakes, using objective feedback, which should be given solely after students have tried their innovative ideas, under close supervision so that they do not hurt themselves or others. In this way students are encouraged to re-create the knowledge they acquire, and to use their creativity. They are taught solely what they can create.

8. There should be no time constraints whatever on the educational process; students should move at the pace which is most satisfying to them. Slow students should be free to move at their own pace without feeling rushed. Fast students should be free to move at their own pace without feeling bogged down by others.

The most creative thing we do is to educate ourselves and our children so that we can all express our maximum creative potential. Every school in the world is at least somewhat destructive to the creativity of its students. Until the Ethical State is completely sovereign, it should concentrate its activities on education, and not on protecting the civil rights of its citizens, although the latter should not be ignored. Toward this end, it should begin by creating and operating schools for teaching the Evolutionary Ethic to young children, while helping these children and their parents to become maximally creative during the rest of their lives. The Epilogue provides an

John David Garcia

outline for creating this school, beginning as a nursery school and then expanding to educate optimally all the children and citizens of the Ethical State.

CHAPTER ONE

BACKGROUND

This is my fourth book on evolutionary ethics. It covers the essential ideas of my other books together with some new ideas, primarily in the first chapter. The other chapters focus on the application of evolutionary ethics to political systems and methods of implementation.

It seems that most people cannot understand a rational system of ethics unless they fully share its values, no matter how intelligent and well-educated they are. The ethical values that I am trying to communicate in all my books are the natural universal values with which we are all born. They were the ethics taught by Moses, Jesus, and Spinoza. But as Nietzsche said, "There has been but one Christian, and he died on the cross." I would correct Nietzsche and say, "There has been at least one other Christian; he was a Spanish-Jew accused of atheism, despised by the Jews and Christians of his time; and deprecated, but ever less so, by academics up to the present; his name was Baruch de Spinoza."

Many great minds have read and appreciated Spinoza, but few have understood him well. Among the greatest minds who have commented on Spinoza is Leibnitz, who appreciated him intellectually without sharing his ethics, and as a consequence did not understand him well and, in fact, attacked him publicly, while privately incorporating Spinoza's ideas into his own philosophy (358). This line of misunderstanding led to a series of further misunderstandings of Spinoza's philosophy that through Kant, Hegel, Marx, Engels, and others eventually led to Lenin and the Soviet Union, possibly one of the most evil systems of government in the history of the world.

The second line of misunderstanding of Spinoza by great minds went from Locke, Hume, Voltaire, Rousseau, Diderot, and others to Thomas Jefferson, and the United States' Declaration of Independence and Constitution, which represents among the best systems of government in the history of the world, at least in theory. However, this system, it is now obvious, is filled with errors and inadequacies and is breaking down. The governmental ethic of Jefferson, as well as some of the other Founding Fathers, that freedom is the greatest good and tyranny is the greatest evil is ethically only partially true. Freedom is necessary, but not sufficient, for ethical government.

In the United States, and almost all other countries, the concept of "democracy" has been corrupted to mean "majority rule." "Democracy" means "the rule of the people," not "majority rule." However, the notion of "democracy" to mean "self-government," as well as the democratic ethic, is ethical but incomplete.

By "democracy" I mean solely "self-government" without any form of tyranny, without anarchy, and without bureaucracy. This will be seen to be a radical new concept of government never before tried on a national level, although it has been used effectively within small groups. Theoretically, this concept of "self-government" is the concept of government originally entertained by the Founding Fathers of the United States and still advocated by the Libertarian Party in the United States. However, it has never been made functionally practical. It is my intention to do so.

Every form of tyranny is unethical. Majority rule is inherently unethical, because it is, at best, a tyranny of the majority over minorities; at worst it is a tyranny of a plutocratic few over an ignorant majority, which is manipulated to exploit the most creative minorities that a nation can produce. The manipulation is done by telling the ignorant majority the comforting lies that they wish to hear, and by confiscating the fruits of the labor of the most creative minorities and then redistributing them among the majority, with large commissions to the plutocratic minority and to the bureaucrats and politicians who support this system.

The third line of great minds who misunderstood Spinoza stemmed from Moses Mendelsohn, the grandfather of the composer. This line led to what today is known as Conservative, Reform, and secular Judaism. This line preserved Jewish ethics within a modern social context, but it could not preserve Judaism itself, or its ethics, for long, since the descendants of these Jews were quickly assimilated into modern society, and within a few generations lost their Jewish ethics along with their Jewish identity. It was thus a political failure, although it was an intellectual success.

The ethics of Spinoza and Reform Judaism are preserved within a non-Jewish context by religions such as the Unitarians, the Universalists, and the more secular Ethical Culture Society, but they seem to be having ever less impact on modern life, as more and more people become ethical hedonists and/or followers of the consumerist ethic, wherein material wealth is the greatest good, and poverty is the greatest evil. Spinoza's ethics are theoretically correct, but have not been very effective. I will make the ethics of Spinoza practical and effective.

The best summary I have ever read of Spinoza and all philosophy is in Russell's *History of Western Philosophy* (358). I recommend that everyone who wishes to understand Spinoza begin with this summary; however, the entire *History* should be read in detail, cover to cover. It was this summary which kept me coming back to Spinoza and forcing me to try to understand him better. I am still doing that today. The great thinker who had, in fact, the greatest impact of all on my life was Pierre Teilhard de Chardin. I first read his book, *The Phenomenon of Man* (438), in English translation, at the age of thirty-four; it changed my life forever. However, I recommend that all who can, try to read Teilhard in the original French (431–439). His language is gorgeous.

My goal is to help you, and me, to understand well the ethics of Spinoza, as well as to implement them practically in a viable, ethical government. The best way for you to begin is to give a quick reading to what you can understand of Spinoza's major works without trying to follow his proofs. Then do your best to acquire the best broad background you can in mathematics and science (1–600), while reading all you can of Bertrand Russell's many excellent books (347–358), but focusing on his *History of Western Philosophy* (358), and particularly focusing on his summary of Spinoza's philosophy.

The next step is to read as much as you can of Pierre Teilhard de Chardin (431–439), focusing on finishing and understanding *The Phenomenon of Man* (438). Then see how the philosophies of Spinoza and Teilhard fit together. Few people can see the connection between the two. My own books will help you in accomplishing this task. I now realize that the major value of my life is bringing together these two apparently disparate systems of values and philosophy. To the best of my knowledge no one else has done this.

With Teilhard I share the love and understanding of Jesus, Darwin, and the Evolutionary Process itself, which I, and others, call God. This is the God of Spinoza and Einstein. It is also the God of Moses and Jesus. This God is truly our Father.

Once you have read the aforementioned books, the goal is then to understand my last book, *Creative Transformation* (115); give this book a quick reading. If you understand it well, then read it again together with this book, and read my other books solely to see how my ideas developed. If you do not understand it well, then read first my other books in any order you wish. Then make sure you read some of the books by David Bohm (31–35). Some of Bohm's books require a graduate level knowledge of physics to understand, but some, such as *Science, Order, and Creativity* (33), are relatively easy and philosophically sufficient, requiring no mathematical sophistication.

Next to Russell, Teilhard, and Spinoza, the thinker who had the greatest impact on my understanding of Spinoza was David Bohm. Although I do not know of Bohm ever mentioning Spinoza, I believe he must have read him. Bohm, like his mentor Einstein before him, has Spinoza's spirit and ideas throughout all his writings, most of which I read after writing my last book.

In my last book I integrated the philosophy of Spinoza, Teilhard, and myself through an early, imperfect understanding of Bohm's model of nature and quantum mechanics. Bohm's model implies that the underlying ultimate reality in nature is not energy or matter, but information. And furthermore that there is a universe of infinite true information at our finger tips, which is the ultimate, unifying cause behind all physical, biological, mental, and spiritual phenomena. This model enables us to unify true science with true mysticism. There can never be a conflict between true science and true mysticism; when there is, either the science, the mysticism, or both are wrong.

I recommend that you begin a study of Bohm by first reading his *Science, Order, and Creativity* (33), which he co-authored with F. David Peat. If you cannot understand it, I recommend that you go back and study more physics. The book is written for a general audience.

If you already know physics well, I recommend that you then try Bohm's last and best book, *The Undivided Universe*, which he co-authored with Basil Hiley in 1993. It was published shortly after Bohm's death. This book is written for professional physicists. Bohm has written many excellent books for professional physicists, as well as for the general public (31–35).

Bohm is somewhat difficult to read and understand, but he is much easier to understand than is Spinoza, although not easier to read. Although Bohm was a great physicist, he was, unlike Spinoza, not a great writer. Bohm is easiest to read and understand when he writes in collaboration with an excellent writer of English, such as F. David Peat or Basil Hiley.

My own opening to true mysticism, through an appreciation of modern quantum mechanics, came from an interaction I had with Amit Goswami, then a professor of physics at the University of Oregon. Although I know physics well, my understanding is less than that of some professional physicists such as Amit Goswami, F. David Peat, Fred Alan Wolf, and much, much less than David Bohm. Both Amit and Bohm are totally mystical in their science, and totally scientific in their mysticism. Amit is a thoroughgoing mystic, born in India. Bohm was a student and collaborator of the Indian mystic Krishnamurti.

Amit Goswami is also my friend. He articulated his basic ideas in an excellent book, *The Self-Aware Universe* (123). Although there is some conflict between Amit's and Bohm's models of quantum mechanics, as well as with my synthesis of the two, the three models all have much in common. Someday there may be a single, information-based model of quantum mechanics which resolves all the differences between them and unites their large areas of commonality. I recommend reading Amit's books (121–123).

In this book, *The Ethical State*, I unify all the important concepts and ideas from my previous books (115–117) that still seem correct, primarily in this first chapter, together with all the new ideas and concepts that I have developed since 1990, when I finished writing my last book. My basic conclusions follow.

The sole true ethic in the universe which does not lead to its own contradiction when it is applied to society and government is the Evolutionary Ethic, which is summarized in the following statements.

1. We should do our best to maximize the creativity of every person in the universe, including our own, without ever decreasing the creativity of any person, including our own.
2. We fulfill our moral obligation to maximize creativity by giving first priority to our children, then to our spouse, then to ourselves,

then to our friends in proportion to the friendship between us, then to our neighbors, then to our fellow citizens, then to our fellow humans, then to other species in proportion to the ethical development of the species.

3. Creativity is the process of increasing ethical truth for at least one person without decreasing ethical truth for any person.
4. Ethical truth is information which increases the intelligence or ethics of at least one person without decreasing the intelligence or ethics of any person.
5. A person is ethical if, and only if, he or she values truth more than happiness.
6. Information is true if, and only if, believing this information enhances our ability to predict and control some aspect of the total environment, physical, biological, and/or psychosocial, without decreasing this ability in any other aspect of the total environment for anybody.
7. The first obligation of any ethical government is never to decrease ethical truth for anyone.
8. Any government that decreases ethical truth for even a single person has behaved unethically, no matter how many other people are allegedly to be benefited by this "sacrifice." Unethical means can never achieve ethical ends. The ends never justify the means. It is unethical to ever unnecessarily harm a single person. "Harm" is any decrease in ethical truth or creativity for any person.
9. A government can be ethical if, and only if, it limits its activities to protecting well the life, liberty, property, and privacy of its citizens without ever imposing undeserved harm on anyone, or ever trying to do good for those with special needs at the cost of its other citizens.
10. No government can do good, outside of protecting basic human rights, for anyone without in the process imposing undeserved harm on someone.
11. Since harm is the decrease in ethical truth for anyone, undeserved harm is imposing unnecessary harm on anyone against the will of the person harmed. Solely the minimum harm necessary to defend life, liberty, property, and privacy against an aggressor can ever be ethically justified; this is a deserved harm.

12. No government can be ethical if it is anarchistic, bureaucratic, tyrannical, or inadequate in protecting the life, liberty, property, and privacy of all its citizens and their dependents, or is in any way subject to majority rule.

13. The basic human rights of life, liberty, property, and privacy cannot be maintained without an absolute right to private property (309).

14. A person's life and property belong solely to that person; no person has a right to any part of another person's life or property, except, possibly, by prior mutual, voluntary contract, which is kept by at least one of the parties to the contract. When someone violates his or her contract with us, that allows us, at our discretion, to abrogate our obligations to that person under this same contract. This is true no matter how great the need of anyone for the life or property of another.

15. Every form of socialism is unethical, unless it is totally voluntary by unanimous consensus between all the persons involved in producing wealth, redistributing it, and receiving it; charity must be entirely voluntary and not imposed by government; otherwise charity becomes evil and destructive.

16. In order for any system of government to be ethical and effective, the unit of autonomy and sovereignty cannot be larger than five men and five women, nor much smaller than four men and four women, which is optimal.

17. There should never be more men than women in the unit of sovereignty, called an "octet," if it is to be effective and remain ethical.

18. The optimal size for a unit of sovereignty is four men and four women, not the nation state, however small. If an organization has any unethical persons in its membership, and this membership is greater than ten persons, it shall become increasingly bureaucratic and unethical until it reaches the potential to become totally unethical and completely destructive, at a membership of sixteen or more persons.

19. Men and women are neurologically, as well as sexually, complementary to one another; all decisions of government at all levels, including the family, are better made by consensus between at least one man and at least one woman who share a common set of true ethical values and voluntarily choose to work together

(115–117, 527–600). This unit is called a "complementary pair." Complementary pairs need not be married to one another, and, in fact, may be married to, and have families with, persons who are not their complements, although a good marriage will always be between persons who are a complementary pair.

20. The most creative interactions between complementary pairs are achieved within octets, which work by consensus among the complementary pairs that compose the octet.

21. There exists a technology of creative synergy between complementary pairs and within octets, called "autopoiesis," which facilitates consensus and amplifies individual and collective creativity. This is described in detail within my book *Creative Transformation* (115). This is a generalization of a much more specific biological term coined by Varela and Maturana (462). It would be better to call this process of creative information exchange between complementary pairs of entities simply "creative synergy." Otherwise it produces confusions with persons who have used the term its original sense.

   "Autopoiesis," in its more specific, biological sense, basically means creative synergy between DNA and Protein within a living cell. I believe that my definition of "autopoiesis" includes the concept originally conceived by Varela and Maturana. I was trying to honor them, and instead I produced confusion. This confusion will not occur in persons who even partially share the Evolutionary Ethic. It is too late to change my use of "autopoiesis," which I have now communicated to many thousands of people. I apologize to Varela and Maturana for usurping their word and to all the people who have been confused by this.

22. The closest approximation to ethical government is given in the draft of the Declaration of Independence as originally written by Thomas Jefferson (229). This version of the Declaration was never adopted. Almost every other aspect of American Government has diminished the ethical principles of the original Declaration of Independence, except for the Bill of Rights, as well as the Thirteenth, Fourteenth, Fifteenth, and Nineteenth Amendments to the U. S. Constitution, the checks and balances system, and other features which protect basic human rights and somewhat limit government corruption.

23. How to understand and apply practically the fundamental Moses, Jesus, Spinoza, Teilhard, and Jefferson is part of the goal of this book.

24. A reading of Thomas Jefferson's writing on ethics and government (176–179), particularly the original Declaration of Independence and his book known as *The Jefferson Bible: The Life and Morals of Jesus of Nazareth* (176), is a good way of beginning to see how Judaism, Christianity, Spinoza's Ethics and the ethical foundation of true democratic government are all interrelated.

25. Whoever does not share and understand Judeo-Christian Ethics and the ethical foundations of truly democratic government will neither share nor understand the ethics and governmental concepts to be developed in this book; such a person is neither a good Jew, Christian, nor democrat.

26. No one can intellectually understand an ethical system that he or she does not intuitively share at the unconscious or mystical level.

27. The understanding of ethics inherent in Judeo-Christian ethics is more mystical than intellectual.

28. The greatest mystical understanding of ethics is the understanding of Jesus.

29. The greatest intellectual understanding of ethics is the understanding of Spinoza.

30. This book is an attempt to combine the mystical understanding of Jesus with the intellectual understanding of Spinoza, and to make it all practical and understandable to an intelligent high school graduate.

31. No one who does not already share the Evolutionary Ethic with me will ever understand this book or any of my other books at any level, no matter how intelligent and well-educated they are.

32. Every healthy human being is born ethical, with the potential to understand the Evolutionary Ethic and all of its implications.

33. Human beings lose their innate ethics and capacity to understand the Evolutionary Ethic only because they are punished when they behave ethically and/or rewarded when they behave unethically.

34. Every institution of government and society in every nation in the history of the world eventually punishes ethical behavior and rewards unethical behavior; this happens in the home, the school,

the economy, and the government; it is the sole, legitimate function of ethical government to prevent this harm when it is undeserved; otherwise, unethical people should be allowed to harm themselves; they deserve it.

ETHICS AND HISTORY

"Ethics" is defined by the dictionary as "the study of what is good" or as a set of normative principles. The philosopher Wittgenstein showed, quite convincingly, that there cannot be a scientific ethics, because we can never infer "ought" from "is" (1, 93, 496–499). I believe that Wittgenstein was wrong.

It is a well-known theorem in mathematics that one can never optimize a function on more than one variable at a time, although other variables may be constrained. If there were an infinity of normative criteria, as most academic philosophers believe today, then Wittgenstein would be correct, and there could be no absolute criteria of good and evil. However, I believe that there is a single normative principle in the universe that can lead to a logically consistent system of ethics (115–117). Furthermore, the use of any other normative principle will lead to a logically and scientifically inconsistent system of ethics.

This normative principal is implicit in Judeo-Christian ethics as expressed in the Bible and the teachings of Jesus, and was first made explicit by Baruch de Spinoza (410–412). It is possible, through the use of modern quantum mechanics, to integrate and scientifically explain the notions of scientific ethics, creativity, true mysticism, and traditional religious ethics, particularly Judeo-Christian ethics (115).

At the core of any civilization is a system of values or ethics together with assumptions about reality. The European civilization, out of which America emerged as a new civilization, had at its core what was long held by the Christian churches: "the natural, hierarchical order of things, Christian ethics, and a notion of the hereditary superiority of some people over other people." This system was highly compatible with the hierarchical order of the Catholic Church, extending beyond this world all the way to God, but less so with the new Protestant sects, which claimed, and occasionally tolerated, respect for individual conscience, so long as this conscience was compatible with the prevalent interpretations of the locally accepted Protestant Bible.

The scientific revolution, which began at about the same time as the Reformation, and had common causes behind it, showed any rational person that almost all the Christian religious authorities were wrong about nearly everything in the natural world from astronomy to zoology; it was reasonable to assume that the same religious authority was probably wrong about the psychosocial and ethical world as well. Therefore, rational people began to look to reason and science to guide them in moral philosophy (ethical behavior and psychosocial sciences) as well as in natural philosophy (physical and biological sciences).

The pioneers in this approach were humanists, such as Francis Bacon and Thomas Hobbes in England and Michel de Montaigne and René Descartes in France (358). The culmination of this new approach was achieved in Holland, perhaps the freest and most ethical society in the world at that time, in the *Ethics* of Baruch de Spinoza. Spinoza was to moral philosophy what his contemporary Isaac Newton was to natural philosophy. Spinoza was the first scientific philosopher of ethics.

Other ethical philosophers such as Buddha, Confucius, Socrates, Averroes, Aquinas, and Maimonides tried to be completely rational, but Spinoza was the first to integrate ethics with mathematically based modern science. As a consequence, Spinoza, whose family had fled first Spain then Portugal to escape the Inquisition, was excommunicated by the Jews of Holland and persecuted by Jews, Catholics, and Protestants. It seems he had something to offend everyone. Religious authorities up to the present time have condemned his work, although the State of Israel, much to its credit, readmitted him into Judaism three hundred years after his death. Maimonides was also, more briefly, excommunicated (228).

Bertrand Russell, a totally secular, anti-religious, but humane, philosopher, referred to Spinoza as "the noblest and most lovable of all the great philosophers ... ethically he is supreme" (358). Goethe so admired Spinoza that he claimed to read him every day as an ethical exercise. When a Rabbi asked Albert Einstein if he believed in God, Einstein answered that he believed in the God of Spinoza. Einstein carefully studied the ethics of Spinoza, which have implicit in them the concepts of relativity, as well as many of the fundamental concepts of modern quantum mechanics, such as the wholeness and unity of God and the Universe (412).

Science tries to be a model of objective reality, although it does not always succeed. Any true system of ethics must also be in full correspondence with objective reality. Which is to say that it must bear up well, according to its own criteria, to scientific scrutiny. There can be no contradiction between true science and true ethics. False ethics will ultimately always conflict with reality.

In the modern world there have been two major experiments designed to create new, ethically based civilizations. Both of these experiments were based on a distortion of Spinoza's ethics. The most recent experiment was the Soviet Union; the first was the United States of America.

American majority rule resulted from a distortion of Spinoza's ethical and political philosophy produced by the line of thinkers—Locke, Hume, Voltaire, Rousseau, Diderot, and others—leading to Thomas Jefferson. Jefferson may be the most brilliant, ethical, and creative leader any nation ever had (177–179, 229), although like any ethical human he had many ethical flaws (89). He, not Washington, is the ethical father of the United States, although Tom Paine might have been the midwife. Tom Paine's pamphlet *Common Sense,* which contained many of the ethical principles of the Declaration, was more widely read and more influential in creating the American Revolution than the Declaration itself. In fact, the Revolution was always a minority movement; only about a third of the adult population supported it.

Yet, although (1) Jefferson clearly wanted an ethical society, based on the Democratic Ethic that freedom is the greatest good and tyranny is the greatest evil, and (2) he and his two closest disciples Madison and Monroe were Presidents for twenty-four consecutive years, they produced instead an increasingly unethical society that has been destroying individual freedom, almost since its inception.

The Democratic Ethic is self-contradictory; it seeks to maximize freedom, but instead it diminishes freedom through a tyranny of the majority. It is a gross form of self-deception to believe that decisions reached by large majorities are automatically ethical and correct. Remember that although Hitler was originally democratically elected only by a plurality, he was able to develop overwhelming majority approval and support for himself and his policies, almost to the end of his regime.

The Democratic Ethic says that the greatest good is that which makes for the greatest liberty or welfare for the greatest number, that it is right and proper for a sufficiently large majority to take away some of the liberty or welfare of a sufficiently small minority, if it will greatly increase the alleged liberty or welfare of the majority. For example, three-fourths of the U.S. State legislatures could ratify a Constitutional amendment abolishing the Bill of Rights, thereby taking away everybody's civil rights (56).

Implicit in the Democratic Ethic is the notion that decisions reached by large majorities are always ethically superior to decisions reached by small minorities. This is clearly false. Jefferson tried to compensate for this deficiency in democratic government by advocating and eventually getting a strong Bill of Rights to protect ethical minorities from unethical majorities and from government in general.

Yet, the history of the United States is the history of the ever growing power of government and the destruction of individual liberty for the alleged benefit of the majority. This began with the toleration of slavery in the United States for four-score-and-seven years, followed by government imposed racial segregation for five score more years. Majority rule led to the military draft, the income tax, the blatantly unconstitutional detention of Japanese-Americans in concentration camps during World War II, the allegedly anticommunist witch hunts of the McCarthy era, the nurturing of a huge, parasitical military-industrial complex, and finally to outright confiscation of private property through land use laws and to gross government interference with private voluntary behavior, such as anti-drug laws, and to the constant attacks on the Second Amendment by a large majority of Democrats, again for the alleged benefit of a willing, frightened majority. Therefore, the Democratic Ethic is a false ethic that, in trying to maximize freedom, ends up destroying freedom. A true criterion for good must not lead to its own contradiction.

The most recent ethical system used to form a new civilization was the Materialistic Ethic of socialism, expressed in its most extreme form in the Soviet Union, which was in such conflict with true ethics and reality that it destroyed itself in only seventy years. The socialistic paradigm is that the greatest good is government redistribution of the wealth of a society so that there is equality of wealth independent of merit, and that the government guarantees the necessities of life to every accepted member of the society. The extreme Materialistic Ethic is "from each according to his ability; to each according to his need" (233–235).

The socialistic distortion of Spinoza's philosophy was produced by the line of philosophers—Leibnitz, Kant, Hegel, Marx, Engels, etc.—leading to Lenin and undemocratic, completely tyrannical socialism (388, 450). All forms of tyranny are unethical. The racist National Socialism of Adolf Hitler was another unethical spin-off from Hegel.

The Soviet Union, by its own criterion of good, material security, ended up impoverishing its own people by destroying their freedom and creativity, thereby contradicting its own alleged ethical purpose. This happens in all socialistic countries; it merely happens faster when they violate the criteria of the one true ethics, which were clearly articulated over three hundred and thirty years ago, when Spinoza simply made explicit what was implicit in the traditional Jewish studies that he undertook as a young man.

Spinoza said that the ultimate good was what he called "the intellectual love of God." According to Spinoza, we love God by understanding and emulating Him. To paraphrase Spinoza, "we understand God through intuition, art, science and technology, since God is the infinite totality of all that exists." The most outstanding attribute of God is creativity. Therefore, we emulate God by maximizing creativity (see *On Improving the Understanding* (412)). This same notion of emulating God as ethical duty ("walking in His ways") is in the Bible (Deut. 11:22).

True ethics are based on the notion of maximizing creativity. "Good" is whatever increases "creativity"; "evil" is whatever decreases "creativity." I call this the "Evolutionary Ethic." In my books I argue that any ethical system based on any other notion of good will lead to its own contradiction, as has clearly been shown for the Materialistic Ethic. It is currently being shown for the Democratic Ethic, which has turned out, at best, to be a tyranny of the majority, thereby contradicting its own fundamental ethical premises.

I derived the Evolutionary Ethic independently of Spinoza, with the advantage of more than three centuries of scientific progress, by first observing that the only common denominator in the evolutionary process is ever increasing intelligence. The biosphere becomes collectively increasingly intelligent. The protozoa are more intelligent than the bacteria; the metazoa are more intelligent than the protozoa; the vertebrates are in general more intelligent than the invertebrates; the reptiles are in general more intelligent than the fish; the mammals are in general more intelligent than the reptiles; and humans are in general more intelligent than all other mammals. Furthermore, this is the order in which the biosphere has evolved. However, intelligence is independent of ethics in the evolutionary process, up to a point.

We all know highly intelligent people who are highly unethical. The two most notorious examples in the last hundred years are Hitler and Stalin. Therefore, the maximization of intelligence is not an adequate ethical criterion. What we wish to maximize is creativity. Creativity grows out of intelligence together with ethics, but it is not identical to intelligence. Creativity will be shown to be a transcendence of intelligence.

"Intelligence," as I will use the concept, is "the ability to predict and control the total environment—physical, biological, and psychosocial." This ability is what is growing in the biosphere. Eventually this ability grows to the point where we have intelligence of our own intelligence. That is to say, "we can predict and control our own ability to predict and control." When intelligence passes this threshold, then the species begins to be ethical and as a consequence becomes creative, thereby transcending intelligence by adding a new dimension to itself. Creativity (C) is a direct interaction of Intelligence (I) and Ethics (E), which may be expressed intuitively in the equation $C = IE$. This is the fundamental process equation of Creative Transformation (115–117).

Intelligence can be used to increase intelligence (good, ethical, creative) or to diminish intelligence (evil, unethical, destructive). Therefore, intuitively, "ethics" are equal to our desire to increase intelligence minus our desire to diminish intelligence, the result divided by our total desire to both increase and decrease intelligence. Everything we do is done either to increase or decrease intelligence, or it is trivial, although we may not be conscious of this. Subhuman (pre-ethical) animals neither increase nor decrease intelligence; they are merely a natural part of the world which may have stopped evolving.

This definition of ethics gives us dimensionless numbers between minus one and plus one (-1,1) as a measure of ethics. There is no practical way of measuring desire. However, there are practical estimators of ethics, **E**, one of which is the following: $\mathbf{E = (T - F)/(T + F)}$, where **T** is an equivalent sampling of all the true information we believe and **F** is an equivalent sampling of all the false information we believe.

But why would anyone seek to destroy intelligence and believe false information, if he or she can otherwise create intelligence and believe true information? Before answering this question, let some terms be defined.

"Information" is the symbolic representation of events and their relationships.

"Truth" is information that when it is believed increases the ability of the believer to predict and control reality, i.e., the total environment—physical, biological, and psychosocial—without decreasing the believer's or anyone else's ability to predict and control the total environment.

"Falsehood" is information that when it is believed decreases the ability of the believer to predict and control reality, i.e., any aspect of the total environment—physical, biological, and psychosocial.

These notions of truth and falsehood are part of a scientific epistemology that leads to the scientific paradigm, which includes scientific method. The essence of scientific method is the experimental testing of hypotheses and theories about reality to see if they are true or false. It is assumed that all hypotheses are probably false until proven true. Science is based on doubt rather than on belief.

Reality is both objective and subjective. Science deals well with objective reality, but not so well with subjective reality. The existence of subjective reality will lead us later to consider mysticism, religion in general, and Judeo-Christian ethics in particular.

We return to considering the phenomenon of evil and why some persons choose to believe falsehood. I say, "choose," because we do not have to believe anything; we can function quite well on the basis of probabilities. A belief is a certainty about the truth or the falsehood of some proposition about nature. We choose to believe because belief makes us happy, although not necessarily more intelligent or more creative.

"Happiness" means many different things to different people. I define "happiness" as "a state of mind in which we believe that our desires are being fulfilled." Desires that have been fulfilled do not make us happy. Only desires that are being fulfilled make us happy. We all have simultaneous desires that are both being fulfilled and being unfulfilled. Unfulfilled desires make us unhappy. Therefore, we are all simultaneously happy and unhappy. If the strength and number of desires being fulfilled is greater than the strength and number of desires being unfulfilled then the net result is happiness. The converse produces unhappiness.

Intuitively, creativity is the process by which we discover scientific laws, invent machines, produce works of art, and help others do these things. The most creative thing we can ever do for ourselves is to help maximize the creativity of another. This is what in fact maximizes our own creativity.

More formally, a creative act is any act which increases "ethical truth" for at least one person, including oneself, without decreasing "ethical truth" for any person, including oneself. "Ethical truth" is any information which increases our ethics or our creativity, the latter by increasing the ethics or intelligence of at least one ethical person, without increasing the intelligence of any unethical person.

It is unethical to increase the intelligence of unethical persons, because their ethics are negative, which makes them more destructive than creative. But it is ethical to increase their ethics by communicating ethical truth to them. Everybody is benefited by the increase in anybody's ethics.

THEOREM 1: People are unethical if, and only if, they value happiness more than creativity.

Happiness and creativity are not mutually exclusive. But neither are they the same thing. Creativity is an objective act of increasing ethical truth for oneself or for another person. Happiness is a subjective state of mind that can be induced just as easily by false as by true beliefs.

THEOREM 2: If we seek to maximize happiness, we minimize it and have neither happiness nor creativity in the long run, although unethical people can have a transitory minimal happiness.

THEOREM 3: If we seek to maximize creativity, we always succeed, and trivially also maximize happiness.

A "trivial" entity or act neither increases nor decreases creativity. Trivia is a set of measure zero; almost all acts and entities in the Universe are either ethical or unethical.

Corollary 3.1: There are many more ethical entities in the Universe than trivial or unethical entities.

Corollary 3.2: There are more angels (to be defined later) *than humans, although, at this time, there are more unethical than ethical humans, and most humans may appear trivial.*

People choose to believe falsehood solely because it makes them happy, and in so doing they are behaving unethically, because $E = (T - F)/(T + F)$ and our ethics are directly related to the proportion of our desire for creativity over our desire for happiness. Note again that creativity and happiness are not mutually exclusive, but neither are they identical. This will be elaborated later.

Subhuman (pre-ethical) animals, with a very few minor exceptions, can be motivated solely by their desire for happiness, because they do not yet have intelligence about their own intelligence and do not yet have an ethical component which can produce creativity. These animals have zero creativity. That is why only humans are systematically creative within the biosphere. That is also why only humans, within the biosphere, can be systematically unethical and destructive. What makes us human and ethical is our unique ability to ethically choose creativity over happiness.

THEOREM 4: Humans have only two primordial desires, happiness and creativity; all other desires are means for achieving the two primordial desires; by maximizing creativity with no concern for happiness, we maximize both happiness and creativity (115, 116, 117).

Therefore there exists a single ethical criterion by which all ethical decisions may be made, which is valid at all times, under all conditions for all ethical beings anywhere in the universe. It is eternally valid. This is what I call the "Evolutionary Ethic"; it is expressed as follows.

WE SHOULD ALL DO OUR BEST TO MAXIMIZE CREATIVITY WITHOUT EVER DECREASING ANYONE'S CREATIVITY ...INCLUDING OUR OWN.

From this single, simple, but very deep, ethical imperative, we may derive a complete system of ethics to structure any society or government, to make individual decisions, to start and run a business, to educate ourselves and our children, to guide us in sexual relationships, and to relate to unethical governments, which do not follow or even pretend to follow the Evolutionary Ethic. The entire ethics of the Bible may be so derived.

An ethical government is, therefore, the organizational structure of a society dedicated to maximizing its collective creativity without ever decreasing the creativity of any entity in the universe. Such a society has never existed; the closest approximation was Judaism under the early kings. More will be said of this later. To create an ethical government we must preserve what has been shown to work in the past, such as Judeo-Christian ethics, the Declaration of Independence, and the Bill of Rights, and eliminate all superstition that does not work, such as religious ritual, bureaucracy, and majority rule. We can then restructure everything within the scientific paradigm of the Evolutionary Ethic. Furthering this end is the purpose of this book.

Such an ethical system is derived in stages, going always from more general to more specific situations. This is the same as the relationship between the Old Testament and the teachings of Jesus. From the Evolutionary Ethic, the preceding considerations, and scientific reality we derive a second stage of eight ethical principles:

1. Any act which increases anyone's creativity, including our own, without decreasing anyone else's creativity, including our own, is ethical. (This is the essence of the meaning of "good." To be "good" is to knowingly and deliberately behave ethically, whatever the consequences.)

2. Any act which decreases anyone's creativity is unethical. (This is the essence of the meaning of "evil." To be "evil" is to knowingly and deliberately behave unethically, for whatever reason.)

3. Unethical means can never achieve ethical ends.

4. Means which are not ends are never ethical.

5. It is unethical to tolerate unethical or destructive behavior.

6. It is unethical to be certain about any cause and effect relationship concerning objective reality; only probabilistic beliefs about objective reality are ethical. We can never deny the reality of our own thoughts or perceptions, our subjective reality; we err solely when

we are certain about the causes in objective reality of our subjective thoughts or perceptions.

7. It is ethical to doubt.

8. Inaction is unethical.

These eight ethical principles are derived and discussed in more detail in my previous books (115–117). They can be used extensively to derive the same norms of behavior as in the Bible, Mishnah, Talmud, and Jewish tradition in general, leading eventually to the teachings of Jesus, but not necessarily to other parts of the New Testament. The essential ethical teachings of Jesus, stripped of superstition and distortion, are best summarized in the Jefferson Bible (176). For making any ethical decision, we must consider all eight ethical principles, all of which are entirely scientific and secular.

As a third stage derivation, we may directly and quickly derive the Ten Commandments from these eight ethical principles. The Ten Commandments are the ethical core of Judeo-Christian ethics. Using the Ten Commandments and the eight ethical principles we can, with varying degrees of difficulty, derive all the ethical norms of the Bible and reach many and perhaps all the ethical conclusions of the teachings of Jesus. (I suspect that the early Catholic Church, established by St. Paul, not Jesus, distorted the true teachings of Jesus.) If the entire ethical message of the Bible, and the way of life that it implies, may be derived solely from the Evolutionary Ethic, then this ethic too is God's message to humanity, and reflects the ultimate reality of the Universe and its fundamental ethical structure.

This is not true for any other system of religious ethics, although there is some overlap in the ethics of almost all major religions. One may say that Jewish ethics and the true teachings of Jesus represent a super-set of ethics, which contains all the true ethics of all other religions but excludes all the false ethics. However, all paradigms are false or incomplete. Therefore, Jewish ethics together with the teachings of Jesus, although true, cannot be complete. We must forever expand all ethical systems. The Old Testament together with the teachings of Jesus provides the mystically revealed set of ethical norms for maximizing the long-term creativity of any people who follow them. The Evolutionary Ethic is implicit in these norms.

Therefore, there is a connection in the world between ethics, religion, superstition, and spirituality. Although all the major religions, not just Judaism and Christianity, have a strong ethical base, almost all religions, particularly the so called "cults," degrade their ethical base by gradually substituting ritual for ethical action, thereby becoming saddled with ever increasing superstition.

RELIGION, SUPERSTITION, AND SPIRITUALITY

Superstition has been defined as "other people's religious beliefs." Similarly a "cult" may be defined as "other people's organized religion." A more precise way of defining "superstition" is "a belief in cause and effect relationships which leads to systematic, repetitive behavior which is totally ineffective in accomplishing what it claims it can accomplish, and which system of belief and behavior is never subjected to scientific scrutiny by those who believe and repeatedly practice it." Superstition is the basis of almost all organized religions, except perhaps your own.

Organized religions usually have "authority figures" who claim to know what is right and what is wrong within the religion and what kinds of behavior should be condemned or lauded. These notions usually have to do with institutionalized superstition, which apparently is a characteristic of almost all organized religions, and is usually called "ritual."

Those who practice popular ritual are often considered "spiritual." In organized religions, the nonobservance or the defiling of ritual is almost always regarded as the greatest sin. That is why in many Christian religions the devil and his worshipers are almost always portrayed as defiling some sacred ritual. The worst thing that happens in ritualized religions is that superstitious ritual, "false spirituality," comes to replace ethical action, "true spirituality." This tends to destroy creativity among the adherents of that religion.

As a general rule, it can be stated that the more concerned a religion is with ritual, the less concerned it will be with true ethics, and the less creative its adherents will be. "Fundamentalists," whether they are Jews, Christians, Moslems, Hindus, Buddhists, or the adherents of any other religion, are militant superstitionists; they are the least creative humans. It is unethical to be certain about any religion.

John David Garcia

Superstition and ritual are practiced because they make their practitioners happy through conformity with the prejudices and unquestioning beliefs of a tightly knit group which approves of this behavior. They then have a very strong sense of belonging and community. Loneliness seems to be the greatest source of human unhappiness.

To be highly ethical in a superstitious society is to be a creative, unbelieving member of a tiny minority, which is condemned, and often persecuted and even killed, by the vast superstitious majority. The ethical persons are a minute, unorganized minority, which is sparsely distributed among the superstitious majority in all nations. This is a very lonely type of existence.

Those who see the contradictions and the hypocrisy of the majority religions often compensate for it by forming new quasi-religions of their own, such as the organized militant atheists under Madeleine Murray, the socialists under Marxist ideology, or the many so-called "cults" of the minority religions such as the Moonies, the Hare Krishnas, the Scientologists, and all minor sects of mainstream religions in general. All of these persons have substituted one set of superstitions for another, and they have compensated for their loneliness by forming another religion, which gives them a sense of belonging, community and "spirituality."

True spirituality is based on dedication to both true mysticism (to be defined later) and true ethics, independently of how lonely or unhappy it might make us. The truly spiritual person is dedicated to maximizing creativity above all things, including self-preservation. The truly spiritual person, or Esprital, as my old friend Henri Lurié might have said, is prepared to stand alone all his or her life rather than subscribe to any form of superstition in order to find fellowship and acceptance in a group. Constantin Brunner distinguished between true spirituality, which he called *Geistigkeit*, and false spirituality, which he called *Geistlichkeit,* and I call "superstition."

Because of their uncompromising attitude, Espritals are extremely rare and can rarely organize themselves into a cohesive group, because they lack a common system of belief. The Esprital acts without believing. All Espritals do the best they can, knowing that they may be completely wrong.

The sole common belief that all Espritals might share is the belief in the notion that the greatest good is to maximize creativity, and that

42

we should all act and interact with one another on the basis of what maximizes our common creativity, without ever reducing the creativity of single person. However, almost all Espritals will differ on how best to do this.

I spent the thirty years of my life after age thirty-five in learning how to identify Espritals and to help them organize themselves in such a way that they could all maximize their creativity through unanimous consensus. My findings are that this will occur solely in small, autonomous groups of eight to ten ethical, cooperative, free men and women, called "octets," as described in my last book, *Creative Transformation (115)*.

It is extremely difficult to find and organize the Espritals, because they seem to be less than .01%, and possibly less than .001%, of the human species. Furthermore they are not concentrated in any part of the earth. They are a tiny minority because, although almost all humans may be born ethical, almost all aspects of every culture destroy ethics by punishing creative, ethical behavior and rewarding unethical, destructive, superstitious behavior.

A very small minority of humanity has the innate courage and ethics, as well as the fortunate environment, to remain ethical in the face of constant punishment, threats, and loneliness. Almost everyone ultimately succumbs to superstitious conformity and surrenders to their own fear (115).

Espritals are most noted by their significant creativity. But what distinguishes the Espritals are their ethics, not their intelligence. If the Esprital is highly intelligent, he or she will be a creative genius. But not all Espritals are geniuses. They are merely highly ethical and mystical. The great mystics have been the major contributors to human ethics. But many of the great creative geniuses in art, science, and technology are also Espritals. The mythical and metaphorical Adam may have been the first Esprital (377, 378).

All humans may be born ethical, but humans are never born moral. Morality must be deliberately created by ethical choice. Morality begins when we become aware of our own ethics and deliberately and knowingly choose to become maximally ethical, and as a consequence maximally creative. We usually have more of a choice over our ethics than we have over our intelligence, if we know what our true ethics are.

The early hominids became ethical when they achieved intelligence about their own intelligence, and as a consequence could predict and control their own ability to predict and control. But humans did not become moral until they had intelligence about their ethics, and as a consequence could predict and control their own ethics, i.e., they could predict and control their ability to predict and control their ability to predict and control.

According to the Bible, this occurred when God breathed a human soul into the man he had made from matter. This is to say that after humanity had evolved from matter, individual cells, and more primitive animals, this ethical animal developed intelligence of its own ethics, and as a consequence became a moral being. Again, according to the Bible, this occurred six thousand years ago. This was the time at which humans created the first great civilization with a true ethical base, Sumer. Therefore, the Biblical Adam is a metaphor for the beginning of morality in the human species and the beginning of the Espritals (378). Adam spoke Sumerian.

More historically-accurate examples of Espritals are Moses, all the Hebrew Prophets, Buddha, Confucius, Thales, Socrates, Jesus, the ethical apostles of Jesus, many of, but perhaps not all, the Christian Saints, Hypatia, Mohammed, Avicena, Averroes, Maimonides, Saint Thomas Aquinas, Hildegard von Bingen, Saint Francis of Assisi, Saint Ignatius, Michelangelo, Shakespeare, Giordano Bruno, Spinoza, Sor Juana Inez de la Cruz, J. S. Bach, Beethoven, Thomas Jefferson, Goethe, Mary Ann Evans (George Elliot), Emily Dickenson, Van Gogh, Mary Cassatt, and in our own time possibly Marie Curie, Lisa Meitner, Mahatma Gandhi, Albert Schweitzer, Unamuno, Dieter Bonhoeffer, Chaim Weizman, Pierre Teilhard de Chardin, Bertrand Russell, Einstein, Andrei Sakharov, Barbara McClintock (577), David Bohm, Mother Teresa, the anonymous woman who wrote *A Course In Miracles (510)*, and among the living, the great composer Penderecki and the great biologist Lynn Margulis (582–584).

There are many other Espritals who have never become well-known, but the total sum of all living Espritals is always a very small minority among humanity. They almost never meet one another, and rarely, if ever, seem to work together. It took Jesus his first thirty-three years to put the twelve Apostles together. One of them betrayed him, and the rest did not seem to have understood his teachings well enough to prevent Saint Paul and the succeeding Catholic Church from corrupting them.

The real problems are how best to find the very few Espritals and then how to put them in touch with each other and bring them together. This is further complicated by the apparent fact that no true Espritals ever consider themselves Espritals. The Espritals are always aware of their moral imperfections. It is the followers of the Espritals who mythologize them by stripping them of their ethical flaws.

If a few Espritals can work together, they may catalyze the creation of an ethical government that can maximize the creativity of all humanity. It will be very difficult for humans who are merely ethical but not yet Espritals to create an ethical government from scratch, as is shown in the later chapters, although they may become citizens of an Ethical State. An ethical government will never come about through majority rule. Unethical means can never produce ethical ends.

Because there are so few Espritals, and they themselves do not know who they are, conventional means, such as advertising in the mass media, are inadequate ways of locating the Espritals at any reasonable cost. Writing books of relevance to the Espritals is also inadequate, since the mass media and the academic community will at best ignore books they are ethically incompetent to understand; at worst they will condemn them ethically and intellectually, as has been the case for Spinoza's writings for well over three centuries and was often true for Bertrand Russell's writings.

Therefore, the Espritals do not know about each other's existence. They only know that they do not seem to fit in very well anywhere, and that they have met few or no persons who seem fully to share their values or their ethical courage.

The only common feature of Espritals, at every stage of their development, is that they lead creative lives. They are usually ethical mystics. Sometimes they are scientific mystics. Because creativity is an interaction of intelligence and ethics, $C = IE$, not all creative persons are Espritals, although all creative persons are ethical. It takes a very high level of ethics to be an Esprital. The critical level of ethics for an Esprital seems to be the level at which someone is ready to die, or at least greatly suffer, before decreasing anyone's creativity, including his or her own.

Therefore, persons who are highly intelligent but only marginally ethical may be highly creative without being Espritals. What every Esprital does, perhaps unconsciously, is to courageously search out the most creative community that can be found, or to try to create such a community from scratch. Jesus tried to create such a community with the twelve Apostles, but failed after Saint Paul took over the Christian movement. Moses, Buddha, Confucius, Socrates, Mohamed, Saint Ignatius, Lenin, and Hitler did the same, but they all failed in one way or another, Lenin and Hitler in particularly horrible ways.

However evil you may consider these last two men, you should understand that their evil came from a perverted sense of ethics, not a lack of intelligence, or even a lack of what might be called "moral commitment."

A true Moral Community, however small, is essential to create an ethical government, which can never come about under majority rule. No one person alone, no matter how genuinely ethical, can ever successfully create a Moral Community. It will take, at least, four male and four female Espritals, as we shall see later in this book. How to find and create such a community will also be discussed later.

Almost all current and historical human organizations and communities that were intended to be creative have become bureaucracies. A bureaucracy is an organization which convinces its members that they are parasites and can be secure solely by living parasitically off the creativity of others. A human parasite is someone who has transformed himself, or has been transformed, so that he or she will do few or no creative acts for the rest of his or her life, and will survive by exploiting the creativity of the more creative people. An exploitive exchange occurs when we destroy more creativity in others than we create in others.

Organizations such as most schools, universities, not-for-profit foundations, businesses, and the agencies of the Federal, state, and local governments are organizations that were originally intended to be creative, but became bureaucracies. Within any bureaucracy, the Espritals usually become quickly dissatisfied with the organization and leave. Almost all persons who remain behind usually become parasites themselves, although they may have been creative when they joined the bureaucracy.

Espritals eventually discover that the only way that they can live a purely creative life without ethical compromises is to be self-employed in some creative endeavor as varied as medicine, engineering, carpentry, machining, mechanics, art, music, farming, and many other fields, although not even a small minority of the people in these fields are likely to be Espritals. Similarly, Espritals are not likely to be employed as lawyers, bureaucrats, politicians, or people who live parasitically off other people's creativity without creating something of their own equal in value to the resources that they are consuming. This knowledge enables us to know something about where to look for Espritals, and where not to look for them.

Espritals will usually find that earning substantial amounts of money will require ethical compromises. These compromises will usually include nurturing totally uncreative parasites. It is always unethical to nurture parasites. Human parasites are those who traffic in money, or bureaucrats who redistribute the wealth that is extorted from ethical citizens by unethical government. Bureaucrats and governments do this without in any way being creative themselves. Financiers and bureaucrats are often biased against financing Espritals, because they can usually earn more money and/or be more secure by financing marginally ethical persons who take few or no risks, and by earning most of their money not by creative action but by buying low and selling high, which for Espritals is a trivial form of commerce.

Espritals, once they are fully developed from less ethical but still creative children and young adults, always courageously choose to work in an environment which maximizes creativity, rather than in an environment which maximizes income or gives them security. This does not, necessarily, mean that Espritals are poor.

Since Espritals are creative, and creativity is the basis of all wealth (115), Espritals will always have all the resources they need to maximize their creativity and that of those they most love, although they may not have any surpluses. The Esprital usually discovers that he or she is better off economically by not making any ethical compromises and by refusing to cooperate with any persons who are systematically destructive to themselves or others, directly or indirectly. As a consequence, eventually all Espritals who survive will try to make themselves and all those they love as self-sufficient as possible.

Therefore, the best place to search for Espritals is in a community which is highly ethical and creative in many fields and which simultaneously promotes self-sufficiency for itself and others. A few Espritals, if they are extremely brilliant and ethically naive, may survive within the academic community, although the academic bureaucracy is already highly destructive.

At one time I thought that the Libertarian Party in the United States might be a community with a concentration of Espritals. However, I soon found that the Libertarians, who have the only political philosophy that is ethically compatible with that of the Espritals, include many persons who are Libertarians primarily because of a desire to use drugs or to maximize their discretionary income, because of hatred of government bureaucrats, or simply because of a love of liberty. None of these are primary motivations of Espritals, though love of liberty is fully compatible with Esprital values, since liberty is a necessary, but not sufficient, condition for maximizing creativity, which is the sole goal of Espritals.

The best place to look for Espritals in the modern world is the Internet. The Internet is the only forum in the world for the free exchange of all information. As a consequence, every government in the world is trying to exercise control over the Internet. This is done in blatantly unethical ways in Communist and Islamic countries, and more subtly in the democracies. However, this book and my other writings will be on the Internet for as long as possible, in the hope of eventually being able to bring together at least four Esprital males and four Esprital females, even if this does not occur in my lifetime. If you are not by now totally bored or outraged by this book, you may be an Esprital and not know it. I do not regard myself as among the Espritals, but merely as their willing servant.

In the democracies, the governments use the excuse of controlling pornography, or even of protecting the Internet itself, as their reason for exercising control over it. All types of control over the Internet should be vigorously opposed by all ethical people, particularly the Espritals. The Internet is the best chance in history for unifying the Espritals, but it will not be easy.

All the great religions of the world, although major repositories of true ethics and true mysticism, have become so bureaucratized and obsessed with ritual that they are also unlikely to lead to a community of Espritals. However, both the ethical foundations of Western Civilization and true ethics are to be found within Judaism and Christianity. We will, therefore, consider and incorporate Judeo-Christian ethics into the model of an ethical government to be developed in the later chapters.

JUDEO-CHRISTIAN ETHICS

The great Jewish sage Maimonides (228) observed that Islam is closest to Judaism ritualistically and theologically. But Christianity is closest to Judaism ethically, because Christians accept the entire Bible as divine truth, particularly the Ten Commandments and the teachings of Jesus, which are pure ethical Judaism, although Christians may often misinterpret the meaning of the Bible and the teachings of Jesus. I would add that Jews also often misinterpret the true ethics of the Bible.

The greatest ethical error in Christianity, and there are many though the basic ethics are sound, is the notion that one should behave ethically in order to avoid hell and to secure heaven. This same ethical error exists in Islam. The Jewish notion of ethical obedience to the Bible is that one should behave ethically solely because it is God's law. This is similar to the Hindu concept of Karma Yoga: that one should behave ethically as an end in itself without fear of punishment or expectation of reward.

The fatal flaw in Orthodox Judaism is that ritual laws, such as dietary laws, are given the same weight as ethical laws, such as the Ten Commandments. Spinoza first showed in his *Theological-Political Treatise* (412) why Jewish ritual is, in part, a mistake. This does not mean that all Jewish ritual is an ethical mistake, but merely that ritual is at best a metaphor for ethical behavior. Art associated with ritual, such as Jewish liturgical music, is an even deeper metaphor for ethical truth.

Thus, Jewish rituals and kosher laws concerning hygiene, diet, slaughter, and even animal sacrifice can be seen as metaphors related to the ethics of good health. Maintaining good health is an ethical obligation.

Jewish sexual rituals say that a man may not have intercourse with his wife until seven days after she has stopped menstruating. Furthermore, he must stop having intercourse with her once she starts to menstruate, but he must have intercourse with her, at proper times, when she demands it. He must never have intercourse with her when she does not desire it. His sexual obligations to his wife are all further governed according to the stress and requirements of his occupation. These rituals are metaphors for sexual ethics, which basically say that a man should first love his wife and, secondarily, have sex with her primarily to please her and to have children with her.

It is unethical to have sexual relations with someone we do not love. We never love someone with whom we would never wish to bear children and whose essential characteristics we would not wish in our children. This does not mean that every sexual act must lead to reproduction. The desire to have children with a spouse, even when this is not possible, is a measure of the love that exists between the spouses. Loving spouses assume full responsibility for maximizing the creativity of each other, and of their children, and of never decreasing the creativity of their children or each other. This notion of sexual ethics is something that many women can probably relate to, but it is probably not acceptable to many men who are not Orthodox Jews.

Great religious art, such as the Kol Nidrei and the Shabat Shalom in Judaism, and the even greater religious compositions of Bach, such as the *Mass in B Minor*, the *Saint Matthew Passion*, the *Cantatas*, and above all *The Art of the Fugue*, are musical metaphors for the deepest and greatest ethical truths. In the plastic arts, there is no greater religious metaphor for Judeo-Christian ethics than the art of Michelangelo, such as the frescoes of the Sistine Chapel, the *Last Judgment*, and his *Pieta*. The metaphorical expression of ethics in art goes back to the works of Atonism in Egypt and the cave paintings of the Cro-Magnon. All great art is the metaphorical expression of great ethical truth. Artistic and personal freedoms are essential if great art is to flourish, as it should.

Although in the Bible God promises the Jews certain rewards for accepting His laws, these are usually long-term rewards, rarely short-term rewards. The basic reward for obedience to the Bible is that any people who practice the Evolutionary Ethic, implicit in the Bible, will in the long run maximize the creativity of their progeny and the creativity of the people with whom they freely interact. This is borne out by history.

Twenty-five hundred years ago the Jews were highly ethical, but not very creative except in the field of ethics. At the same time the Greeks were highly creative in all fields, but not very ethical when compared to the Jews. The classical Greeks were primarily motivated by their desire to dominate others. However, they were ethical in being sincere seekers of the truth, as a means of dominating others. Nevertheless, within less than one thousand years the Greeks had virtually destroyed themselves, and they ceased to be significantly creative in virtually all fields.

The Jews, in the meantime, continued to grow in significant creativity in virtually all fields, while maintaining their ethical creativity, although they were constantly persecuted and had no country of their own after Christianity began. The flaw in Orthodox Jewish ethical evolution, in addition to compulsive ritualism, is that it gave overwhelming weight to studying the Bible and its ethical and ritualistic ramifications, but gave very little weight to studying science. It is ethical and good to study the Bible, but it is unethical to remain deliberately ignorant of science. Ethics may be more important than intelligence, but we have an ethical obligation to maximize both our ethics *and* our intelligence. Although we may remain ethical, we can not be maximally intelligent while choosing to be a scientific illiterate. A knowledge of science is absolutely essential to being maximally creative in the modern world. We separate truth from falsehood solely through the use of the scientific method. This notion is actually in the Bible, in Deuteronomy and the Book of Jeremiah.

Maimonides and Spinoza had both taught that science was the essential method for understanding God. But it was not until the nineteenth century, when the largely secular Jews of Germany, the United States, and other European cultures began to study science and technology, that the Jews became highly creative outside of the field of ethics, although they had begun to be highly creative in mathematics, science and technology in Spain before their expulsion. Modern science, which is one of the most creative consequences of Judeo-Christian ethics, was mainly a Christian invention until the nineteenth century.

That is why, in order to create an ethical political system, we must combine true Christian and true Jewish ethics into a single, coherent, secular system based on the Evolutionary Ethic. Neither Conservative, Reform, nor secular Judaism seem to have the ethical power of Orthodox Judaism, although they are much more accepting of the scientific method and are more likely to produce creative scientists, engineers, and artists than is Orthodox Judaism. But secular, Reform, and Conservative Jews become assimilated in a few generations into gentile society and lose their Jewish identity along with their Jewish ethics. The same happens to the children of their Christian counterparts in the Unitarian and Universalist churches, and to the children of their secular counterparts in the Ethical Culture Society.

Today the Jews, at about one quarter of one percent of the human species, are about fifty percent of the winners of Nobel Prizes in science and economics; they do almost as well in social science, technology, literature, and the other arts and humanities. In the United States, the Jews at less than three percent of the population, are over thirty-five percent of the people listed in *Who's Who*. The Jews get into *Who's Who* almost entirely through their creativity. Before the Soviet Union began to persecute the Jews in a major way, it was estimated by a leading non-Jewish scientist, personally known by me, that the Jews produced three-fourths of the major creativity in the USSR. The same phenomenon occurred in fifteenth century Spain and early twentieth century Germany.

The Jews today are, relative to their numbers, by far the most creative people on earth. However, unethical Jews are no more creative than are unethical gentiles; they are both destructive. Judeo-Christian ethics are a system for maintaining ethics within a people, but they are not entirely effective because we all have free will to reject the ethics of the Bible. Almost by definition, fewer Jews than gentiles reject the ethics of the Bible. This is particularly true of Orthodox Jews. The reasons are ethical choice and natural selection, although the Jews are not a race or even a genetically homogeneous nation (115, 116, 119, also see the work of Dobzhansky), and although the Orthodox, along with other Jews, produce unethical persons.

The Jews are a genetically heterogeneous people bound together by a spiritual and ethical code that transcends race and nationhood, although, through ignorance, there clearly exist chauvinistic and racist Jews. All branches of Judaism are open to all humanity, although the Jews have almost completely stopped proselytizing for over one thousand years, due to Christian and Islamic persecution. It is possible to prove, through blood typing and DNA analysis, that Jews alive today are much more the descendents of converts to Judaism from many nations than exclusively descendents of the ancient Hebrews. Judaism is based much more on memes, transmittable ideas, than on genes, transmittable biological information.

This state of affairs has come about because the two major religions derived from Judaism, Christianity and Islam, have persecuted the Jews. The persecutions within Islam were usually, although not always, relatively minor. They primarily took the form of extra taxes, until the twentieth century and the beginning of Zionism. The persecutions within Christendom were major, and included periodic pogroms, expulsions, the Inquisition, and the Nazi Holocaust. Therefore, there was an enormous practical advantage to the Jews, particularly within Christendom, to convert to the dominant local religion. The sole reason for not converting was because of the higher ethical standards of Judaism, which are more akin to Karma Yoga. Therefore, solely the highly ethical Jews remained Jews, and solely the even-more-ethical Christians converted to Judaism under the threat of death for them and the Rabbis converting them. Unethical Jews, in turn, eventually converted to the dominant local religions for practical personal advantage.

At the same time in order to survive as Jews, the Jews had to be highly intelligent. Stupid Jews, even when highly ethical, were either exterminated or at least put at a reproductive disadvantage by the persecutions of the dominant religions. Therefore, solely persons who were both highly ethical and highly intelligent could survive as Jews. Because $C=IE$, the Jews, through ethical choice and natural selection, became highly creative over the last two thousand years and lost their Hebrew and racial identity from a genetic point of view, although it has survived as a cultural trait. Judaism would be far more effective ethically without this trait.

Modern Jews are much more the ethical and spiritual descendents of Abraham, Aaron, and Moses than their genetic descendents. Although there are purely European Jews, (such as the Ashkenazim),

John David Garcia

Chinese Jews, black Ethiopian Jews, and purely Negroid Jews in southern Africa (the Lemba Tribe), there is some genetic evidence that many Jews can trace their ancestry to Aaron, the Biblical brother of Moses, because of a genetic marker that Jewish men of the priestly class, the Kochanim, carry on their Y chromosome. However, all their other genes seem to come much more from the many other races that converted to Judaism.

Through their creativity and their ethics, the Jews have had throughout history the same kind of growing, creative, catalytic effect as in the twentieth century, but to a much lesser degree: first in ancient Egypt, then in Babylonia, then in Persia, then in Greek Alexandria, then in Islam, then in Spain, then in Germany, then in the United States and the Soviet Union, as well as in other countries to a lesser degree. With the exception of the United States, every civilization that was significantly catalyzed by the Jews eventually became the worst persecutor of the Jews. This speaks well for basic American ethics. As we shall see in the next chapter, the ethical aspects of American Government are fully compatible with the Evolutionary Ethic, the Eight Ethical Principles, the Ten Commandments, and the teachings of Jesus. American Civilization is a spin-off from Christianity, as was first noted by Jefferson (177–179). And Christianity is a spin-off from Judaism.

The nations and civilizations that were significantly catalyzed by the Jews eventually all began to lose their creativity in bureaucratic, apparently irreversible decline. That is because the Jews become the ethical conscience of the nations which they catalyze. When such nations become unethical, they ruthlessly persecute the Jews. This may happen in the United States, even though today it may seem very unlikely. It is part of a historical pattern that has repeated itself many times in the past, most recently in Spain, Germany, Russia, and Islam. The Jews catalyze other nations through their creativity, but it is easier to increase intelligence than to increase ethics.

High intelligence with low (negative) ethics leads to self-destruction, $C = IE$. It is more important to maximize ethics than intelligence, if we must choose solely one of these attributes. It is suicidal to increase intelligence without increasing ethics, or to increase the intelligence of persons who have negative ethics. The Jews have often increased intelligence more than ethics in their host cultures, although they normally do both, at least for awhile until they become assimilated.

A final observation is that the Jews have been most creative within Christian cultures. They have been much less creative within Islamic cultures, although until recent times the Islamic cultures were much more tolerant and less repressive of the Jews than were the Christian cultures. The reason for this is, as Maimonides first observed, that Christianity is closer to Jewish ethics than is Islam, and as a consequence Christianity is more creative than Islam. Furthermore, the teachings of Jesus add a new and very important component to Jewish ethics, the concept of Christian love. The Jews are catalysts, not ethical masters, of their host cultures.

The Jews have grown in ethics because they were able to survive as a persecuted ethical minority without a government, i.e., bureaucracy, of their own. They were persecuted because of their ethics, and they survived in spite of the governments and societies that persecuted them.

The "intelligence" of a culture, i.e., its total collective capacity to predict and control its environment, is directly proportional to the ethics, intelligence, and number of its members and its wealth. One thousand years ago Islam was collectively more intelligent and dynamic than Christianity, but less ethical. Although the intelligence of individual Jews may seem high, the Jews have traditionally had low collective intelligence because of their very low numbers compared to the populations of the empires and nations among which they lived.

THEOREM 5: The more ethical a culture, the less attractive its values will be to persons who are unethical, although these same people will be attracted to the wealth of an ethically superior culture.

Recall that all wealth comes from individual and collective creativity. This is why Christianity and Islam attracted many more adherents than Judaism, although the Jews were very active proselytizers at the beginning of the Christian era. Note that for many years Islam was the fastest growing major religion on earth. The many sects of Christianity may now be collectively overtaking Islam in their rates of growth.

Corollary 5.1: There are more unethical than ethical adults in almost all the cultures of the world.

Corollary 5.2: All the sects of Judaism, such as Christianity, Islam, Reform, and Conservative Judaism, are imperfect bridges for gentiles more easily to learn and accept Jewish ethics, as well as for the Jews to become assimilated into the dominant cultures.

Corollary 5.3: It is the ethical duty of all Jews to communicate their ethical system to all humanity without having to dilute it.

This is very difficult, but clearly not impossible, within the constraints of traditional, Orthodox Judaism. (Until this century almost all the converts to Judaism were converted to Orthodox Judaism.) The main problem is not to confuse ritual with ethics.

Ritual is not ethics. However, many of the ethical norms of Judaism are within metaphoric rituals and art, because the ethics upon which these rituals and art were based were too abstract to explain three thousand years ago to a group of ignorant former slaves. The Bible communicates primarily through metaphors, although it also contains explicit ethical norms, e.g., the Ten Commandments. Many of the 613 commandments of God are also explicitly ethical. Spinoza, although he was a mystic, was the first Jew to totally secularize Jewish ethics, through the imperfect, but mystically true, application of modern science.

Although the Book of Jeremiah as well as other parts of the Bible (e.g., Deut. 13:2) clearly describe scientific method as the means for distinguishing true prophets from false prophets, Judaism is not based on science, but is a mystically revealed religion based on metaphor. If such profound ethical truths as are contained in Judaism and the teachings of Jesus evolved mystically with little or no benefit of science, then mysticism must be accepted and understood as part of the process for maximizing creativity and discovering truth.

THE MYSTICAL PARADIGM

Mysticism means many different things to many different people. As a young man I considered mysticism a form of pathological self-deception, in which people, in order to be happy, choose to deceive themselves increasingly, until they learn to predict and control their own thoughts and perceptions (subjective reality) independently of objective reality. I would often ask the mystics who exhorted me to open myself to mysticism and religion, "What can I predict and control in objective reality by accepting your mystical or religious model of the universe that I cannot predict and control without it?" I never received a satisfactory answer to this question. Therefore, I continued to regard mysticism as a pathology which decreases creativity. I was, at the time, an anti-mystical, antireligious logical positivist (116, 117).

As I grew older, I noticed that the most creative scientists known to me tended to be highly mystical, e.g., Einstein, Bohr, de Broglie, Pauli, Heisenberg, Schrödinger, Jeans, Edington, and more recently David Bohm and Fred Hoyle, among many others (488). The atheistic, non-mystical scientists tended to be much less creative. Therein I had the answer to my question.

When true mysticism is combined with true science, creativity is maximized. However, there is also an anti-scientific, happiness-producing false mysticism which leads to a form of self-deception, and which is commonly called "superstition." Recall that idolatry is a metaphor for superstition, and that "superstition" may also be defined as "other people's religious beliefs."

What enables us to separate truth from falsehood is scientific method, as previously discussed. Therefore, in order to maximize creativity we must combine true mysticism with true science, and be both thoroughly scientific in our mysticism as well as thoroughly mystical in our science. In order to do this we must distill the notion of mysticism down to its essentials. This is what all true mystics, or as Jeremiah would say "true prophets," i.e., Espritals, have as a common belief system. This gives us the following four-part paradigm of true mysticism.

1. The universe has an ethical structure to it; it is neither random, nor chaotic, nor absurd.

2. Within the universe there exists at least one intelligence superior to humanity's which is, at least in part, responsible for the ethical structure of the universe, e.g., God and the angels, or more scientifically and for those less inclined to work with religious metaphors, an infinite hierarchy of Moral Societies (115, 116).

3. It is possible for humanity to communicate with this higher form of ethical intelligence: e.g., Moses and the quantum metaphor

of a bush that burned without being consumed, or the metaphor of the ethical communications between Lot and the angels sent to destroy Sodom and Gomorrah. Prayer is the traditional way of communicating with God, but any creative or ethical act, i.e., any *mitzvah*, is a communication with God. There are many specific, secular ways of communicating with the higher intelligence of ethical order (115).

4. Behaving ethically enhances this communication by creating an open communications channel with God of ever greater bandwidth and ever less noise or randomness. The more ethical our behavior, the better our communication with God, and the more creative we are. *All truth comes from God. God is truth.*

This is the paradigm of true mysticism, which when fully integrated with the scientific paradigm produces scientific mysticism, which enables humanity to be maximally creative.

An Esprital is someone who has had a true mystical experience, believes in the Mystical Paradigm, and is highly ethical in his or her personal behavior. A true mystical experience comes from the insight that comes from a true communication with God that reveals to us a significant new truth previously unknown to us. This manifests itself in a deep ethical truth, a great work of art, a new invention, or the discovery of a scientific law. Yet many Espritals do not know that they are mystics who believe and practice the Mystical Paradigm.

An Esprital does not need to be proficient in science. When an Esprital is not proficient in science, he or she is usually a creative artist, as in the case of Michelangelo, J. S. Bach, or Mary Cassatt, or an ethical teacher, as in the case of Moses, Buddha, Jesus, Saint Francis, Mother Teresa, or the Jewish woman who anonymously authored *A Course in Miracles (510)*. However, when an Esprital is proficient in the science or philosophy of his or her time, then the Esprital is a full scientific mystic who greatly contributes to human evolution and/or material progress, as did Thales, Hypatia, Hildegard von Bingen, Maimonides, Spinoza, Sor Juana Inez de la Cruz, José Ortega y Gassett. Teilhard de Chardin, Barbara McClintock, and Lynn Margulis.

There is a pattern in nature, and in the latest findings of quantum mechanics, which shows us how to be a maximally creative scientific mystic. This does not guarantee that we will be an Esprital. One who has contributed greatly to scientific mysticism is Amit Goswami, a Hindu and former Professor of Physics at the University of Oregon (121–123). However, many of the contributors to this field are Jews. Foremost among them is David Bohm (31–35).

The essence of scientific mysticism is that one must be fully scientific in one's mysticism and fully mystical in one's science in order to maximize creativity. To see that this is the case, and to achieve this apparently paradoxical state of mind, it is essential to thoroughly understand quantum mechanics as it eventually became understood by David Bohm. Bohm was raised as an Orthodox Jew but became a secular Jew and a Marxist as a young adult, although he felt compelled to eat kosher food all his life. He became a complete scientific mystic later in life (302, 598).

Although quantum mechanics is among the most mathematically rigorous of subjects and among the most conceptually abstruse, David Bohm's model is quite simple and easy to understand without using any mathematics or advanced physics. A good knowledge of mathematics and physics will, however, deepen our understanding (31–35, 302, 598). Bohm's model follows, together with my own speculative extrapolations of this model.

QUANTUM MECHANICS

Quantum mechanics is based on the discovery by Max Planck in 1900 that energy is not infinitely divisible, but that it can be transferred solely in discrete units called "quanta." In other words, there is a minimum unit of energy, the quantum. Einstein used this notion in 1907 to explain the photoelectric effect, for which he received the Nobel Prize. (Einstein's greatest contributions, special and general relativity, were not so honored.)

Although Einstein was a major contributor to quantum mechanics, he refused to accept what came to be the conventional interpretation of quantum mechanics. Namely, (1) that the universe was at its core random and unpredictable (contrary to the first part of the mystical paradigm); and (2) that the structure of the universe was holistic, such that it was impossible to observe anything in the universe without changing what we are observing by the very act of the observation (contrary to other parts of the mystical paradigm).

Einstein responded to the first premise by saying, "God does not play dice with the universe"; he responded to the second by saying, "God is subtle but not malicious." Remember that Einstein was a scientific mystic who believed in the God of Spinoza, a single God of deterministic universal order and ethical coherence.

As Einstein grew older, he was increasingly in conflict with the physics establishment over the interpretation of quantum mechanics. The establishment interpretation was called the "Copenhagen interpretation," because it was formulated by Niels Bohr, a Dane who was another secular Jew. The physics establishment was particularly disturbed by the fact that Einstein kept bringing God into the argument. Bohr, in exasperation, finally told Einstein to stop telling God how the universe should be structured. Both sides of the quantum argument were dominated by Jews and scientific mystics, e.g., Bohr and Einstein.

Einstein kept coming up with incredibly ingenious thought experiments, which he called "Gedanken experiments," to disprove the Copenhagen interpretation. Max Born, another Nobel-Prize-winning Jewish physicist, who defended the Copenhagen interpretation, said that every time he received one of these thought experiments from Einstein he knew that he had many weeks of work ahead of him to be able to convince Einstein that the Copenhagen interpretation was not invalidated by his Gedanken experiments.

Finally, in 1935 Einstein and two of his post-doctoral students at Princeton came up with the ultimate thought experiment, which Einstein believed proved that the Copenhagen interpretation was an incomplete description of reality and that there were hidden variables in nature ignored by the Copenhagen interpretation. If we could discover and measure these hidden variables, then the universe would be shown to be properly deterministic, and we could observe without changing what we are observing. This thought experiment is known as the Einstein, Podolsky, Rosen paradox, or EPR, after Einstein and his two young Jewish students (88).

What EPR pointed out is that the Copenhagen interpretation predicts that when two electrons are quantumly correlated, e.g., by originating at a common source, though we send one to the Moon and the other to Mars, the act of observing the electron on the moon will instantaneously, not at the speed of light, disturb the electron on Mars. This contradicts the Special Theory of Relativity (87, 136), which says that a signal cannot be sent anywhere in the universe faster than the speed of light. Therefore, according to Einstein, the Copenhagen interpretation is an incomplete description of reality, and there have to be other, hidden variables in nature.

Quantum mechanics passes the test of science because it is a practical predictor and controller of reality. Quantum mechanics enabled us to develop lasers, holography, super conductors, super fluids, and microelectronic devices, to predict the chemical behavior of elements and molecules, and to do many other practical things according to the formulations of Heisenberg, Schrödinger, Dirac, and Feynman (another secular Jew). Therefore, quantum mechanics is valid. However, the EPR paradox remained.

Bohr resolved the paradox by categorically stating that, in this case, quantum mechanics, not relativity, made the correct prediction, because of the holistic structure of the universe. Naturally, Einstein could not accept this, and he and Bohr stopped talking to each other about these matters, and their previously warm friendship cooled. It turns out that both were right and both were wrong.

In 1965 an Irish physicist by the name of John Stewart Bell, deeply influenced by David Bohm, showed that, given the validity of the EPR paradox, there might indeed be hidden variables, but they must be non-local (25, 26). "Locality" implies a universe where things are tied together in such a way that they cannot interact faster than the speed of light. To say that things are non-local is to say that they are outside of our time and space, and may interact instantaneously at some level, no matter how large the distances between them. This implies action at a distance, which Einstein called "a spooky concept."

Finally, in 1982 a team of French physicists led by Alain Aspect (7) showed that EPR and Bell were both right. Therefore, Bohr was right, but Einstein was also right about hidden variables, though they are non-local (25, 26). (Einstein believed all variables to be local.) From this, David Bohm was able to show that there is infinite true information in a universe outside of our time and space (32, 33, 35).

Early in his career, David Bohm had shown that the EPR paradox applied to other quantum objects, such as photons and neutrons, and not solely to electrons (31). Therefore, the EPR paradox is now referred to as the EPRB paradox. It was so referred to by Bell and the Aspect team. After being exiled from the United States because of his extremely ethical, courageous, but misguided, stances against the McCarthy-era witch hunts, Bohm worked in Brazil, Israel, and England, where he made many discoveries in physics, such as the famous Aharanov-Bohm effect, discovered while working with some Israelis in England (302).

In 1951, under the close, personal influence of Einstein, David Bohm began developing a new hidden-variables model of quantum mechanics while he was still an instructor at Princeton. He continued this development for the rest of his life; it led to him to become a very profound mystic as well as a highly creative physicist. This model was validated by the Aspect experiments; it is known as the holographic or implicate-order model of the universe (32–34). I accept it as true, although a large majority of contemporary physicists are leery of it.

The Copenhagen model, further removed from mysticism, is much more comfortable to conventional scientists. However, within the framework of the Copenhagen interpretation, two very great Jewish scientists, mathematical genius John von Neumann and Nobel-Prize-winning physicist Eugene Wigner, proposed as early as the 1930's that quantum phenomena were due to the direct interaction of the human mind with material reality (142, 487). They recognized that human consciousness and quantum reality were inextricably interconnected (487).

The holographic model, as I interpret it (115), says that there is an infinite, non-local holographic universe that, in a sense, contains our local finite universe as well as an infinity of other universes. This infinite universe is a universe of pure, true information. Quantum phenomena in our universe are an expression of the implicate order of the holographic universe manifesting itself in the explicate order of our local universe. *God is truth.*

The holographic universe, in my interpretation, contains all of its information at each point, as does a regular hologram. Therefore, our local universe contains all the information of the holographic universe at each local point. The hidden variables are non-local quanta of information which pass through the quantum field from the implicate order of the holographic universe to the explicate order of our local universe. Matter in our local universe is transformed by this information in direct proportion to its degree of evolution. These concepts (115–117) lead to my generalized model of evolution.

QUANTUM EVOLUTION

Evolution occurs through a growing hierarchy of ever more complex and intelligent species incorporating ever more information from the implicate order into their genetic and/or neural structures, thereby transforming themselves into still more intelligent species within the explicate order of our local universe.

An electron represents a very low level of material evolution, and it essentially responds randomly, but coherently, as it receives information from the implicate order. A cell is more intelligent and less random in its responses to quantum information than any form of nonliving matter; as a consequence it evolves faster than matter. A metazoan is still less random in its response to quantum information, and it evolves even faster than the cell. This process continues in harmony with the evolution of the nervous system from simple metazoan to fish, fish to amphibian, amphibian to reptile, reptile to mammal, thereby creating the collective intelligence of the biosphere, until humanity begins to respond ethically to the information from the implicate order, thereby catalyzing its own evolution by becoming ever more creative.

I point out in *Creative Transformation* (115) that this quantum hierarchy of evolution proceeds in systems of complementary pairs and hierarchies of four complementary pairs. For example, the first jump in atomic evolution occurs in a hierarchy of four complementary pairs of electrons and protons that constitute four hydrogen atoms, which when fused give us a helium atom. Protons and electrons are complementary in their charges, masses, and atomic cross sections. Therefore, an electron and a proton form a complementary pair, which we call a hydrogen atom. Hydrogen atoms evolve into all the other atoms through fusion in the stars and other physical processes.

The fusion of helium atoms produces a carbon atom, which is the most chemically generalized atom, in being equally an electron donor and an electron receiver. Furthermore, a carbon atom is a system of four complementary pairs, in having four active protons and four active electrons which enables it, with oxygen, nitrogen, phosphorous, hydrogen, and other abundant light elements, to begin to form all the organic compounds leading to chemical evolution and the beginning of life.

Furthermore, life begins when there is a new chemical hierarchy of four complementary pairs of nucleotides: cytosine, guanine, thymine, and adenine. These in turn form new complementary pairs in the DNA molecule, which in turn forms new systems of complementary pairs with protein, which produces the phenomenon we call *life* from non-living matter. Varela and Maturana have called this process, by which protein and DNA interact synergistically within the cell to produce the epiphenomenon of life, *autopoiesis*. I have generalized this term in *Creative Transformation* (115), using it to refer to any creative exchange of complementary information in a system of complementary pairs.

This process of generalized autopoiesis leads to metazoa and other multicellular life forms, where there is autopoiesis among cells. Then there is autopoiesis among neurons, which leads to the brain in the lower animals. This process continues all the way to the human brain, which is a system of four complementary pairs of brains. The left brain is a complement to the right brain. Within the human brain there is the brain of a fish; then the brain of a reptile, the R complex; then the brain of a primitive mammal, the limbic system, which we share with all mammals; and finally our highest brain, the neocortex, which we share with the higher mammals. Within the neocortex we have those characteristics of mind that make us ethical beings and uniquely human.

As I have indicated in *Creative Transformation (115)*, the next stage of evolution is a new higher form of autopoiesis between four complementary pairs of human brains. Men and women can be shown to be far more complementary in their neural structures than in the rest of their bodies (527–555). Therefore the way to maximize human creativity is in a new form of autopoietic organization among four complementary pairs of men and women, i.e., four men and four women who are ethically committed to maximizing each other's creativity. I call these basic new forms of human organization "octets." Octets and super-metazoan autopoiesis will be discussed later in this book.

The same process which produces benign mutations, through new hierarchies of autopoiesis which increase the genetically determined intelligence of ever more new species, produces, in ethical beings, creative ideas which increase the collective, extra-genetically determined intelligence of the species. Reality is based on true information, not on energy or matter. The emotional, personal God of the Bible is a metaphor for the creative, impersonal universe of infinite truth beyond our time and space; therefore, as the Bible says, "God is a spirit" (Gen. 1:2).

In accordance with the mystical paradigm and my model of the nature of the holographic universe, the more ethically we behave, the more quantum information flows into our consciousness from the implicate order, and the more creative we become. However, there is a quantum quarantine in the universe (115) such that unethical persons become closed to this higher quantum information; they cannot create no matter how intelligent they are, so long as they remain unethical. The quantum quarantine also inhibits the ability of ethically immature species, such as humanity, to travel between the stars (115).

Humans, and other ethically immature species, using classical technology based on Newtonian and Einsteinian physics, cannot even begin to imagine how it may be possible to travel between the stars in a lifetime at any reasonable cost and using a feasible amount of energy. However, there is a quantum type of technology, suggested by the physics of David Bohm, which can be used to engage in virtual travel between the stars, by using quantum coherence between moral beings in different star systems to ethically transfer true information (115).

True information is the basis of all existence and the evolution of matter, life, and mind. Quantum technology, still to be developed, may enable us to transfer information instantaneously, as in the EPRB paradox, between the stars, but not to move physical objects between the stars. Classical information cannot be exchanged except within certain quantum limits. Solely quantum information can be exchanged without limits between coherent moral beings. If humanity can ever develop this quantum technology, it will have become a Moral Society. The major purpose of an ethical government is to help humanity evolve from an Ethical State into a Moral Society (see Glossary). These concepts are discussed in a previous book (115).

Because **C=IE**, an ethical person, no matter how low his or her intelligence, will be creative, because of positive ethics. However, an unethical person, no matter how great his or her intelligence, can never be creative, because his or her ethics are negative; such persons will in fact be destructive in direct proportion to their intelligence. When ethics are negative, creativity is negative, i.e., unethical persons produce more destructive acts than creative acts; ethical persons do the opposite. Negative creativity is destructiveness. However, it is unethical to be certain about who is ethical or unethical (EP 6). The cosmic quarantine protects all ethical beings from the intelligence of unethical beings.

There exist techniques, given in my previous book, for stimulating the flow of quantum information into our consciousness (115). The most powerful of these techniques is simply to behave as ethically as possible in every situation we encounter, without expectation of external reward and without fear of punishment. This is in harmony with the Talmud and the teachings of Jesus, which say we should expect no reward from doing a *mitzvah* (an ethical act) other than the opportunity to do more *mitzvahs*. Although there may be external rewards for doing a *mitzvah*, we should be satisfied with the knowledge that the more *mitzvahs* we do, the more *mitzvahs* we can do. Hindu scriptures say the same.

In harmony with Judaism, Jesus, Spinoza, and quantum mechanics, God, the spirit, may be seen as the infinite, quantum process, outside of our time and space, by which the universe grows forever in creativity. Each evolving creature chooses to become closer to God, by growing in intelligence, ethics, and creativity in ever greater quantum leaps of four complementary pairs, which for humans are octets.

The simple choice to innovate superior behavior randomly, which any living creature, even a bacterium, can choose to do, catalyzes the transfer of true quantum information from the implicate order to the explicate order of the genes, thereby producing a benign mutation

(115). Humans now do this by behaving ethically and creating new extra-genetic information which they teach to other ethical beings.

Evolution through purely random mutations can be shown mathematically to be impossible, using conventional probability theory (155). To produce creative results from purely random processes requires an additional source of information, the implicate order. Perhaps solely the implicate order may make the evolution of the biosphere possible, through punctuated equilibrium (115). Evolution is the mechanism by which God creates creative mind from uncreative matter.

God as an infinite, abstract, spiritual process cannot be represented by visual imagery. Therefore, as the Bible says, we must reject all forms of superstition, for which idolatry is a metaphor. God may be seen as the abstract infinite process that engenders both evolution and personal creativity throughout the universe. We worship the one true God by learning, teaching, and creating new truth to the maximum limits of our capability, while never decreasing truth for anyone (115).

When we receive information from the implicate order, so that we may perform a creative act, we are communicating with God. When we have only a little scientific information, the quantum information is communicated mainly metaphorically. As we grow in ethics, intelligence, and scientific information, this communication is ever less metaphorical. A major prophet is someone who creatively derandomizes the ethical information from the implicate order and communicates it to humanity, as did Moses with the Torah and as did Isaiah, Elijah, Jeremiah, Jesus, and the other major prophets. Minor prophets engage in minor creativity. But as Jesus said, "Beware of false prophets. By their fruits you shall know them." We should never trust people who are uncreative in direct proportion to their intelligence.

The highest form of creativity is the communication of divine ethics. That is why the Bible as well as the ethical scriptures of all the major religions are a repository of true information from the implicate order, which in both metaphorical and non-metaphorical ways tell a people how to become ever more ethical, and as a consequence ever more creative. This is particularly true of Judaism. That is why the Jews, who are not a race or even a genetically homogenous nation, have continued to grow in creativity, while many powerful nations who tried to dominate and exterminate the Jews have collapsed and ceased to be creative or even to exist.

JEWISH GOVERNMENT

The initial Jewish Government as described in the Bible was a combination of elected kings, true prophets, and priests. No one could become or remain king without approval of the prophets and priests. This gave effective feedback to the government and kept it ethical, since the prophets and priests had moral authority but no temporal power. It was their form of checks and balances. As the priests acquired temporal power, and the prophets were no longer true, the system became corrupt, as was first shown by Spinoza (412). These corruptions were the equivalent of "campaign contributions."

In his *Theological-Political Treatise* (412), Spinoza shows why this form of government was originally ethical, why it became corrupt, and why it is no longer possible. Instead, we have the example of modern Jewish Government in the State of Israel.

Changes in Jewish ethics may be produced by the State of Israel, which provides Jews with a national instead of an ethical identity. Over the last two thousand years the Jews were able to evolve ethically, in part, because they had no government of their own and consequently no bureaucracy, although they had the moral authority and wisdom of the Rabbis. The State of Israel and the assimilation of non-Orthodox Jews to their host cultures, not the legacy of the Holocaust, will be the major influences upon Jewish ethics in the future.

Nation states, even when governed by a majority of Jews, tend to put short-term political gains ahead of long-term ethical gains. Not all Jews are ethical, since we do not inherit all of our ethics solely from our mother. (Most forms of Judaism, except for some of the ultra-Orthodox, define a "Jew" as a convert or as someone who has a Jewish mother.) As with other nation states without ethical government, a majority-ruled Jewish state will become ever more dominated by unethical politicians, while its most creative citizens constantly lose power. My Israeli friends all insist that the most corrupt political parties in Israel are the religious parties. Israel is already highly bureaucratic.

Israel is bureaucratic, socialistic, and inherently unethical because it has a majority-rule form of democratic government. Recall that majority rule is inherently unethical and cannot produce, or even maintain, an ethical government, because it is at best a tyranny of the majority. At worst it is a tyranny of a minority that manipulates the majority through comforting, but self-serving, lies that the majority delights in hearing. Such is the case in the United States, Israel, and other democratic nations under majority rule. All forms of tyranny are unethical, including the so-called "benevolent tyrannies."

Nations which have been catalyzed by the Jews, when they reject the ethics of the Bible, persecute the Jews and fall into irreversible bureaucratic entropy. In relatively recent times this happened to Spain, Germany, and the Soviet Union. It may happen to the United States. However, an ethical person's loyalty is first to the Evolutionary Ethic, which is to say to God, not to an ethically corrupt nation state or empire, much less to an individual tyrant.

Judaism transcends nationhood. That is why the Jews continued to grow in creativity without a nation state or bureaucracy of their own, while many mighty empires that persecuted them have crumbled first to bureaucracy, and then to uncreative nothingness. But the Jews could not create an ethical government through majority rule.

The development of an ethical alternative to all forms of tyranny is the goal of this book. But this takes more than Jewish ethics. It takes a combination of true Jewish ethics and true Christian Ethics, without Orthodox or Christian superstition, plus Evolutionary Ethics and science.

Evil will always destroy itself, but it can in the interim destroy much that is good. Jesus taught that we should suffer evil, but the Old Testament is uncompromising and ruthless about dealing with evil. The Evolutionary Ethic implies that it is always unethical to tolerate evil (5th E.P.).

Christianity is much more tolerant of evil than Judaism, because Jesus taught, correctly, that evil will always destroy itself. However, this does not mean that we should tolerate evil. How to deal with evil is a basic problem for ethical government. We must neither tolerate nor ignore evil, nor use evil means to combat evil. Although all people may be born ethical, many become unethical through the actions of unethical government, which rewards evil and punishes ethics. The world will either become ethical or destroy itself.

The future of Judeo-Christian ethics is to become completely integrated with the Evolutionary Ethic and science, and thereby clearly to communicate its ethical message to all humanity. This message is best communicated through ethical and creative example by Jews and Christians, while encouraging converts and becoming friendlier to them. A Jew, as well as a Christian, should be redefined as a person dedicated to living an ethical life without expectation of external reward or fear of punishment. All unethical "Jews" and unethical "Christians" are apostates.

CHAPTER TWO

KEEPING WHAT WORKS

The Evolutionary Ethic is a revolutionary new concept which leads directly to the political system to be developed in the next chapter. However, the essence of Judeo-Christian ethics, as expressed in the Ten Commandments and the teachings of Jesus, are implicit in the Evolutionary Ethic. The ethical essence and the practical reality of political ethics as expressed in the Declaration of Independence and the Bill of Rights, together with the Thirteenth, Fourteenth, Fifteenth and Nineteenth Amendments to the U.S. Constitution, are also implicit in the Evolutionary Ethic, although no democratic constitution is intrinsically ethical if it leads to majority rule. Solely the concepts of self-government and maximum respect for the individual are intrinsically ethical. In this chapter we will show how these more familiar ethical concepts of Judeo-Christian ethics and the political ethics of the Declaration of Independence and parts of the Constitution of the United States relate to the Eight Ethical Principles, the Evolutionary Ethic, and the political principles and system to be developed in this book.

We should note that having a partially ethical constitution does not necessarily produce an ethical government. The Government of the United States stopped even having a pretense of being ethical long ago. In fact, it has become increasingly, but not monotonically, unethical since the end of the Monroe Administration. But it is only in the last hundred years that each succeeding President has usually, not always, been significantly less ethical than the previous President, with the notable exceptions of Harry Truman and Jimmy Carter. The latter was clearly an ethical, but ineffective, President. Without the short-lived revulsion against the Nixon Administration, a man like Jimmy Carter would never have been elected President. Bill Clinton and Al

Gore were as unethical, or worse, than Nixon ever was, but they covered their tracks more effectively.

THE TEN COMMANDMENTS

Although there are 613 divinely ordained commandments in Judaism, some Orthodox Jews believe that all 613 commandments can be derived from the Ten Commandments. As was mentioned in the previous chapter, the Ten Commandments can be derived from the Evolutionary Ethic and the Eight Ethical Principles. From the Evolutionary Ethic, the Eight Ethical Principles, and the Ten Commandments all the *ethical* commandments of the Bible may be derived as well as the metaphorical ethical implications of the ritualistic commandments, but not, to the best of my knowledge, the ritual itself.

Therefore, I reject Jewish ritual, but not its ethics, both explicit and metaphorically implicit. But along with Spinoza I believe we should be respectful of other people's rituals, if they are not overtly unethical, but merely trivial to our perceptions. That is how I feel about both Jewish and Christian ritual. I personally find most forms of ritual obnoxious. But the Ten Commandments are explicitly ethical, although they all require rational interpretation in order to apply them properly in our personal lives as well as in ethical political systems, such as in the Ethical Constitution to be developed in the next chapter. Later, practical methods to implement such a constitution will be suggested.

The Ten Commandments are common to both Judaism and Christianity and are the core of Judeo-Christian ethics, although the early Catholic Church revised the Ten Commandments, as well as the teachings of Jesus, in order to make its form of idolatry acceptable and to justify its bureaucratic structure. Most Protestant sects have translated the Ten Commandments more correctly, but also with errors. We shall use mostly the Revised American Standard Version of the King James translation to express the Ten Commandments.

The teachings of Jesus are extremely anti-bureaucratic and have added a new dimension to Jewish ethics. Jewish ethics are based on a universal sense of justice. Jesus' interpretation of Jewish ethics emphasizes universal love over justice, although universal love is also within Jewish ethics. Therefore, purely Christian ethics will be discussed separately, after first analyzing the rational and political implications of the Ten Commandments, which we now consider.

FIRST COMMANDMENT

First Part. I am the Lord your God who brought you out of the land of Egypt, out of the house of Bondage.

Second Part. You shall have no other Gods before me.

Third Part. You shall not make for yourself a graven image, or any likeness of anything that is in heaven above, or is in the earth beneath; you shall not bow down to them or serve them, for I the Lord your God am a jealous God, visiting iniquity of the fathers upon the children to the third and the fourth generation of those who hate me, but showing steadfast love to those who keep my commandments.

Interpretation of the First Commandment

First Part: The concept of an emotional, personal God, as we saw in the previous chapter, is a metaphor for the impersonal quantum universe of infinite truth outside of our time and space. God is not an anthropomorphic being, but is rather the process of ever increasing creativity throughout the universe. Solely processes are infinite, never anthropomorphic beings. We are created in God's ethical image, not His physical image, which does not exist.

All creative changes in the universe, such as Moses leading the Jews out of Egypt, occur solely through the intervention of God through His true messengers, e.g., Moses, or His angels. Anthropomorphic angels are metaphors for higher stages of evolution, for ethical beings who have become moral (see Glossary: Moral Societies), i.e., highly, but not yet irreversibly, ethical. Solely God is irreversibly ethical (115, 116, 117).

Second Part: We cannot put any person, principle, or thing before God. We must worship solely the one true God, i.e., the quantum universe beyond our time and space that is the root cause of all evolution and each creative act in the universe. We worship the one true God by learning, teaching, and creating objective truth to the limits of our capability, not rejecting the subjective message of true mysticism out of hand, but rather testing it scientifically. This is the Evolutionary Ethic.

Third Part: The one true God is a spirit, i.e., an infinite, non-local process of infinite complexity beyond our time and space, and cannot be truly represented by any graven, earthly, or finite image. If we hate the one true God, i.e., behave unethically and decrease anyone's creativity including our own, we shall destroy our own creativity and that of our children unto the third or the fourth generation. Therefore, ethics are partly hereditary and are not determined entirely by our environment, but our descendants can recover their ethics after several generations. If we follow the commandments of God, i.e., behave ethically, we shall be loved by God, i.e., we shall enhance our creativity, that of our children and potentially of all our future progeny.

SECOND COMMANDMENT

You shall not take the name of the Lord your God in vain; for the Lord will not hold him guiltless who takes His name in vain.

Interpretation of the Second Commandment

The name of God is a description of an infinite process infinitely complex. Our knowledge is always finite. Therefore, we never know the true name of God; i.e., a finite being can never fully understand the infinite process that is God. To take the name of God in vain is to speak falsely in the name of God. Since, according to Spinoza and to Bohm's holographic model of the universe, all of nature and everything in it is a part of God, to say anything false about nature is as much a taking of the name of God in vain as is swearing an oath falsely. This is the ethics of science.

Since the universe is an interconnected whole, as in David Bohm's holographic model, we can never fully understand any part of the universe unless we understand all of it, and we will never understand all of it. But we can grow in knowledge and creativity forever, becoming ever closer to God by understanding Him and emulating Him, i.e., by following the Evolutionary Ethic. Therefore, it is unethical to be certain about any aspect of nature, because our knowledge is always at best incomplete, and at worst false. We are believing falsely and speaking falsely when we are certain and express certainty about any aspect of nature. To be certain about nature is to take the name of God in vain.

We must never say anything that is false under the name of God, i.e., swear an oath falsely, fake a scientific experiment, or express certainty about nature or anything in nature other than our own mind, which is the only thing in the universe about which we have direct certain knowledge. We can be certain solely about having our thoughts and perceptions, but never about their causes, since all truth comes from God.

God is infinite. Completely true information about any part of the infinite holographic process which is God is also infinite. We are finite, and all the information we will ever have will be finite. Therefore, we can never be certain about any aspect of nature, except our own thoughts and perceptions. This is the Sixth Ethical Principle, and it implies the Seventh Ethical Principle, that it is ethical to doubt. So long as we doubt, we are open to the truth that comes solely from God.

THIRD COMMANDMENT

Remember the Sabbath day to keep it holy. Six days shall you labor and do all your work; but the seventh day is a Sabbath to the Lord your God; in it you shall not do any work, you, your son, or your daughter, your manservant or your maidservant, or your cattle, or the sojourner who is within your gates; for in six days the Lord made heaven and earth, the seas, and all that is in them, and rested the seventh day; therefore the Lord blessed the Sabbath day and hallowed it.

Interpretation of the Third Commandment

The natural cycle of creativity for all ethical beings and processes is that of seven time periods. For humans a time period for creativity is twenty-four hours. For God these time periods may be very different, since He exists outside of our time and space (377, 378).

In order to maximize our creativity, we must always rest for a full time period after six consecutive creative time periods, as well as during every individual time period by sleeping. Therefore resting is not doing nothing. Rest is essential to maximize our creativity. We must sleep every day, and sleeping is a creative act necessary to maintain our intelligence and maximize our creativity. The most creative thing we do while sleeping is to dream.

After six creative time periods we rest for a full time period in order to maximize our overall creativity. While awake, the most creative way to rest is to contemplate the nature of God and God's ethics (the Evolutionary Ethic, the Eight Ethical Principles, the Ten Commandments, and other ethical principles tested by time, such as the Declaration of Independence and the Bill of Rights.) Therefore, on the Sabbath we do no remunerative work, and we devote our day to contemplating God and His ethics. We do this by ourselves if we must, but we are obligated to share these contemplations first with our families and second with our friends and neighbors. On the Sabbath we neither work nor cause anyone else to work. This is how we maximize creativity on the Sabbath.

Since we have an ethical obligation on the Sabbath to our family, friends, and neighbors, it is optimal for any creative society to have a consensus on which day of the week shall be the Sabbath. The Jews have for over three thousand years chosen Saturday. The Christians for almost two thousand years have chosen Sunday. The Muslims for about thirteen hundred years have chosen Friday. What is essential on our Sabbath is the contemplation of the nature of God and His ethics without doing any directly or indirectly remunerative work, not the practice of some particular ritual. The more compulsively ritualistic a religion, the less ethical and creative its adherents will be.

FOURTH COMMANDMENT

Honor your father and your mother that your days may be long in the land that the Lord your God gives you.

Interpretation of the Fourth Commandment

We have ethical obligations to all humanity, including our enemies. However, we must always behave ethically toward our parents and always treat them with love, respect, and honor. We do this by never doing or saying anything that will diminish their creativity, and by always seeking to increase their creativity, always speaking the truth to them in the most loving way possible. We must do this no matter how unethical or trivial we may perceive our parents to be, because we can never be certain about these things, and we should always treat all persons with love, respect, and honor. We begin with our parents.

However, we are not obligated to stay in the household of our parents if they are destructive to us, and we are, in fact, obligated to leave unethical parents. However, so long as we live in their household, we are ethically obligated to honor and obey them. We must always honor our parents.

If we do not honor our parents, our own creativity will be diminished, because we shall have behaved unethically. We owe our life, our intelligence, our ethics, and our original creativity to our parents. That is why we must always honor them as an ethical obligation. It is always unethical to display any form of disrespect toward our parents, and they should not tolerate it. If parents do tolerate disrespect from their children, then they are diminishing their own children's creativity, which is an unethical act. It is always unethical to tolerate destructive behavior (5th E.P.).

FIFTH COMMANDMENT

You shall not kill.

Interpretation of the Fifth Commandment

The Fifth Commandment is more than an admonition not to murder. Neither shall we kill except when absolutely necessary to defend our creativity, that of our children, or of our friends and neighbors from unethical assault. Both Judaism and most forms of Christianity recognize the right to self-defense. But self-defense should not be lightly undertaken.

By the Fifth Ethical Principle, it is always unethical to allow our creativity or that of our children or other ethical persons to be diminished, and we are justified, if we are very careful, in using deadly force to defend the creativity of all ethical persons. This is the case because it is unethical to tolerate destructive behavior. But since it is also unethical to be certain, we must be extremely careful not to apply any kind of force to others unless it is to relieve immediate, unethical danger to someone's creativity. Therefore, it is unethical to impose the death penalty on deadly criminals who are already restrained and under control, but we also have the obligation to protect the creativity of society from such dangerous persons. Prison is an unethical way of doing this.

Prisons, as currently constituted in most parts of the world, degrade the prisoner and do not give him an adequate opportunity to rehabilitate himself. A more ethical alternative to deal with all criminals, not just murderers, is to exile them to a carefully guarded island with other prisoners of the same kind, where they will not be brutalized by unethical bureaucrats, but will be given an ethical opportunity to rehabilitate themselves if they wish it. If they do not choose to rehabilitate themselves, they should remain in exile until they do so choose. It is ethical to increase the ethics of criminals. How to rehabilitate criminals ethically is a topic beyond the scope of this book.

A final observation on the Fifth Commandment is that we cannot murder another even to protect, but not defend, our own life. This is to say that we cannot save our own life at the expense of another innocent life. We can take the life of someone solely when that person is in the act of unethically diminishing someone's creativity and he or she will not cease without the use of deadly force.

We cannot take the life of another, even to save our own life, if that person is innocent of any unethical action against our life. If we ever take another's life, we must never lose sight of the fact that we might have been mistaken in our action, since we are never certain. We can take a life solely when absolutely necessary in defense of the ethical life of another. It is unethical to unnecessarily degrade, in any way, the life of another or to tolerate the degradation of life by anyone.

Sixth Commandment

You shall not commit adultery.

Interpretation of the Sixth Commandment

Among Orthodox Jews, the Sixth Commandment is interpreted to prohibit all illicit sexual relationships, which, in addition to adultery, include rape, incest, homosexuality, and bestiality. Given that the ancient Jews were polygynous, the concept of adultery is quite complex in Judaism, and involves primarily married women and men who have sexual relationships with a person married to another. The Jewish concept of incest is equally complex. There are many conflicting schools regarding exactly what is an illicit sexual act.

According to the Second Ethical Principle, to never decrease anyone's creativity including our own, the Sixth Commandment means never having a sexual relationship that will lead to the decrease of anyone's creativity, including our own, even at the cost of our own life.

In Orthodox Judaism there are only three sins which we must always avoid, even at the cost of our own life: idolatry (superstition), murder, and illicit sexual relations. Public idolatry is considered the worst kind of idolatry because it may contribute to the ethical degradation of another. We should, at all costs, avoid communicating superstition or the illusions of certainty to others.

The Evolutionary Ethic says that we should die before deliberately reducing anyone's creativity, including our own. It is unethical to allow anyone to degrade another human being, which can be done sexually. According to the Evolutionary Ethic, the most creative form of sexuality is ethically committed, heterosexual monogamy. The Evolutionary Ethic is somewhat more rigorous in regard to sexual ethics than is the Sixth Commandment, but they are similar.

SEVENTH COMMANDMENT

You shall not steal.

Interpretation of the Seventh Commandment

The Evolutionary Ethic and the Fifth and Seventh Commandments say that a person's life and property belong entirely to him or herself. Furthermore, no one has a right to any part of another person's life or property without his or her consent. Therefore, taxes imposed on minorities by majorities are inherently unethical. They are a form of theft. Taxes, to be ethical, must be fair and must not favor one group over another. We shall see how this can be made practical within the concept of an Ethical State.

A person's life and property are a part of his or her intelligence, i.e., ability to predict and control the total environment, and as a consequence part of his or her creativity. Therefore, stealing any part of someone's life or property diminishes his or her creativity and should never be done.

EIGHTH COMMANDMENT

You shall not bear false witness against your neighbor.

Interpretation of the Eighth Commandment

In Judaism the notion of "neighbor" refers to a fellow Jew. Recall that we use this notion differently, i.e., to refer to any ethical person. The Commandments still apply with our broader notion of "neighbor." The worst lie we can tell is a lie that leads to the false conviction of another. The Evolutionary Ethic says we should never tell a lie to anyone about anything, because that will diminish truth for them and as a consequence diminish their intelligence and their creativity. Therefore, a lie of any kind is always unethical, but the worst lie is knowingly and falsely to convict another of a crime he or she did not commit. This does not mean that we always have to speak the truth to everyone.

We should always speak the truth, or not speak at all. To persons we believe to be engaged in unethical activity we should not lie, but instead remain uncommunicative, except as to ethics. The general principle is that we should increase the intelligence solely of ethical persons; it is unethical to increase the intelligence of unethical persons because C=IE. Thus, increasing the intelligence of people with negative ethics will only increase their destructiveness. As it is unethical to be certain about who is ethical or unethical, we should always begin our communication with the communication of true ethics. This is always ethical, whether our audience is ethical or unethical. As Patanjali said, we should begin every new conversation by speaking about God (298).

Persons who are not interested in true ethics should not have their intelligence increased. However, when in doubt, in an emergency, we should always assume that persons are ethical and should communicate the information that is necessary to save a life or preserve an intelligence, without going through a test of ethics. We should always be very careful in going beyond this limit in communicating truth to others.

When persons ask us to teach truth of any kind to them, we may carefully assume that they are truth seekers, and as a consequence ethical, if we have no evidence that they are systematically destructive to themselves and/or to others. The safest course, to avoid engaging in a destructive act, is always to begin our communications with a brief discussion of ethics, and to stop discussion if there is no interest. This principle is one reason why many great spiritual teachers end up living as hermits.

NINTH AND TENTH COMMANDMENTS

You shall not covet your neighbor's house, you shall not covet your neighbor's wife, or his manservant, or his maidservant, or his ox or his ass, or anything that is your neighbor's.

Ninth Commandment

You shall not covet any part of your neighbor's life or property.

Interpretation of the Ninth Commandment

Recall our broader use of "neighbor." It is not sufficient merely not to steal your neighbor's goods because that diminishes his creativity. Neither must you even covet his property or any part of his life or of his property rights, for that diminishes your own creativity and may induce you to steal or even to kill. All that we have in life should come from our creative actions. It diminishes our creativity to value the fruits of our creativity more than the creativity itself; it diminishes our creativity even more to value the fruits of someone else's creativity more than we value our own creativity.

81

In order to maximize our creativity, we must cease valuing the fruits of anyone's creativity, including our own, and learn to take creative action as in end in itself, without expectation of external reward or fear of any punishment.

It is an ethical duty to seek creativity as an end in itself. It is at best trivial to behave ethically in exchange for external rewards. Both trivial and unethical behavior are destructive to our creativity. Therefore, we are behaving destructively and unethically when we covet our neighbor's property or any of his or her rights to his or her own life and property.

Tenth Commandment

You shall not covet your neighbor's wife.

Interpretation of the Tenth Commandment

Recall that for us "neighbor" is any ethical person. Not only is adultery unethical because it is destructive to you and to your neighbor's marriage and, as a consequence, to society, but the coveting of your neighbor's wife is also unethical, because it shall also diminish your creativity and put you in peril of committing adultery. Although your neighbor's wife is not his property, a committed relationship between two people, whether it has been formalized by marriage or is less formal, is a holy relationship, and you should not even lust in your heart after your neighbor's spouse, for when you do you are behaving unethically, diminishing your creativity, and putting your neighbor's marriage in peril.

We should seek our sexual partners solely from unattached persons who truly love us for our creativity, and whom we in turn truly love and value for their creativity. There is never any true or ethical love without a commitment to the creativity of our partner.

If you should ever feel lust for your neighbor's spouse, you should meditate on this, and do your best to overcome it, and discreetly avoid your neighbor's spouse until you have overcome this lust. Otherwise, you are heading down the path of destructive behavior. By the Fifth Ethical Principal you are ethically obligated to be intolerant of destructive behavior or its precursors in yourself as well as in others. *What God has joined together, let no man put asunder.*

CHRISTIAN ETHICS

Although the Sermon on the Mount is normally considered the best summary of Christian ethics, as distinct from purely Jewish ethics, the simplest, clearest, and most concise summary of Christian ethics is in the Gospel of John. When Jesus is about to be led away to be crucified, the Apostles ask him, "Master, what commandment do you leave us." Jesus immediately replies, "My sole commandment is that you love one another, as I have loved you." Then almost immediately Jesus repeats himself, for the sole time in the Gospels, and says, "My sole commandment is that you love one another." This is the essence of Christian ethics as distinct from Jewish ethics.

In the Sermon on the Mount, Jesus went so far as to say we should also love our enemies, in contradiction to the Jewish admonition to hate our enemies. Therefore, the essence of Christian ethics is that we must try to maximize the creativity of everyone, including our enemies. Note that neither Jesus' sole commandment, nor the Sermon on the Mount, nor the Ten Commandments have anything to do with ritual.

An enemy is any unethical person who systematically decreases the creativity of anyone, including himself. However, we can never be certain about who is an enemy. Therefore, the sole way to behave ethically toward a potential enemy who appears systematically destructive is to communicate true ethics to this possible enemy in the most loving way possible.

By "love" Jesus clearly did not mean sexual love, which the Greeks called "eros." Saint Paul used another Greek word to denote the notion of Christian love. The word he used was "agape." This is a spiritual notion of love which does not involve sexuality, although it may exist in conjunction with sexuality. Sexual attraction can easily exist without love. Sex without love is unethical.

The definition of love which emerges from the Evolutionary Ethic and the Eight Ethical Principles is that love is the desire to maximize, and the act of maximizing, the creativity of another. This is the meaning of true love or ethical love.

Self-love is maximizing our own creativity.

There is also a perverse love based upon the desire to maximize, and the act of maximizing, the happiness of another. Paradoxically, parents who sacrifice their own creativity in order to maximize their children's happiness only succeed in destroying their children's ethics, without necessarily increasing their happiness.

The Evolutionary Ethic says that we should treat all persons with true love. The minimum love we should express toward every person we meet is to do our best to communicate true ethics to that person. But we are ethically constrained not to increase the intelligence of unethical persons, because if their ethics are negative, we only increase their destructiveness by increasing their intelligence. Remember, **C=IE**. But we can never be certain about who is ethical or unethical. We can only do the best we can, by beginning with true ethics. And this is ethically sufficient.

It is not a legitimate function of government to try to increase anyone's creativity. The maximization of creativity must be an act of individual ethics, not of government intervention. The sole legitimate function of any ethical government is the protection of people from having their creativity involuntarily diminished. No government in history has been more successful in this latter function than the Government of the United States of America, but this is a rapidly diminishing truth.

THE ETHICAL FOUNDATIONS
OF DEMOCRACY

The ethical foundations of America, and all modern democracies, are in the Declaration of Independence, the Bill of Rights, and the Thirteenth, Fourteenth, Fifteenth, and Nineteenth Amendments to the Constitution. The rest of the Constitution is at best an ethical mistake; at worst it is an overtly unethical act, although the basic principles of American Government, such as the system of checks and balances, equal protection under the law for all citizens, and maximum respect for the individual, are completely ethical. The Government of the United States has been straying ever further from these ethical principles, almost from its inception.

All the considerable evil that has been done by the U.S. Government has been allegedly done to do good for someone. The problem is that since governments are inherently uncreative, they can never increase anyone's creativity without decreasing someone else's creativity. Governments usually do this by confiscating the fruits of the creativity of their most creative citizens, and then redistributing them to their least creative citizens. This is done through forced taxation, which, as we have seen, is a form of theft. Solely taxation by consensus is ethical taxation.

No government should ever try to do good, other than protecting the civil rights of its citizens, for it shall always fail by doing evil instead, i.e., shall decrease the creativity of its most creative citizens and, at best, merely increase the intelligence of its least creative citizens. Remember that, according to the Third Ethical Principle, unethical means can never produce ethical ends.

Therefore, an ethical government must never decrease the creativity of a single human being, no matter how many other human beings might, allegedly, be benefited by this "sacrifice." However, an ethical government will never try to prevent its citizens from doing evil to themselves, since evil must be allowed to destroy itself, as Jesus taught. That is why Jesus taught that we should love our enemies and suffer evil.

The main function of ethical government is to avoid doing evil, and to prevent evil from being done to its unwilling citizens. Therefore, the sole legitimate function of government is to protect its citizens from having their creativity diminished without their consent by the evil actions of others or by ecological or natural catastrophes. Therefore, the public health functions of government to prevent the spread of infectious diseases or the pollution of the natural environment are ethical methods for preventing ecological catastrophe. An ethical government may also evacuate and render emergency assistance to its citizens when they are ravaged by earthquakes, floods, hurricanes, and other natural catastrophes. But ethical governments must not go beyond these limits, attempting to do good for some of their citizens by doing evil to other citizens. Any government that acts beyond these limits is unethical.

Two of the most evil governments of modern times, Nazi Germany and the Soviet Union, justified their existence and all their horrendously evil acts by claiming they were doing good for their citizens, as do all the tyrannies of today, such as all the remaining Islamic and Communist governments, some of which were, and still are, just as evil as the Nazis, but by the grace of God less powerful. The same can be said for all the other tyrannies, including some of the democracies, which claim to do good for some by doing evil to others. As the Third Ethical Principle tells us, the ends never justify the means. Unethical means can never produce ethical ends.

For reasons given in the previous chapter, the Founding Fathers did the best they could with what they had and knew. Not even Jefferson could foresee the bureaucratic structure and the tyranny that would emerge from majority rule. But Jefferson knew about the foundations of ethical government. He expressed these in the Declaration of Independence, which he wrote, and the Bill of Rights, which he inspired and guided James Madison to write.

The Declaration of Independence went through several drafts, primarily to delete Jefferson's caustic references to slavery, but also to delete another very important passage. In the original draft of the Declaration of Independence Jefferson had said, "...all men are created equal *and separate"* (229, my emphasis). By "separate" Jefferson meant that no one had a right to any part of another person's life or property, as implied by the Ten Commandments, without that person's consent.

The *separate* reference was deleted at the insistence of John Adams, who was terrified of anarchy, as were many of the other Founding Fathers. The compromise that was finally reached was to delete "separate" and to create a representative republic where the representatives were elected democratically, although suffrage was far from universal. For example, solely property owners could vote at first, because solely they paid taxes. However, the democratic basis of government was to spread until today there is universal suffrage for all citizens of the United States, with minimal requirements for citizenship; the sole voting requirements, for the native-born, are to be 18 years of age and not to have been convicted of a felony. The native-born do not even have to pretend that they are dedicated to the ethical principles upon which the United States was founded.

The United States was thereby given a truly democratic Government, which has claimed that its main function is to do good for its citizens, thereby violating a fundamental principle of ethical government. The majority of citizens, in turn, have become ethically corrupt, expecting nothing from the Government but that it do good for them, and tolerating the most egregious unethical behavior from the elected leaders. This complicity will last as long as they believe that Government is doing material good for them.

Among the greatest evils that is done today by the Government of the United States and all other governments in the world is the violation of the principle not to diminish the creativity, or violate the basic human and civil rights, of a single human in order to benefit other humans. All the evil that government does is done in the name of doing good for its citizens.

THE DECLARATION OF INDEPENDENCE

In order to put the Declaration of Independence in a modern, evolutionary, ethical context, it will now be rewritten in terms of the Evolutionary Ethic, with the advantage of almost two hundred and thirty years of successful and failed experimentation with democratic government. This is what I believe Jefferson would say if he were alive today, although he would clearly say it better; wherever possible I have kept and/or used the original words of Jefferson.

Any group of people, no matter how small, who jointly choose to live by the ethical principles of the Second Declaration of Independence have created an ethical government for themselves. They are living in, and are citizens of, an Ethical State. An Ethical State evolves and becomes a Moral Society and then goes on evolving forever (115, 116, 117). An "angel" is a metaphor for a Moral Society.

A Second Declaration of Independence

Inspired by Thomas Jefferson

Unanimously Agreed to by
All Citizens of an Ethical State

When, in the course of human events, it becomes necessary for one people to dissolve the political bands which have connected them with another, and to assume, among the powers of the Earth, the separate and sovereign station to which the laws of nature and of nature's God entitle them, a decent respect to the opinions of humanity requires that they should declare the causes which impel them to the separation.

We hold these truths to be self-evident: that humanity is equal, but *separate*, before God in being endowed by the Creator with certain unalienable *individual* rights; that among these are life, liberty, property, privacy, and the maximization of creativity according to the dictates of one's own conscience. That to secure these rights, governments are instituted among humanity, deriving their just powers from the consent of the governed; that whenever any form of government becomes destructive to these ends, it is the right of the people to alter or abolish it, and to institute new government, laying its foundation on such principles, and organizing its powers in such forms, that creativity shall be maximized.

Prudence, indeed, will dictate that governments long established should not be changed for light and transient causes; and accordingly all experience has shown that persons are more disposed to suffer, while evils are sufferable, than right themselves by abolishing the forms to which they are accustomed.

But when a long train of abuses and usurpations, pursuing invariably the same object, evinces a design to reduce them under any form of despotism, *it is their duty to throw off such government*, and to provide new guards for their future creativity.

Such has been the patient sufferance of the subjects of this Government, and such is now the necessity which constrains them to alter their former system of Government. The history of the Government of the United States is one of repeated injuries and usurpations, all having in direct object the establishment of tyranny over these once-free people. Let the facts be submitted to a candid world.

The Government of the United States, in collusion with the vassal governments of States, Counties, and Municipalities, have usurped the power originally granted by God and the Constitution of the United States to the people, and imposed destructive taxation, an inequitable legal system, an oppressive, compulsory educational system, theft of property rights, gross violations of privacy, and insufferable interference in private lives.

The elected officials have repeatedly lied to and misled the public in order to obtain its support in further reducing its liberty. A majority of the electorate has repeatedly shown itself willing and anxious to be deceived, by voting for the most deceitful of the political candidates before them. A majority of the electorate has repeatedly rejected ethical candidates who refused to lie to them. The Government of the United States and a majority of the voters have shown that the United States' system of government by majority rule is a failed ideology which leads to the concentration of power in the hands of the most destructive liars that the society can produce. The possibility that all other systems of government have, in the past, been even worse, does not justify any form of destructive tyranny. We seek the best possible form of Government, and not merely the lesser of popular evils.

The Government of the United States has shown its moral bankruptcy in recent times by squandering the wealth of its people in supporting some of the most corrupt, destructive, evil tyrannies in history. Among these have been the governments of the Soviet Union between 1941 and 1945, the Republic of China (now in Taiwan) since 1941, the regime of the Shah of Iran from 1953 to 1978, South Vietnam from 1954 to 1975, the Somoza dictatorship in Nicaragua from 1933 until 1979, the dictatorship of Ferdinand Marcos in the Philippines from 1966 to 1986, many despotic Islamic states in the Middle East and other parts of the world from 1948 to the present, plus many evil, destructive dictatorships in Africa, Asia, and Latin America whenever it seemed politically expedient.

This destructive expediency has been allegedly practiced to inhibit the deleterious spread of even greater evils, particularly Communism. But it is self-evident that unethical means can never achieve ethical ends. Confiscatory socialism and other evils have steadily spread and become worse through the unethical acts of the United States Government. This Government has given aid and support to the largest Communist tyranny in the world, the People's Republic of China. Humanity is now closer to self-annihilation than at any time in history.

The Government in its alleged attempt to benefit its people has taken away their liberties and has almost succeeded in destroying them along with the rest of the world. The Government and a majority of the electorate of the United States have engaged in gross fiscal mismanagement. They have produced a huge national debt of many trillions of dollars. At the same time, they have impoverished the most creative people of the United States by confiscating their wealth and redistributing it to the most destructive persons in the nation, thereby spawning a new parasitical class of politicians, bureaucrats, corporate monopolies, oligopolies, and their clients, who further destroy the creativity of the nation.

The Government of the United States has constantly expanded its police powers, through the Central Intelligence Agency, the National Security Agency, the Federal Bureau of Investigation, the Internal Revenue Service, the Immigration and Naturalization Service, the Drug Enforcement Agency, the Secret Service, and other bureaucracies, to spy upon and harass its ethical citizens with police-state methods, while selectively aiding and abetting the ever more destructive organized crime syndicates at home and the tyrannies abroad (511–526).

In gross violation of their civil and human rights, the Government has made it increasingly difficult for ethical citizens to arm and defend themselves, while simultaneously contributing to the proliferation of vicious criminals by supporting and expanding a legal system that punishes the ethical and rewards the unethical. These destructive practices are exacerbated by the rulings of the Supreme Court, which constantly take away individual liberty for the benefit of the police bureaucracies and for political expediency, by catering to popular fear and prejudice, while protecting criminals at the expense of the innocent.

The legal system itself is dominated by parasitical lawyers who corrupt the law to serve solely their own power-seeking and money-making purposes, by constantly eliminating all vestiges of truth and justice from the legal process and replacing them with legal technicalities, bureaucratic procedures, and the deception and manipulation of ignorant, fearful jurors. In the current legal system, a combination of money, deceit, and/or a clever, unscrupulous lawyer can almost always prevail over truth and justice.

The Government of the United States, with the criminally negligent acquiescence of an electoral majority, has plundered the wealth of its citizens, imposed upon them an ever growing oppressive government, exacerbated the pollution and destruction of the environment, destroyed the creativity of its youth through a malignant educational bureaucracy, and made it ever more difficult for individual creativity to express itself. The Government has greatly endangered the very survival of humanity and life on earth. The political leaders of the United States, and those who vote for or in any way support them, have shown themselves unwilling to provide for the common welfare and to prevent the destruction of the people's God-given creativity.

In spite of all its faults, we recognize that the Government of the Unites States is among the least evil governments on earth. But just as the United States was originally created when an ethical minority of its inhabitants revolted against what was then the least evil and most powerful government on earth in order not to be forced to accept the lesser of evils, so now must a new ethical minority revolt against the least evil and most powerful government of today. For evil in any form, no matter how powerful, must not be tolerated. We recognize, along with those who signed the original Declaration of Independence, that all current governments are inherently evil; only that government which governs least, governs best. We have used the remaining liberty in the United States to warn our American brethren and the rest of the world of these dangers through our words and our actions; we have given alternatives. They have chosen to continue on the path of self-destruction.

We, the People of the Ethical State, choose life over death. We choose creation over destruction. In ethical self-defense, we declare ourselves a free and sovereign people, no longer bound by ties to any government other than our own. We welcome those who choose to join us in a creative, free society. The Ethical State begins. We shall create a Moral Society.

Before the world and the God who created all, we declare ourselves an Ethical State, dedicated to the maximization of creativity and bound by no other law. We declare the inviolate liberty of every human being to do and say what he or she pleases, as long as he or she does not impose undeserved harm on another. We declare that harm to another is deserved solely when necessary in defense against an aggressor who intends to harm an innocent person.

A person's life, liberty, property, and privacy belong entirely to him or herself; no one has a right to any part of another person's life, liberty, property, or privacy. Solely mutually voluntary transactions by unanimous consensus can ever be ethical or creative. The tyranny of any majority over any individual is hereby denounced. We, the

People of the Ethical State, swear eternal hostility against every form of tyranny over the mind of any ethical being. We declare all persons ethical until proven otherwise.

Upon these principles we shall henceforth govern ourselves and interact with others. We shall do our best to maximize creativity. Toward this God-inspired end, we, and all future citizens of the Ethical State, pledge our lives, our fortunes, and our sacred honor.

CITIZENSHIP

A citizen of an Ethical State is anyone who understands the Evolutionary Ethic well and sincerely commits to implement it by living in accordance with the ethical principles expressed in the Second Declaration of Independence. It is not necessary to agree with any of these criticisms of American political history to be a citizen of an Ethical State. However, all citizens of an Ethical State must be fully committed to its ethical principles.

The ethical principles of an Ethical State are further clarified by seeing the correspondence between the Evolutionary Ethic and the Bill of Rights and the other ethical Amendments to the Constitution of the United States of America. The following section relates these Amendments to citizenship in an Ethical State and the Eight Ethical Principles.

THE ETHICAL AMENDMENTS

FIRST AMENDMENT

Congress shall make no law respecting the establishment of religion, or prohibiting the free exercise thereof; or abridging the freedom of speech, or of the press; or the right of the people peaceably to assemble, and to petition the government for a redress of grievances.

Interpretation of the First Amendment
Religion is a question of personal, private morality, and, as we have seen, this should not be a concern of the government. It is clear that

there exist destructive religions; however, so long as these are freely chosen by their adherents and are privately practiced and do not impose any undeserved harm upon any other citizen, the Government should remain entirely neutral in questions of religion and other aspects of personal, private morality. This is supported by the Ten Commandments, the Second Declaration of Independence, the Evolutionary Ethic, and the Eight Ethical Principles. Unethical people should be allowed to destroy themselves.

In a free society, ethical children will often reject the unethical religion and behavior of their parents without government intervention. However, the Government has a certain obligation to protect dependent children from unethical parents; some religions are very destructive to children. How ethically to protect dependent children, without having Government unethically interfering with parental rights, is discussed in the next chapter within the context of a Constitution for an Ethical State.

Freedom of speech is also a question of private morality. All truth should clearly be allowed to be spoken, written, or otherwise communicated by anyone; but also lies that are private and do not have to be believed should be allowed to be communicated without any Government intervention. Solely fraudulent, libelous, or slanderous lies are a concern of an ethical government, since the main task of an ethical government is not to allow its citizens' creativity to be diminished involuntarily.

Therefore, false advertisements which induce anyone to harm themselves financially, physically, or otherwise are fraudulent and subject to criminal prosecution if they are deliberate, or to civil action if they are accidental or unintentional. Deliberate lies are now sometimes considered civil fraud rather than criminal, but within an Ethical State any intentional harming of another is a crime. Solely unintentional harm is a non-criminal civil harm. The lies of some religions border on the criminal, but would be difficult to prove in a court of law so long as there is no criminal coercion.

Slander and libel are destructive to a person's reputation, and may therefore diminish creativity. Slander and libel damage the creative potential of a person. Therefore, slander and libel should be subject to criminal prosecution if deliberate, or to civil action if unintentional or accidental.

Peaceful assembly of any group of any size is clearly a basic human right which should not be infringed, so long as this assembly is voluntary among all of the people involved, and it is on private land voluntarily provided for this purpose, or on public land set aside for this purpose and for which permission is given or implied by the branch of Government responsible for the use of this public land. Such permission should not be unreasonably withheld or denied by an ethical government. The people cannot maximize their creativity unless they are allowed to assemble peacefully according to the dictates of their own consciences. However they must not impose any undeserved harm on any non-consenting person by any such assembly.

Therefore, the Government cannot ethically infringe on the right of any voluntary assembly for any purpose, unless it can prove that this assembly is harming someone without his or her consent. Therefore, the Government cannot ethically control schools, theaters, sports arenas, or other places of voluntary assembly, or for that matter any voluntary gatherings for any purpose, such as in hospitals or businesses. The people, however, assemble at their own risk.

The same applies for any use of private property for any purpose by the property owner. The burden of proof is on the Government to show, after the fact, that someone is being harmed. No prior restraint can ethically exist on religion, speech, assembly, or private use of private land. Otherwise creativity shall not be maximized, and the Government shall become destructive. However, the Government is ethically bound to intervene after the fact if someone is being damaged or is recklessly endangered by any of these acts.

As a consequence of the ethics of the First Amendment, anyone may petition the Government for a redress of grievances, and the Government is ethically and legally obligated to respond to these complaints in a timely matter, and to answer the petitioner as to what action is being taken and for what reason. Otherwise, the Government is not ethical, and it shall be destructive and in violation of the Evolutionary Ethic.

SECOND AMENDMENT

A well regulated militia being necessary to the security of a free state, the right of the people to keep and bear arms, shall not be infringed.

Interpretation of the Second Amendment

The right of self-defense is a basic human right. It is our ethical duty to keep anyone from diminishing our creativity, or the creativity of those we love, even through the use of deadly force, so long as deadly force is necessary. Therefore, it is unethical to infringe on the right of any ethical citizen to arm and defend him or herself. To do so shall be an unethical act of Government, in violation of the Evolutionary Ethic and most of the Eight Ethical Principles, as well as the Ten Commandments and the Second Amendment to the Constitution.

A militia is a voluntary group of citizens who have joined together for mutual self-defense, and the defense of their country and its principles, according to the laws of their country. Since peaceful assembly and self-defense are basic human rights, it is unethical to prevent any group of people joining together for mutual self-defense. To do so shall diminish their creativity. No prior restraint may ethically exist on the formation of a militia or on the arming of the citizens of an Ethical State for self-defense. Citizens and a militia may be disarmed solely when it is proved that they have caused undeserved harm to someone, that or they are about to do so by intent or reckless endangerment.

The purpose of the Second Amendment was, when it was originally passed, to permit citizens to defend themselves against criminals and other hostile aggressors, as well as the Government itself if the latter ever became destructive to the human rights and freedoms of its citizens. The Government of the United States has long passed this threshold of harm to its citizens.

Patrick Henry stated that an armed citizenry was absolutely necessary for a people to maintain their freedom, otherwise the Government would infringe upon their freedoms a little at a time until the people were no longer free. This has now been going on for almost two hundred years.

THIRD AMENDMENT

No soldier shall in time of peace be quartered in any house, without the consent of the owner, nor in war, but in a manner prescribed by law.

John David Garcia

Interpretation of the Third Amendment

Maintaining the peace and defending its citizens, both in times of war and of peace, are the primary ethical responsibilities of an ethical government. But even these responsibilities take second place to the basic human rights of its citizens. These rights may be summarized by saying that a person's life, liberty, property, and privacy belong entirely to that person and may not be involuntarily appropriated or infringed upon by the Government, even when it is necessary for the public good. This is in harmony with the Fifth and the Seventh of the Ten Commandments, as well as the Third Amendment and the Evolutionary Ethic. Again, a government may never ethically take any part of any citizen's life, liberty, property, or privacy for any public purpose without that citizen's consent, except when necessary in self-defense against aggression by that citizen.

FOURTH AMENDMENT

The right of the people to be secure in their persons, houses, papers, and effects against unreasonable searches and seizures, shall not be violated, and no warrants shall issue, but upon probable cause, supported by oath or affirmation, and particularly describing the place to be searched and the persons or things to be seized.

Interpretation of the Fourth Amendment

This is another affirmation of the ethical axiom that a person's life, liberty, property, and privacy belong entirely to that person. Furthermore, even when it is necessary to appropriate any part of another person's life, liberty, property or privacy in order to maintain the peace, this may not be done, unless a criminal is caught in the act, without proper safeguards and permission from a court, after sworn testimony has been given that this appropriation or arrest is absolutely necessary to maintain the peace and to protect someone's creativity from criminal infringement.

If false testimony is knowingly given in such a matter, then the person involved is guilty of a crime, and must be prosecuted by the Government. If false testimony is given unknowingly, then the person involved is civilly liable for causing involuntary harm to a citizen, violating his or her rights to life, liberty, property, and privacy.

The Fourth Amendment implies a right to privacy in our life, liberty, property, and communications that are not made public. Since a person's life and property belongs entirely to him or herself, the Fourth Amendment, as the U.S. Supreme Court has correctly determined by a slim majority, also implies the right to privacy, which, in turn, implies the right of a woman to obtain an abortion.

Although an abortion for convenience may be an unethical act, it is an act of private morality and may not be infringed by the Government. A fetus has no right to any part of its mother's life without her consent. However, the Government of the people in an Ethical State should not be involved in abortions or in any way support them. They should not be done as a matter of public health or eugenics.

The Government, however, has certain obligations to dependent children, after they are born, who are not taken proper care of by their parents. How Government may ethically accomplish this obligation, without interfering unethically with the rights of the parents to raise their children according to the dictates of their own consciences, is shown in the next chapter.

Abortion is an act of private morality or immorality, as may be determined by a woman and/or her physician, and is not a matter of ethical concern for the Government or anyone else. Unethical people should be allowed to destroy themselves, but their dependent children have a right to certain ethical protection, solely after they are born, when they are being abused or neglected by their parents.

Dependent children also have no right to any part of their parent's life, liberty, property, or privacy, although parents have a personal ethical obligation, as a first pricrity, to maximize their children's creativity and never to do anything to diminish the creativity of their children. Therefore, for all legal purposes, dependent children should ethically be regarded as the sole exclusive and private responsibility of their parents, without any infringement on this right by Government or anyone else, except for the welfare of the child under the special conditions given in the next chapter.

The Government's first duty is to protect parental rights. Secondarily, the Government has an ethical duty to protect the human rights of all dependents. An ethical balance must be struck between the rights of the parents and the basic human rights of the dependent children. An ethical government will never interfere unreasonably with parental rights.

As a consequence, in an Ethical State parents are each criminally and civilly responsible for any crimes or damages that their dependent children might cause. A child ceases to be an exclusive dependent and responsibility of its parents, if, and only if, the child is adopted by others or qualifies for citizenship. If the child is legally adopted by others, as determined by an impartial jury, then the child becomes the dependent of new parents, and their responsibility.

If an impartial jury determines that a dependent child has qualified for citizenship, then the child shall have all the rights of citizenship, and he or she shall no longer be the dependent of anyone in an Ethical State. At this time the parents or guardians of the child are no longer responsible for his or her acts, and they no longer have any right to any part of the life or property of the child. It is the individual, private responsibility of each parent or guardian to prepare his or her children as soon as possible for citizenship in an Ethical State, and to do nothing to inhibit this preparation.

In an Ethical State, the mother is the sole and exclusive parent of a child unless she declares a man to be the father. The man becomes the legal father of the child solely upon his acceptance of the declaration of the mother or when proved to an impartial jury by DNA matching, if a declaration of fatherhood by the mother is not accepted by the alleged father. Otherwise, a man has no legal rights or obligations regarding a child.

There is a tacit, implicit, ethical evolutionary contract between a man and a woman when they have a child together. This implicit contract has existed for millions of years. The evolutionary contract says that both parents will do their best to maximize the creativity of their children, and each other, and that they will never do anything to diminish the creativity of their children, or each other.

It is the proper duty of an ethical government to enforce contracts and to demand compensation for the complaining party when any contract is violated. Therefore the Government may intervene on behalf of a child, or either parent, to protect their rights under the evolutionary contract. Again, how to protect both the rights of a child and the rights of a parent is shown in the next chapter.

Part of proper compensation for violation of the evolutionary contract is requiring child support from a father who does not wish to assume parental responsibility. However, private, voluntary sexual relationships between mutually consenting citizens of an Ethical State are no concern of the Government, which shall remain neutral in all such relationships, including marriage. Marriage, or its absence, is a private ethical choice of the partners, who may, or may not, form legal and/or religious contracts in addition to the evolutionary contract.

The legal father of a child holds both the rights and the responsibilities of parenthood jointly with its mother, so long as the child is dependent and has not yet become a citizen of an Ethical State. A father loses the rights, but not the responsibilities, of parenthood, if he refuses to assume these responsibilities voluntarily and is later found by an impartial jury to be the legal father.

The mother is the sole responsible parent with rights to a child when she does not declare who is the father. A man who has accepted a declaration of fatherhood, or whom a court has otherwise declared to be a child's father, is responsible for half the costs of supporting and educating the child.

No parent may harm its child without the consent of the other legal parent, if there is one. If any parent or guardian chooses to damage a child without the consent of the other parent or guardian, then the child, the parent, or the guardian may sue the party doing the harm for breach of the evolutionary contract. A party losing such a suit may be assessed damages and/or may lose his or her rights of parenthood. In an Ethical State, a dependent child shall have the right to divorce his or her parents, and to collect damages, when the parents are destructive to the creativity of the child and when the child has other citizens willing to become his or her guardians. All these matters will be adjudicated by impartial juries.

FIFTH AMENDMENT

No person shall be held to answer for a capital or other infamous crime, unless on a presentment or indictment of a grand jury, except in cases arising in the land or naval forces or in the militia, when in actual service in time of war or public danger; nor shall any person

John David Garcia

be subject for the same offense to be twice put in jeopardy of life or limb, nor shall be compelled in any criminal case to be a witness against himself, nor be deprived of life liberty or property, without due process of law; nor shall private property be taken for public use without just compensation.

Interpretation of the Fifth Amendment

This Amendment affirms again that a person's life, liberty, property, and privacy belong entirely to that person. Furthermore, a person's life, liberty, property, and privacy are so much his or her own, that the state, even to maintain the peace, may not appropriate any part of a person's basic civil rights without due process of law. Furthermore, this process must give the benefit of the doubt at all times to the citizen, who is considered innocent until proven guilty by the unanimous consent of an impartial jury.

Therefore, no serious criminal charges may be brought without indictment by a grand jury, where the burden showing justification of the criminal charges is entirely upon the Government. Then there must be a trial by an independent jury, where the jury can convict solely by unanimous consensus, and a person may be tried solely once for a given crime. Furthermore, no one may be compelled to testify against oneself in a criminal trial, and may always simply remain silent, requiring the prosecution to prove its case to the unanimous satisfaction of an impartial jury. The worst thing that Government can ever do is to diminish the creativity of any one of its ethical citizens, and this must always be guarded against.

Furthermore, a person's property, or any of his or her property rights, may not be taken away without due process of law, even when absolutely necessary for the public good, and without just compensation, even when in self-defense against any form of personal or ecological aggression by the person. The latter must be unanimously determined by an impartial jury. Only a compensation to which the property owner agrees can be just. To be ethical, transactions must be entirely voluntary, except in self-defense against an aggressor.

The right to private property is the foundation for all human rights (309). The violation of private property rights always leads to the violation of all other human rights, as has been shown by all the Communist governments of the twentieth century.

100

SIXTH AMENDMENT

In all criminal prosecutions, the accused shall enjoy the right to a speedy trial, by an impartial jury of the state and district wherein the crime shall have been committed, which district shall have been previously ascertained by law, and to be informed of the nature and cause of the accusation; to be confronted with the witnesses against him; to have a compulsory process for obtaining witnesses in his favor, and to have assistance of counsel in his defense.

Interpretation of the Sixth Amendment

All the guarantees of the previous Amendments are not sufficient to protect a person's basic human rights to the exclusive ownership of his or her life, liberty, property, and privacy. The Government must also guarantee the right to a speedy trial, and that the accused shall be judged by an impartial jury and represented by a willing counsel of his or her choice. It is the ethical duty of an ethical government to have enough courts and juries to assure a speedy trial for all citizens. This is a right which is systematically violated by the courts in the United States.

In an Ethical State, juries shall be elected by the unanimous consent of their peers, who have similarly been elected by the unanimous consent of the appropriate citizens. This process shall be elaborated in the next chapter.

SEVENTH AMENDMENT

In suits at common law, where the value in controversy shall exceed twenty dollars, the right of trial by jury shall be preserved and no fact tried by a jury shall be otherwise reexamined in any court of the United States than according to the rules of common law.

Interpretation of the Seventh Amendment

The protection of any individual against civil harm will be guaranteed by a trial by an impartial jury. This extends beyond the needs of the Government to protect its citizens; it extends to any significant suit brought by individuals who have claims of having been civilly harmed

John David Garcia

by another. Furthermore, there shall be no second-guessing of local juries by juries from other locales.

The only ethical and legal appeal is to a higher court with another higher impartial jury. In such an appeal, the facts in the civil case shall not be at issue, but solely the procedures of the lower jury and court, in order to assure proper protection of human and civil rights, as well as due process of law. So shall it be in an Ethical State.

EIGHTH AMENDMENT

Excessive bail shall not be required, nor excessive fines imposed, nor cruel and unusual punishments inflicted.

Interpretation of the Eighth Amendment

A person's life and property are so much his or her own that even when the person is criminally or civilly liable as determined by a grand jury or a local jury, there shall be no excessive bail, fines, or cruel punishment imposed. Bail, fines, and punishments should be proportional to the risk of flight involved and the harm that has been alleged or proven.

Punishment is never an ethical act. Therefore, all punishment imposed by imprisonment, torture, or any degrading of a human being is excessively cruel. However, an ethical government has the duty to protect its citizens when they are likely to be harmed in any way. Therefore, reasonable compensation for undeserved criminal or civil harm should be required of the person who has been found guilty of imposing this harm on the unconsenting person.

Since, by the Sixth Ethical Principle, it is unethical ever to be certain about cause and effect relationships in the natural world, we cannot be sure that a person convicted of a crime is truly unethical, because $C = IE$, and E is never equal to 1 for any finite being. E is, in fact, a random vector, whose components are always less than 1. Therefore, ethical persons can occasionally commit unethical acts, just as unethical persons can occasionally perform ethical acts, depending upon the random fluctuations in their ethics. Therefore, the only ethical treatment of a convicted criminal allowable in an Ethical State, and only in order to defend society, is exile to a place, e.g., an island, where the rest of the society will be secure from further unethical acts by this legally convicted criminal.

Furthermore, it is cruel punishment to put criminals in the company of other criminals who have committed more heinous crimes than they have. Therefore, in an Ethical State the convicted criminals shall be exiled to a place where solely other criminals of the same type shall be located. Furthermore, this place shall be open to businesses as well as individual and organizational volunteers who wish to rehabilitate the criminals, either for profit or as an act of charity. The criminals may choose their rehabilitators. Taxes would not be used to pay commercial rehabilitators; rather, other ethical and proper business arrangements would be made according to law.

Since Government cannot try to do good for anyone without doing evil to someone, the Ethical State shall not be involved directly in criminal rehabilitation, but it shall cooperate with, listen to, and, within reason, protect those involved in criminal rehabilitation, including the criminals themselves. The risk and cost of rehabilitating criminals shall be born entirely by the rehabilitators and the criminals themselves, but not by the citizens of an Ethical State.

It shall be incumbent upon those rehabilitating criminals, as well as the criminals themselves, to convince a court higher than that which convicted the criminal in the first place that the criminal has been rehabilitated beyond a reasonable doubt, and should be given another chance to become a member of society on a probationary basis. The conditions of probation should not be cruel or excessive; they should solely reflect reasonable precautions necessary to protect the rest of society from the criminal that has been put on probation. Exile to any country outside of the Ethical State could be an acceptable form of probation. But it is unethical to dump criminals on the citizens of other countries, as Fidel Castro did to the United States in 1980.

Ninth Amendment

The enumeration of the Constitution of certain rights shall not be construed to deny or disparage others retained by the people.

Interpretation of the Ninth Amendment

The Government may not infringe the rights of the people to life, liberty, property, and privacy in any way, except when necessary in self-defense against an aggressor. However, these rights may be incompletely protected by the Constitution.

Therefore, when in doubt, a person's right to life, liberty, property, and privacy shall be assumed by the Government, which may not infringe upon these rights, but may further protect them. In an Ethical State, the rights to life, liberty, property, and privacy may never be diminished except in necessary self-defense against an aggressor, although they may be strengthened and expanded.

TENTH AMENDMENT

The powers not delegated to the United States by the Constitution, nor prohibited by it to the states, are reserved to the states respectively or to the people.

Interpretation of the Tenth Amendment

The Federal Government is strictly limited in its powers to those powers and rights granted by the Constitution. All other rights not in conflict with the Constitution are reserved to the States or to the people. All rights belong to the people, other than those Constitutional rights given by the people to the States, and these rights may not be reduced without a Constitutional Amendment.

The notion of strictly limited government is essential to any ethical republic. In an Ethical State, the Government is strictly limited solely to protecting the rights of its citizens to life, liberty, property, and privacy from unwanted intrusions and violations by any of the people of the Ethical State, any of the branches of local or national Government, foreign invaders, or the vagaries of human-caused ecological disaster or of natural catastrophe. The Government is strictly forbidden to do good for anyone by confiscating the fruits of the creativity of some through taxes, and then redistributing them to less creative or needier people through bureaucracy, subsidies, or other methods.

Furthermore, all taxes in the Ethical State shall be paid by those who choose to participate in Government. How this can be done practically and ethically is discussed in the next two chapters. Those who pay taxes have certain rights which other residents of an Ethical State do not have, primarily the right to participate in Government. There should never be taxation without true representation of the taxpayer. Under majority rule, taxpayers who vote for candidates not elected are not properly or ethically represented.

THIRTEENTH AMENDMENT

Section 1. Neither slavery nor involuntary servitude, except as punishment for crime, whereof the party shall have been duly convicted, shall exist within the United States, or any place subject to their jurisdiction.

Section 2. Congress shall have the power to enforce this article by appropriate legislation.

Interpretation of the Thirteenth Amendment

A person's life is so much his or her own, that even to pay for civil and criminal damages, unanimously agreed to by an impartial jury, a person may not be subjected to involuntary servitude as collection for debt.

It is not considered a cruel and unusual punishment by the United States' Constitution to subject a convicted criminal to involuntary servitude, but it is so considered in an Ethical State. The only protection against convicted criminals is that they are exiled to a well guarded place where they may not inflict undeserved harm on any of the people of an Ethical State who are not themselves criminals convicted of a similar crime. It is unethical to subject any human being to involuntary servitude under any conditions, even to collect just debts or to receive just compensation for undeserved harm.

The only compensation which is ethical to demand from a person who has harmed us is money or property, not a part of his or her life. Every form of human degradation is unethical and may never be ethically imposed upon another. For this reason, exiled criminals are not imprisoned, but are merely guarded around the periphery of their place of exile, so that they may not again endanger the ethical people of an Ethical State if they remain unrehabilitated.

FOURTEENTH AMENDMENT

Section 1. All persons born or naturalized in the United States, and subject to the jurisdiction thereof, are citizens of the United States and of the State wherein they reside. No State shall make or enforce any law which shall abridge the privileges or immunities of citizens the United States; nor shall any State deprive any person of life, liberty or property, without due process of law; nor deny to any person within its jurisdiction the equal protection of the laws.

The next three sections of the Fourteenth Amendment are not of an ethical nature, but have more to do with bureaucratic requirements for dealing with the aftermath of the Civil War. The ethical implications of the Fourteenth, Fifteenth, and Nineteenth Amendments shall be considered jointly.

FIFTEENTH AMENDMENT

Section 1. The right of citizens of the United States to vote shall not be denied or abridged by the United States or by any State on account of race, color or previous condition of servitude.

Section 2. The Congress shall have power to enforce this article by appropriate legislation.

NINETEENTH AMENDMENT

Section 1. The right of citizens of the United States to vote shall not be denied or abridged by the United States or any State on account of sex.

Section 2. Congress shall have power to enforce this article by appropriate legislation.

Interpretation of the Fourteenth, Fifteenth and Nineteenth Amendments

The ethical essence of these three Amendments is that all citizens of the United States are equal before the law and that no one is above the law, including the highest government authorities. Furthermore the rights of citizenship of any person in an Ethical State are not subject to any vagaries of biology such as race, gender, or health, but are equal for all, based solely upon behavior.

It is reasonable in an Ethical State to require all citizens to understand minimally the Evolutionary Ethic, basic Ethical Principles, plus the Constitution of the Ethical State to be developed in the next chapter. It is also reasonable that all citizens of an Ethical State be required to uphold these ethics, principles, and constitution, as now are Government officials and the military in the United States. But no rights of citizenship may be infringed due to any biological, religious, or ideological differences among persons. Everything else, other than criminal and uncivil behavior, is permitted. The sole ethical criteria for all the rights of citizenship must be entirely behavioral and must apply to individuals; there cannot ethically exist privileged or specially protected classes of any kind.

One of the reasons for the ethical decline of the United States has been that the behavioral requirements for citizenship have been extremely lax. Namely, merely being born within the United States or, for naturalized citizens, a very limited understanding of English, of the Democratic Ethic, and of the history and Constitution of the United States.

The original citizens of the United States were much more committed to the Democratic Ethic than were those who followed. More and more people came to the United States not to be free, but to share in the economic prosperity that comes from freedom. These less ethical people became an ever-growing majority and debased the original ethical principles of the United States by turning it into a socialist democracy under majority rule. The Democratic Ethic led to its own contradiction.

An ethical republic must require for all its citizens, native-born and immigrant, a full understanding of its ethical principles and a personal commitment to them expressed in its official language or languages. English should have long ago been made the official language of United States.

To remain ethical, an ethical state must require of all its citizens, native-born and immigrant, that they fully understand and commit to the Evolutionary Ethic, the Ten Commandments, the ethical teachings of Jesus, the Eight Ethical Principles, and the fundamental ethics expressed in the Second Declaration of Independence, the Bill of Rights, and the Thirteenth, Fourteenth, Fifteenth, and Nineteenth Amendments to the Constitution of the original United States of America. Furthermore, this understanding and commitment must be made in the official language or languages of the Ethical State.

We must learn by experience, keep what works, and eliminate what does not work.

ELIMINATING WHAT DOES NOT WORK

The purpose of this chapter has been to identify all the ethical principles of religion and government that have been shown to work over time and then to show how they relate to the Evolutionary Ethic and ethical government in general. This has been done for the Ten Commandments, the ethical teachings of Jesus, the Declaration of Independence, the Bill of Rights, the Thirteenth, Fourteenth, Fifteenth, and Nineteenth Amendments. However, it is important also to point out what has not worked. This has been shown to be ritual, bureaucracy, and majority rule, but many other aspects of government have also proved to be unworkable. We will consider all the failed government paradigms in order to avoid them in the future, and to make sure that they are not subtly included in what might otherwise be an ethical government.

Winston Churchill once said that democracy is the worst system of government, except for all the other ones, which include monarchy, aristocracy, theocracy, and personal dictatorships. The problem is that democracy has been corrupted to mean "majority rule" rather than its true meaning of "rule by the people." The fact that majority rule seems to be the least evil system of government up to now does not mean that it is a good system, let alone the best system of government possible. In order to devise a better system of government, it is necessary to understand exactly how majority rule functions, and what are both its inherent advantages and its inherent disadvantages.

The main advantage of majority rule is that it tends to diffuse power and, as a consequence, to inhibit, in the short run, the corruption of highly concentrated power elites. Therefore, in the beginning it is usually less tyrannical than the other systems of government tried until now. Eventually however, wealthy power elites, i.e., plutocracies, learn to manipulate the majority with massive, very expensive propaganda which propagates comforting, popular lies, and in effect convinces the majority to cut their own throats, thereby creating a new type of democratic tyranny by an evil minority.

Tyranny, even a "benevolent" tyranny, is always unethical, because it diminishes at least one person's creativity, including the tyrant's, by taking away the right to choose alternative, more ethical courses of action (112, 115, 116).

The majority of all democratic electorates will almost always sacrifice their own, and almost certainly others', personal liberty in exchange for promises of more security from a centralized authority, which in virtually all democracies quickly becomes irreversibly evil and corrupt. Democratic authority, no matter how virtuous and well-intentioned it originally was, becomes corrupted because professional politicians quickly learn that the easiest way to get elected is openly to share the fears and prejudices of the electoral majority, independently of the politicians' true beliefs, and then to manipulate the majority by telling the lies the majority wishes to hear. Solely evil politicians will do this. These evil politicians eventually become the leadership in all democratic countries.

This was understood two thousand years ago by Cicero, who said, "the world wants to be deceived" (351). It was even better understood twenty-four hundred years ago by Socrates, who said that democracy (i.e., majority rule) would never work, because the least creative majority would always choose to live parasitically upon the most creative minority, confiscating their wealth and then redistributing it among themselves. This was the first clear understanding of socialism (311). In time, majority rule will inevitably lead to unethical, confiscatory socialism.

Spinoza rejected majority rule because it was destructive to the individual liberty that was essential to maximize creativity. Spinoza said that majority rule always leads to the imposition of the will of the majority upon minorities, and that this is unethical because the destruction of freedom also destroys creativity (412). A tyranny of the majority is inherently unethical.

As Bertrand Russell eventually learned through personal experience after running for public office, democracies with majority rule eventually become so corrupt that "solely persons who are hypocritical, stupid, or both can be elected to public office" (351, 356). This is the case because the hypocrite has learned how to manipulate the majority by speaking what he does not believe, while stupid politicians may actually believe some or all of what they say. Russell, presumably, considered anyone less clever than himself to be stupid, and he concluded that a majority of the electorate was stupid.

My own observation is that politicians are more hypocritical than stupid, and that the electorate is more lazy and unethical than stupid. Most of the electorate could understand what is going on if they wished to spend any time studying it, simply by reading what has already been published on political corruption (127, 495, 511–526); however, they are too lazy to give up any of their fifty hours per week watching television to study and understand the political process. Furthermore, they are too unethical to reject the blatant lies that they are constantly told by charming but apparently unethical politicians, such as Franklin Roosevelt, Ronald Reagan, and Bill Clinton.

It seems that most people choose to believe what they want to believe, not because it is true but because believing it makes them happy. By definition, someone who values happiness more than truth is already unethical (115–117).

POLITICAL PARADIGMS

Almost all political paradigms fall into one of four classes: conservative, liberal, authoritarian, or libertarian. Conservatives are usually better off economically than the majority and wish no government interference in the economic sector, particularly concerning property rights, or forced government redistribution of wealth from those who have it to those who have less of it. But conservatives wish government to control individual behavior that might be threatening to them, particularly crime, drug use, abortion, homosexuality, and any impediments to the aggressive expansion of their conservative religious beliefs.

In terms of the ideological dichotomies used in my previous book (116), I would call these people conservatives of the right. A "rightist" is defined as anyone who believes that the major cause behind human differences is heredity instead of environment. In the United States most, but not all, conservative-rightists are Republicans. Republican-minded persons represent slightly less than forty percent of the electorate.

The Democrats, or Democratically-minded, are slightly more than forty percent of the electorate. These persons are usually called, incorrectly from my point of view, "liberals," although there are conservative Democrats and liberal Republicans. Again using my previous paradigm, I would call "liberals," "liberal leftists." A "leftist" is someone who believes that the major behavioral differences between persons are due mainly to their environment and not to their heredity.

The scientific evidence is that both heredity and environment determine behavior, but that in a rich, relatively free country such as the United States, heredity is considerably more important than environment (119, 144, 180–182, 346). Since the 1930's, the western democracies have become overwhelmingly biased, particularly in the academic community, toward a false leftist view of society.

This bias has caused the phenomenon of "political correctness" in the United States and other democratic countries, in which rightist views cannot even be mentioned in the academic community or the rest of society without serious social repercussions. However, the leftist bias is scientifically incorrect (116, 119, 144, 180–182, 346). Most ideologues of both the right and the left do not even realize that at the core of their ideology is an unscientific belief about the relationship between nature and nurture and the relative effects of environment and heredity on human behavior.

A "liberal" is a person who is tolerant of change in most aspects of the environment, including those changes which most affect his or her beliefs and paradigms, so long as those changes do not physically affect his or her life.

A "conservative" is a person who is intolerant of change in most aspects of the environment, particularly those changes that affect his or her beliefs and paradigms, even if they do not physically affect his or her life.

All leftists are socialists; but not all socialists are leftists. Liberal socialists are known as "social democrats"; conservative socialists are often called "authoritarians."

About fifteen percent of the electorate in the United States prefers an authoritarian type of government that interferes in people's lives in both (1) questions of personal morality, where authoritarians are usually conservative, and (2) the economic sphere, where authoritarians are usually, but not always, leftists.

Communism, fascism, and Islam provide examples of recent authoritarian societies. In the United States, Ross Perot, Pat Buchanan and many of their followers are today's authoritarians. Sometimes authoritarian political movements are called "populism" or "statism," but in my terms they are "conservative leftism" (116). Nazism was an authoritarian socialism of the right, "radical, socialistic rightism."

The least popular of the four political paradigms in all countries of the world is called "libertarianism." It is most popular in the United States, where libertarianism was the political philosophy advocated by Thomas Jefferson and many of the Founding Fathers. In the United States, the Libertarian Party attracts about five percent of the electorate, although I suspect that if libertarian-minded voters believed that there was any chance of the Libertarian Party winning, the party might draw enough votes from Republicans, Democrats, authoritarians, and possibly others such as nihilists and existentialists, to capture perhaps as much as twenty percent of the electorate.

The libertarian believes that government should not interfere in people's economic or moral lives, except in protecting members of society from undeserved harm, such as from forces which violate their civil rights of life, liberty, personal property, and privacy. Therefore, libertarianism is the only political paradigm in harmony with the Evolutionary Ethic. However, libertarian principles are insufficient to form an ethical government, although they are necessary.

I define libertarians as "radical liberals of the right," according to my previous paradigm (116). A libertarian believes that the only legitimate function of government is in (1) a judiciary and (2) the defense of life, liberty, property, and privacy. The public defense of life against natural catastrophes, pollution, and infectious diseases (though not providing general health care) is also justifiable to libertarians; all other activities, including education, should be left to entirely voluntary associations among private parties, which is to say to the open market and to private charity. Libertarians regard the initiation of aggression by anyone as evil, although the right to self-defense is accepted.

I have indicated in a previous book (115) that all political paradigms other than libertarianism lead to contradictions and are inherently unethical and destructive. Indeed it can be stated as a general theorem that any political paradigm other than libertarianism will lead to the eventual collapse of the society that practices it, as well as to the contradiction of its own ethical principles.

The United States was originally designed by the Founding Fathers, particularly Thomas Jefferson, to be a libertarian society. However, the democratic structure of the United States has led it to majority rule, and then ever closer to confiscatory socialism, extreme leftism, and much less personal freedom. Majority rule leads to its own contradiction. It leads to ever less freedom while advocating freedom.

The basic concept of democracy is simply the rule of the people, which for most persons has come to mean the rule of the majority of the people. There can be democracy without majority rule, through self-rule within the context of a truly libertarian government, as will be shown in the next chapter.

Majority rule is not in itself a political paradigm, but merely a method of implementing one of the previous four paradigms, as is the case for monarchy, biologically based aristocracy, theocracies, and personal tyrannies such as those of Hitler, Stalin, Mao Tse Tung, Pol Pot, the Somozas, Ferdinand Marcos, Saddam Hussein, and Fidel Castro. Some of these personal tyrannies were more like theocracies. All of these political methods are unethical. Remember that unethical means can never produce ethical ends.

Every form of tyranny, including majority rule, justifies its existence by claiming to do good for the people, while actually destroying their creativity and impoverishing them. Creativity is the basis of all wealth and is the only proper criterion for good (115). Governments can never maximize creativity. The best government can do is sometimes to prevent creativity from being destroyed for unconsenting persons.

Thomas Jefferson made the mistake of believing that a majority-ruled, republican form of government was the best way of maintaining a libertarian society. A majority-ruled republic is a nation in which there is not direct democratic rule, as in the Greek city-states, but instead government formed by representatives who are elected by majorities of the citizens, and in which the power of government over individuals is limited by a constitution.

At the beginning of the American Republic, in a society where ninety percent of the electorate were likely to be independent farmers on their own land for the foreseeable future, majority rule seemed a

John David Garcia

reasonable risk to libertarians. Society was greatly enhanced by wide respect for property rights. Of course, almost from the beginning of the nation, the industrial revolution caused ever more people to concentrate in the cities, until today about ninety-five percent of the electorate are urban dwellers and only about five percent are rural, relatively self-sufficient property owners. This ever smaller minority has been economically marginalized as their property rights have been greatly eroded and diminished by Government.

Jefferson despised cities, which he saw as concentrations of parasitical, uncreative human beings who lived off the labor of the more creative, self-sufficient farmers and inventive rural dwellers, whom he saw as much more worthy and creative than the city dwellers. Jefferson lived long enough to see the trend of political dominance in national politics by city dwellers. I believe that Jefferson's dream would still have failed even if a majority of the population had remained self-sufficient, yeoman farmers as Jefferson hoped. He worked very hard to achieve this with his illegal, but not unethical, Louisiana Purchase. Jefferson believed, falsely, that there would be a new bloody revolution each generation in order to maintain a libertarian society: "In each generation the tree of liberty must be watered with the blood of patriots and tyrants; it is its natural manure (229)."

The flaw in the American system of government lies in the very nature of majority rule, as Socrates, Cicero, Spinoza, and Russell have observed. Majority rule will always be, at best, a tyranny of the majority. All tyrannies are destructive. Unethical means can never achieve ethical ends.

There is nothing inherently creative or ethical in having the allegiance of any popular majority. Adolf Hitler, an authoritarian rightist, was democratically elected by a plurality and had overwhelming majority support until he died. Richard Nixon, who almost succeeded in turning the United States into a police state, had overwhelming popular support in the 1972 presidential election. It would have been even higher without discovery of the Watergate incident.

In the United States, the only politicians who can now be elected are those who tell the majority the lies they wish to hear, whether they speak the lies out of hypocrisy or out of stupidity. The 1992 presidential election in the United States and almost all subsequent elections demonstrate this hypothesis.

In the 1992 presidential election, Bill Clinton was the most mendacious of all the presidential candidates, and he received about forty-three percent of the popular vote. George Bush was the next most mendacious of the presidential candidates, and he received about thirty-seven percent of the popular vote. Ross Perot was the third most mendacious of the presidential candidates, and he received about nineteen percent of the popular vote. The only presidential candidates who eloquently spoke the truth at all times and had an ethically consistent political philosophy were the Libertarian Party candidates, André Marrou for President and Nancy Lord for Vice President; they received less than one-half-of-one-percent of the popular vote. Even George W. Bush in 2000 was elected by much less than a plurality of the popular vote over Al Gore, a pathological liar and hypocrite who strongly advocated socialism. A clear majority of the population wanted socialism as advocated by Gore, Ralph Nader, and others. Even George W. Bush had to advocate limited socialism in order to obtain the presidency by a constitutional accident. A majority of the American electorate is now clearly ethically corrupt.

In both 1992 and 2000, the presidential candidates of the Libertarian Party were on the ballots in all fifty states; their message was clearly disseminated for all who wanted to hear it. Yet the vast majority of the electorate preferred to vote for candidates who told them the lies they wished to hear; they voted in direct proportion to the number and magnitude of lies told by each candidate. This same trend has continued in almost all the elections since 1992 and in the primaries of the major parties.

This is the fatal flaw in majority rule: the majority at almost all political levels, and always at the national level, votes not on the basis of ethical principle but on the basis of whose "promises" (i.e., lies) they believe will make them happiest, either by distributing to them the wealth produced by others, or by chastising those who have beliefs, practices, or behaviors that are offensive to them. The reason for this is that at almost all political levels, majorities are not guided by ethical principles but rather by the desire to be happy; most can be made happy by believing comforting lies appealing to their fear, greed, jealousy, hate, or the other negative emotions by which they guide their lives. At the same time, a professional political class is spawned, typified by Bill Clinton, Al Gore, and other career politicians, whose sole loyalty is to the powerful special interests, including foreign enemies of the United States, who bribe them with "campaign contributions." This is why democracy cannot long endure once it has been corrupted into majority rule.

No nation in history has ever been closer to being an ideal libertarian society than was the United States during the twenty-four continuous years that Jefferson and his closest disciples Madison and Monroe were President. The major flaw at this time was slavery. All three of these presidents tried to abolish it, as did John Adams the previous president and John Quincy Adams the subsequent president, both of whom were ethically comparable to the Jeffersonians. They could not accomplish this because of the bureaucratic structure of the Government. It took a catastrophic civil war to abolish slavery, although the major motivation for the Southern Secession was to preserve state rights, not to retain slavery. The North, in turn, fought not so much to abolish slavery, but rather to preserve the Union.

All political paradigms other than true libertarianism lead to ever larger, ever more parasitical tyrannical bureaucracies. And even libertarianism cannot function or long endure under majority rule. Libertarianism can begin and endure solely in a truly democratic society which is founded on the Evolutionary Ethic, with maximum respect for the individual and no tyranny of the majority. The United States has, almost from its origins and because of majority rule, been moving ever further from libertarianism toward increasingly authoritarian, bureaucratic socialism.

Since the end of the Civil War, in contradiction to the Declaration of Independence and the spirit of the early Constitution, the United States has increasingly become a hierarchy of power with the most power in the Federal Government, followed by the state governments, then the local governments, and with the least in the private individual, where the most power was originally supposed to reside. This inverse pyramid of power is the exact opposite of what a libertarian society should be like. A libertarian society can never be produced or even maintained under majority rule, as United States history and the history of every other democracy shows.

There is an ethical alternative to majority rule that not only directly produces a libertarian society as a side effect, but which also produces the freest and most creative society possible. What we wish to achieve is the freest possible society which is orderly, safe, and not anarchistic, but where everyone is free to express themselves creatively without any bureaucratic constraints, and where at the same time there is no type of tyranny, including a tyranny of the majority. Although this may seem impossible, there are several ways to structure such a society.

The first and simplest approach is to turn the Libertarian Party into a libertarian society, which it has never been. The Libertarian Party is a democratic society under majority rule, thus its failure. It is failing for the same reason that the United States could not remain a libertarian society. The Libertarian Party is a contradiction in terms, because it is captive to the concept of majority rule. It should become a living example of a libertarian society, instead of being just one more contradictory example of majority rule, and a rather unpopular one at that. A step-by-step program to turn the Libertarian Party into a libertarian society follows in the next section.

In order to have ethical government, we must have a libertarian society based on the Evolutionary Ethic, where there is complete individual freedom, without anarchy, and an unbureaucratic government whose powers are limited to protecting life, liberty, property, privacy and human rights in general, and which never interferes in questions of individual private morality or in the economy. There can be no majority rule or tyranny of any kind.

How to structure such a society and then bring it about is shown in the next two chapters. As a preliminary to this program, consider how the Libertarian Party may cease being a bureaucratic organization under majority rule and may become truly libertarian. A truly Libertarian Party is something worthy of preservation, and it can pave the way for an Ethical State.

MAKING THE LIBERTARIAN PARTY LIBERTARIAN... AND BEYOND

The following program has the capability of giving the Libertarian Party a truly libertarian structure.

1. Stop electing the leaders of the Libertarian Party by majority rule; instead elect them by hierarchical unanimous consensus.

2. Hierarchical unanimous consensus is established by first organizing Libertarians at the local level into small groups, preferably half

male and half female. For example, Lane County, Oregon has about one thousand Libertarian Party members, but very few are active. Almost all of them would become active if they could be politically and practically effective at the local level, even if they might never be effective at the state or national level.

My observation from interacting with local Libertarians is that there are many more men than women in the Libertarian Party. I suspect that this is true at all Libertarian Party levels. In my previous books (115, 116), I have shown why it is important to have men and women, in approximately equal numbers, work together in small groups to formulate social policy and to produce a maximally creative society. Furthermore, the optimal arrangement for maximum creativity in a small group is that of four ethical men and four ethical women integrated into a working group called an "octet."

3. Octets are formed first by having eight Libertarians who know each other and wish to work together agree to do so and to designate themselves as a Libertarian octet. If all the members of the local Libertarian Party are not integrated into octets by this voluntary joining, then the remaining Libertarians are assigned at random into statistically created octets, such that each octet has an approximately equal percentage of the unassigned women in the local Libertarian Party.

If there are not enough women for each octet to have at least one woman, then women may volunteer to participate in more than one Libertarian octet at the local level, and in effect have more political power, as will soon be shown. This would compensate for the Libertarian Party having too few women. The women who are given this extra political power are obligated to actively recruit more women members for the local Libertarian Party, until the membership is almost equally divided between men and women. If men are in the minority, the reverse of this procedure is to be practiced.

4. Each Libertarian octet agrees to meet at least once per month for at least four hours to discuss Libertarian Party issues among themselves and to decide what is the best course of action for them to take as an octet. Octets do not have to cooperate among themselves except by unanimous consensus of all the octet members. However, they have an obligation to send one man and one woman representing the octet to interact with other male-female pairs of octet representatives. These representatives then form new octets by voluntary association with other

octet representatives at a one-day local Libertarian Convention occurring every three months. My last book shows how this process can be implemented easily and quickly, even with millions of persons (115).

5. The representatives for each octet are chosen by unanimous consensus of all the members of each octet. If they cannot achieve unanimous consensus, then the octet will not be represented and will have no vote at the next level of political organization. However, in my last book (115), I describe a communication technique called "autopoiesis," which almost always quickly produces unanimous consensus on any question which is being addressed by an ethical octet. This is a generalization of the biological process of autopoiesis first discovered by Varela and Maturana (462).

Octets who cannot achieve consensus about who should be their two representatives should restructure themselves with new, more compatible members, and exclude the minority members who are less compatible. The minority octet members may in turn form new octets with other local Libertarians with whom they are more compatible. Eventually all Libertarians at the local level who are capable of ethically cooperating with their peers will be in octets with whom they can work harmoniously by unanimous consensus.

6. At the second level of political organization, the new octets that are formed will, in turn, discuss Libertarian Party issues among themselves and every three months choose, again by unanimous consensus, a male-female pair from the octet to represent them at the third level of Libertarian Party organization. Those octets who cannot achieve consensus again have no representation at the third level of political organization, but they can reorganize themselves, as before, into new second level octets. They have three months in which to do this.

7. This process continues until, at the national level, the highest level octet chooses every four years a male-female pair to represent them. These shall be the next presidential candidates of the Libertarian Party. The members of the immediately lower level octets who participated in choosing the presidential candidates shall be the senatorial and gubernatorial candidates of the Libertarian Party within their respective states, by their own hierarchical choice. The representatives of the next lower octets shall be the House candidates of the Libertarian Party. The representatives of the next lower level octets shall be the candidates for their respective State Legislatures. The next lower

level octet representatives shall be the candidates for county and city governments. All the lower octets shall be grassroots workers.

8. Each member of any octet who is chosen as a representative must agree to occupy the highest office that he or she is qualified for by unanimous consensus within the Libertarian Party. No one should, in any way, campaign to be the representative of any octet, but should always strive to find the best representative other than oneself. Solely when all seven other octet members choose a person must that person accept the position or resign as a representative.

Persons who seek power, even petty power within the Libertarian Party, should never have it (115). People should serve as representatives from a sense of duty rather than a desire for power. No octet member, at any level, should ever vote for a representative who actively seeks the job.

9. The power of this process, in lieu of majority rule, is that each octet representative and political candidate has been chosen all along the way by persons who know him or her personally, and the higher the level of the candidate, the more Libertarians have by unanimous consensus chosen that candidate. Each Libertarian has, in a sense, a veto, so that persons obnoxious to him or her will never rise above his or her highest level in the hierarchy.

The presidential candidates are, in a sense, chosen by unanimous consensus of all members of the Libertarian Party. This is a much more powerful endorsement than the votes of a majority of the Libertarian Party members for someone that most do not know personally, but solely through his or her speeches and writings.

Octets which are incapable of achieving one hundred percent consensus are flawed, and it is best for all that they not participate in higher levels of the Libertarian Party. It is the responsibility of each individual Libertarian at each level of the party to integrate him or herself into an octet with which he or she can work through unanimous consensus. A failure in this task disqualifies the individual party member from further participation in higher levels of the party.

Remember that there is a technique, autopoiesis, given in my last book (115) for greatly facilitating consensus, and this technique optimizes the consensus process within small groups of four men and four women.

The quality of the Libertarian candidates is already the highest among the candidates of all American political parties. This new process will increase candidate quality geometrically. The Libertarian Party is the sole political party of true ethical principle in the United States, with a politically sound, but ethically incomplete, political philosophy. The tragedy is that the Libertarian Party is already a corrupt bureaucracy because of majority rule. But it can be corrected by the party itself.

10. At the lower levels, the octet representatives should pay all of their own expenses. As the octet representatives reach the higher levels of the Libertarian Party, they should be entitled to a campaign contribution to run for political office, but not for participating in the octets.

Each Libertarian should have an obligation to contribute a minimum of $25 per year to the Libertarian campaign fund or a total of $100 every four years; this is in addition to their regular Party dues. If there were 500,000 active Libertarian Party members in the United States, which is not impossible, then the Presidential candidates would receive $25,000,000, the Senatorial and Gubernatorial candidates for each state would collectively receive $12,500,000, the House candidates would collectively receive $6,250,000, the State Government candidates would collectively receive $3,125,000, and the local government candidates would collectively receive $1,562.500. The campaign funds would be stratified according to the Libertarian population in each state and in each locality.

Each candidate would of course be free to solicit more funds for his or her campaign, according to law. This system would enable the Libertarian Party to run outstanding candidates for each election in the nation, and to have their voices heard.

Although a Libertarian President may never be elected, the presidential candidates of the Libertarian Party will be the major vehicle for producing and disseminating information to the American people about Libertarian principles and about the corruption of the current system. All Libertarian candidates shall reinforce this message in every election and jointly achieve economies of scale by sharing their educational materials, a major advantage to a party based on principle rather than the expediency of the Democrats and Republicans.

Americans will have an alternative, even if they never vote for it. At the lower levels, the Libertarian Party might have a chance of electing some of its best members.

11. We note that at each level the octet representative pair is representing four times as many Libertarians as at the previous level.

Therefore level one representatives represent 8 Libertarians; level two represent 32 Libertarians, level three represent 128 Libertarians, level four represent 512 Libertarians, level five represent 2,048 Libertarians, level six represent 8,192 Libertarians, level seven represent 32,768 Libertarians, level eight represent 131,072 Libertarians, and finally level nine can represent up to 524,288 Libertarians.

For the foreseeable future, therefore, there will not need to be more than nine levels of representative octets to represent all the active Libertarians in the nation. At level one, seventy-five percent of the total Libertarian population spends only four hours per month creating the consensus hierarchy; those at level nine will have spent no more than twenty-six hours per month over a period of four years to reach that level in the consensus hierarchy.

12. Each level one octet focuses on how best to choose level two representatives, how best to inform their friends and neighbors about the Libertarian Party and how to get them to join, and in raising money for the Libertarian Party. It would also be worthwhile if the level one octets chose, by unanimous consensus, to engage in creative projects related to Libertarian principles but having to do with local politics, such as defeating all proposed increases in taxes, governmental theft of property rights, or any other government or private threats to personal liberty.

Libertarian octets should engage in creative libertarian projects, such as helping themselves and others to become self-sufficient, avoiding taxes, and circumventing the Government-controlled money system through barter. In this way, the octets can serve as examples of how to create self-sufficient libertarian communities, such as on small farms near their homes, which they could purchase and operate as a corporation or as a partnership, with octet members having equitable shares in the operation. These suggestions are all in the spirit of the vision that Thomas Jefferson originally had for America. Jefferson's mistake was political, not conceptual.

There are many other options for creating practical embodiments of libertarian ethical principles in politics, economics, education, health and social organization. Some of these are discussed in *Creative Transformation*.

A libertarian political system for an entire nation would empower individuals rather than political parties. The whole nation would be organized into voluntary octets to produce the workers at all levels of legitimate government, which would be limited entirely to military, public health, police, judicial, legislative and executive functions, all by hierarchical consensus. A libertarian society would have no need for bureaucracy, lawyers. or a professional judiciary, although lawyers could be voluntarily employed by the citizens if they so wished. There would be neither majority rule, tyranny, nor anarchy. Each octet would be sovereign on its own territory; there would be no public lands, other than those that were declared public parks or dedicated to other public uses by unanimous consensus. The level one octet would be the basic unit of sovereignty.

Octets or individuals who did not wish to pay taxes to support a common defense force, public health organization, or a judiciary consisting entirely of higher level neutral octets, i.e., octets with no connections to either party, for resolving disputes among octets, could secede at any time from the libertarian society and go their own way, without having to pay for any services they do not want and will no longer receive.

The major justification for a massive nation-state is to provide adequate military defense against foreign aggressors. The same can be accomplished by a smaller society that is highly creative and invents weapons and military organization superior to those of the large nation-states. If foreign aggressors could be eliminated, or if there were enough technological superiority among the octets, then it would be possible to have a libertarian society which operates entirely on the basis of voluntary cooperation, with a police force but without need for any significant military organization. Octet consensus hierarchies would exist solely as desired, to accomplish non-governmental goals not readily achievable by single octets; the government would be much more limited than currently.

The Libertarian Party could create a sovereign libertarian society, as a living example of what a libertarian nation would be like, within the confines of the United States, by simply concentrating its members in rural areas suitable for self-sufficiency, self-employment, and voluntary cooperation. Libertarians who share fundamental ethical values and wish to work together could then have the opportunity to do so. Self-sufficiency in cities is more difficult, but not impossible.

The libertarian ethic of maximum liberty for all, without the diminution of the liberty of any for the alleged benefit of anyone else, is an inadequate ethical base for a maximally creative, progressive society. That is one of the reasons that the United States could not remain a libertarian society. A necessary and sufficient ethical system for creating and keeping a libertarian society is one based on the notions that the ultimate good is to maximize creativity and that anything that diminishes even a single person's creativity is an absolute evil, no matter how many other persons are allegedly supposed to be benefited by this "sacrifice."

Ecological ethics can be seen to be in harmony with the preceding notions by recognizing that the only environmental changes that one is entitled to make, including within one's own property, are those changes that do not decrease the creativity of a single unconsenting person. We cannot ethically pollute our own environment if this also produces pollution for an unconsenting person. The environment is best managed to maximize the creativity of all, without diminishing anyone's creativity. There is no reason why Libertarians should not embrace ecological ethics, thereby expanding their appeal and strengthening their ethical base. Currently, almost all environmentalists are socialists.

The best political advice I can give to my fellow Americans at this time is never again to vote for anyone who is actively involved in turning the United States into a socialistic democracy subject to majority rule, as is the agenda of almost all Democrats. Vote solely for the best candidates who advocate libertarian principles and have some reasonable chance of being elected. He or she may not be a member of the Libertarian Party. He or she might be a Republican or even a Democrat, although this probability is very low. But he or she will never be a member of a party that advocates any form of socialism, or of a party, such as the Green Party, which advocates socialism under the cover of environmentalism or any other agenda. Almost nothing is worse than socialism for destroying the creativity of a nation.

The details of how to combine Libertarian principles with the Evolutionary Ethic are given in an ethical Constitution developed in the next chapter. Practical suggestions for implementing these principles are provided in the final chapter.

Chapter Three

AN ETHICAL GOVERNMENT

In this chapter, I speculate about how an ethical government should be structured, given the ethical theory and analysis of the previous chapters and my other books and writings. The basic requirement of ethical government is that all its citizens and government officials must be at least sufficiently creative to understand the Evolutionary Ethic and to affirm and to commit to its ethical principles.

Toward this end, all persons applying to be citizens of an Ethical State should take an oath and sign a contract of citizenship, after objectively demonstrating before a Court that they understand well its Ethical Principles and Constitution. The "Ethical State" is the name that will be used for all persons and societies who govern themselves according to the Evolutionary Ethic. An Ethical State should accept as full citizens all persons who sign this contract and take this oath before one of its Courts, who understand its constitution, and who adequately speak its official language or languages.

Each language is a system for processing information in a unique way. My best languages are English and Spanish. I think and feel in both languages, but I think best in English and feel best in Spanish. I always write my books first in English and then translate them into Spanish. I teach and lecture in both languages, but I am a far more effective teacher in Spanish. I see fundamental value in both languages, but they are optimal for different purposes. No one language is uniformly superior to all other languages, and there is an overlap in the ability of all languages to process information. Consensus of the citizens of an Ethical State for any written language(s) would suffice, although, if we follow Spinoza's example, there is probably an advantage to simultaneously speaking Spanish, Hebrew, Aramaic, Latin, and a Germanic language such as Dutch, English, or German itself.

English is unique in combining some of the best aspects of the Germanic languages, through Anglo-Saxon, with some of the best aspects of the Latin-based languages, first through Old French, after the Norman conquest, and later through Latin directly. Therefore, English may be the single best language to know, if we are to maximize creativity and use solely one language. English is also among the most widely spoken native languages, and it is the most widely spoken language as a second language. It has twice the vocabulary of any other European language. For many reasons, a synthesis of English and Spanish, like that currently happening in the United States, might give us the single best language, as Spanish is also one of the most widely spoken languages.

I recommend that a newly formed Ethical State use both English and Spanish as its official languages. This means that anyone may use either one of the languages to interact with the Government. It does not mean that someone has to be fluent in both languages. Such a system may be optimal, but it is not necessary; any single written language will do.

Some day there may be many independent Ethical States, speaking many different languages, but they shall all speak the same language at an ethical, spiritual level. There are no such nations today.

An Ethical State will exist when any number of men and women, however small, make a commitment to uphold its Ethical Principles and Constitution.

An autonomous, self-governing octet shall exist when exactly four men and four women agree to work together by unanimous consensus for the mutual benefit of maximizing creativity. Thus begins an ethical republic. All citizens of an ethical republic must have made the same commitment of citizenship and must share a single constitution, all by unanimous consensus.

What follows is an example of one such commitment and one such constitution. Other better commitments and constitutions are possible. This is merely the best I can do at this time. Better alternatives should be developed by persons and octets who feel they can do so. If you cannot give a better alternative in harmony with the Evolutionary Ethic, it is best that you study, and ask questions about these matters, until you can give a better alternative.

The wisest statement I know of political ethics is in the Declaration of Independence, as originally written by Thomas Jefferson. I make this wisdom an integral part of the contract that I now make with the Ethical State.

PROPOSED OATH OF CITIZENSHIP

Upon my honor, I promise to do my best to maximize the creativity of my children, my spouse, myself, my fellow citizens of the Ethical State, and the rest of humanity in this order of priority. Toward this end I shall never knowingly decrease the intelligence or the ethics of any sentient being, except in necessary defense against an aggressor. I pledge my life, my fortune, and my sacred honor to defend my family, myself, and all citizens of the Ethical State from all enemies, foreign and domestic, who threaten their creativity.

PROPOSED CONTRACT OF CITIZENSHIP*

When, in the course of human events, it becomes necessary for one people to dissolve the political bands which have connected them with another, and to assume, among the powers of the Earth, the separate and sovereign station to which the laws of nature and of nature's God entitle them, a decent respect to the opinions of humanity requires that they should declare the causes which impel them to the separation.

We hold these truths to be self-evident: that humanity is equal, but separate, before God, in being endowed by the Creator with certain unalienable individual rights; that among these are life, liberty, property, privacy, and the maximization of creativity according to the dictates of one's own conscience. That to secure these individual rights, governments are instituted among humanity, deriving their just powers from the consent of the governed; that whenever any form of government becomes destructive to these ends, it is the right of the

---

* To be signed before the court granting citizenship, after testing the candidate for an adequate understanding of the evolutionary ethic, its applications, and the constitution of the ethical state.

people to alter or abolish it, and to institute new government, laying its foundation on such principles, and organizing its powers in such forms, that creativity shall be maximized.

Prudence, indeed, will dictate that governments long established should not be changed for light and transient causes; and accordingly all experience has shown that persons are more disposed to suffer, while evils are sufferable, than right themselves by abolishing the forms to which they are accustomed.

But when a long train of abuses and usurpations, pursuing invariably the same object, evinces a design to reduce them under any form of despotism, it is their duty to throw off such government, and to provide new guards for their future creativity.

We, the People of the Ethical State, choose life over death. We choose creation over destruction. In ethical self-defense, we declare ourselves a free and sovereign people, no longer bound by ties to any government other than our own. We welcome those who choose to join us in a creative, free society. The Ethical State begins. We shall create a Moral Society.

Before the world and the God who created all, we declare ourselves an Ethical State dedicated to the maximization of creativity and bound by no other law. We declare the inviolate liberty of every human being to do and say what he or she pleases, so long as he or she does not impose undeserved harm on others. We declare that harm to another is deserved solely when necessary in defense against an aggressor who intends to harm an innocent person.

A person's life, liberty, property, and privacy belong entirely to him or herself; no one has a right to any part of another person's fundamental, unalienable civil rights. Solely mutually voluntary transactions by one hundred percent consensus can ever be ethical or creative. The tyranny of any majority over any individual is hereby denounced. We, the People of the Ethical State, swear eternal hostility against every form of tyranny over the mind of any ethical being. We declare all persons ethical until proven otherwise.

Upon these principles we shall henceforth govern ourselves and interact with others. We shall do our best to maximize creativity, and never knowingly decrease the creativity of anyone. Toward this God-inspired end, we pledge our lives, our fortunes, and our sacred honor.

I fully understand and completely commit to these ethical principles and to the Constitution which upholds them. I pledge my full loyalty to the people of the Ethical State, its Constitution, and its principles. I promise to always do my best, according to the true dictates of my own conscience alone, to maximize my creativity and that of those I love, in direct proportion to my love for them.

I further promise to do my best never to decrease the creativity of anyone by imposing undeserved harm upon them. If I should ever impose undeserved harm on anyone, I fully accept that the people and Government of the Ethical State are entitled to receive just compensation from me, and, if necessary, exile me according to law or restrict my freedom according to law, in self-defense against me and any future destructive acts I may commit.

I further promise not to tolerate destructive acts in others, including my dependents, and, as a minimum, to do my best to prevent such acts by identifying them, and their perpetrators, to the appropriate officials and citizens of the Ethical State; I will do this in good faith, expecting help in defense against these destructive acts and in eliminating them in the future.

I accept full criminal and civil responsibility for all crimes and other destructive acts that my dependents may perpetrate, and I shall seek help from the appropriate officials of the Ethical State if I cannot prevent the citizens of the Ethical State from having undeserved harm imposed upon them by my dependents.

I accept as dependents all of my biological children and any biological children that any of my dependents shall have while they are still dependent upon me. I accept as dependents all persons I adopt with the consent of a full Court. I assume full responsibility for all of my dependents, so long as they remain dependent on me or until they become citizens or until they are legally adopted by other parents, either with my consent or as the publicly expressed wish of my dependent sworn before a Magistrate.

It shall be the proper function of a Court to determine who are the legal parents of a dependent. This shall always be done according to law, while fully preserving the rights of all parents. I also recognize that my primary obligation as a parent, to all my dependents, is to do my best to love, nurture, and educate them, so that they may themselves become free, independent, and maximally creative citizens of the Ethical State as soon as possible.

As further obligations, I will do my best to maximize my creativity and defend myself, my family, my neighbors, my fellow citizens, and the principles and people of the Ethical State. I will, when necessary, and according to the dictates of my conscience alone, arm myself and join any militia that my representatives may form for the defense of my fellow citizens. I will respect all the laws of the Ethical State so long as I choose to remain one of its citizens.

So long as I choose to be a citizen of the Ethical State, I shall obey all its laws, keep my contracts, pay all my fair, legal taxes, do my best to participate in Government, and do my best to make sure that the Government and citizens of the Ethical State act in accordance with its ethical principles of truth, justice, freedom, and the maximization of creativity, according to law and the Constitution.

I recognize that I may secede from the Ethical State and renounce my citizenship whenever I wish, and that I have an ethical obligation to do so when I believe its laws to be unethical or its taxes unfair. I further recognize that upon seceding I may live wherever I wish, keep title to all my land and property within the territory of the Ethical State, and take all my personal property with me wherever I go.

If I ever believe that the Ethical State does not treat me or anyone else ethically, with honor, respect, and justice, I shall do my best to remedy the situation according to law. If I do not believe that I can succeed in this endeavor, I shall denounce the Ethical State publicly and renounce my citizenship as soon as possible, giving my full true reasons for this renunciation. Upon so doing, I shall promptly secede from the Ethical State and go anywhere I wish outside of its territory, taking title to all my land and property with me even if I seek the protection of other nations or societies. I accept fully all the obligations of citizenship in the Ethical State solely upon condition that it shall keep good faith with me, treat me with justice, and always grant me the full rights of citizenship.

My rights of citizenship may not be suspended or infringed upon, except upon my conviction of a crime by two independent Courts in accordance with the laws and Constitution of the Ethical State. My rights of citizenship may not be temporarily suspended except on indictment or arrest for a crime. I may not ever be legally arrested except on probable cause for a crime, and the indictment process against me must be begun within twenty-four hours of arrest, unless the indictment has been earlier handed down by a full Court of independent jurors in accordance with the laws and Constitution of the Ethical State.

All previous agreements and contracts which conflict with this contract are now null and void.

Signed and Affirmed before a full Court of Justice according to the Constitution of the Ethical State.

Date, Description of the Court Granting Citizenship, and Place of Signing.

Signatures with Dates for each of the Eight Members of the Court Granting Citizenship.

PROPOSED CONSTITUTION OF AN ETHICAL STATE

Citizenship

All persons who prove, according to law and before a Court of the Ethical State in its official language(s), that they understand the Ethical Principles, Laws, and Constitution of the Ethical State, who take its Oath of Citizenship, and who sign the Contract of Citizenship shall be full citizens of the Ethical State and entitled to the full rights, privileges and protection of its Constitution, Government, and People.

No restrictions may be placed on citizenship due to age, national origin, place of birth, race, gender, ethnicity, beliefs, or religion. The criteria for the rights of citizenship shall depend entirely on intelligence and ethics. The criteria for accepting a new citizen within the Ethical State shall never exceed, nor be less than, an adequate understanding of its ethical principles and Constitution, together with taking the Oath of Citizenship, signing the Contract of Citizenship, and then obeying its laws, unless it is unanimously decided by the citizens of the Ethical State that they wish different citizenship criteria.

Territory

All land and other resources owned or leased according to law by citizens of the Ethical State, and accepted under the protection of the Ethical State, shall be regarded as being within the territory of the Ethical State. Such land and resources shall cease being within the territory under the protection of the Ethical State when its owner publicly renounces citizenship and secedes according to law. Should a lessor secede from the Ethical State, his or her person and personal property, and that of his or her dependents, shall cease to be under the protection of the Ethical State, but any leasehold property owned by a citizen of the Ethical State shall remain under its protection.

The Ethical State may not generally own land or natural resources, except land reserved for permanent national parks and exclusive Government functions. All land and natural resources which do not lend themselves to private ownership, such as the electro-magnetic spectrum, atmosphere, oceans, and ocean floor, shall be managed and held in trust by the Ethical State for the equal and maximum benefit of all its citizens. All such land and resources shall be considered to be within the territory of the people of the Ethical State.

All land and resources held in trust may not be leased, sold, or traded by the Government of the Ethical State without full approval of all the citizens of the Ethical State or by unanimous consensus of their 128 highest elected representatives, as determined by law.

When citizens secede from the Ethical State, they and all their legally owned land and property shall cease being within the territory of the Ethical State, and shall no longer be under its protection. The Ethical State will, in general, evolve to govern territory that is coextensive with territory owned by its citizens.

BILL OF RIGHTS

1. Right To Life, Liberty, Property, and Privacy

Each person has an inviolable right to his or her own life, liberty, property, and privacy, and may dispose of them as he or she wishes, so long as he or she does not impose undeserved harm on another by infringing on that person's right to life, liberty, property, or privacy. Such undeserved harm, when it occurs, shall be determined and remedied by the Courts of the Ethical State according to law.

A person's life is entirely and solely his or her own forever. No one ever has a right to any part of another person's life for any reason other than self-defense. People's needs or the needs of the Ethical State give them no right to any part of another person's life.

A fetus has no right to any part of its mother's life, and any woman has the absolute right to abort any fetus or embryo that is entirely dependent on her for life, since she is the sole owner of her life and body. Although this may be a destructive, evil act, it is a completely private and legal act, allowable under the Constitution of the Ethical State. The rights of the mother are always absolutely superior to the rights of the fetus, but this changes once a child is born.

Once a dependent is born, it acquires an absolute right to its own life, but it has no liberty, property, or privacy that is not given by its parents. These rights are acquired gradually as the dependent matures, until it qualifies for the absolute rights of a full citizen of the Ethical State.

Dependents have no right to any part of their parents' life, liberty, property, or privacy. However, parents who neglect their children by denying them proper care and education are violating their oath of citizenship. They may be found guilty of dependent abuse and subject to remedial counseling at the discretion of a Court and jury who find, by unanimous consensus, that the parents are guilty of dependent abuse.

Parents have a vested right to care for their children as they see fit. The Ethical State may interfere in a parent's child rearing solely after the parent has been found guilty of dependent abuse by one independent Court.

A Court may then recommend, but not force, parents into remedial counseling. If the parents refuse this counseling, or if they continue systematically to abuse their dependents, then the Ethical State may revoke their citizenship upon conviction of dependent abuse by two additional independent Courts, and send the parents together with all their dependents into non-criminal exile to any nation or region that will accept them.

A sentence of exile for dependent abuse shall be enforced solely after the parents have been found guilty of dependent abuse by the two independent Courts, and after at least one of these same Courts recommends exile as a necessary remedy for the well-being of the other citizens of the Ethical State. The Ethical State should never tolerate citizens who abuse their dependents, but protecting the rights of both parents and dependents is the responsibility and obligation of the Ethical State.

The resolution of conflicts between the rights of parents and the rights of dependents is the ethical, moral, and legal issue to which the Ethical State shall give its most careful attention. But the rights of parents shall always come before the rights of dependents.

The Ethical State shall not tolerate parents who severely or systematically abuse their dependents, since the Ethical State is also obligated to protect the life, liberty, property, and privacy of dependents But the Ethical State is also obligated to protect the rights of parents to care for their dependents according to the dictates of their consciences alone. Therefore, if this conflict in obligations cannot be resolved by voluntary counseling, all such dependent abusers shall be subject to exile, but not as ordinary criminals.

All such parents may simply secede from the Ethical State, keeping title to their land and property and voluntarily leaving the Ethical State, or may be exiled to the territory of other nations. Whenever possible, exiled parents and their dependents shall be exiled to a nation or region of their choice.

The Ethical State and its agents may never forcibly remove a dependent from its parents' custody, except by the lawful request of either the dependent or the parents.

Dependents shall increase their own rights to life, liberty, property, and privacy as they become less dependent. Any dependent may petition any Magistrate for complete independence from his or her parents if, and only if, the dependent is able to make the petition, qualifies for citizenship, or has found another set of parents willing to adopt him or her.

A dependent may not be adopted by new parents without the explicit consent of either the dependent or the previous parents. Such adoption must be approved by the unanimous consent of an independent Court and jury, whose main focus must be in serving the best interests of the dependent. Otherwise the parental rights of the original parents shall control.

After adoption, the new parents shall assume full legal responsibility for the dependent, and the former parents shall no longer have any liability, responsibility, obligations, or rights with respect to the adoptee.

A person's rights to liberty, privacy, and property may not be infringed, except upon indictment for a crime or as part of a just and proper investigation of a crime or civil offense, as determined by law, and after sworn testimony that this infringement is necessary, given before a Magistrate. Such infringements must be temporary, conditional, just, proper, appropriate, and according to law as determined by a Magistrate after the sworn testimony is given. The giving of knowingly false testimony before a Magistrate or a Court shall be treated as a serious crime by the Ethical State.

Private property may not be permanently taken or in any way infringed upon, except for just compensation to remedy an undeserved harm that was done to another. Such permanent takings and infringements must be first unanimously approved by two independent Courts and juries according to law.

Any property, or any rights to property, which may be required for the public good may not be taken or used except after just compensation. Such compensation shall be deemed just if, and only if, it is acceptable to the property owner. Restrictions on property use shall be considered a taking unless it can be proved beyond a reasonable doubt before two independent Courts that such restrictions are necessary to prevent harm to, or the reckless endangerment of, others.

The right of the people to privacy is inviolable, except when absolutely necessary in the investigation or prevention of a crime. The people's right to be secure in their persons, houses, papers, and effects against unreasonable searches and seizures shall not be violated, and no warrants shall issue but upon probable cause, supported by oath or affirmation, and particularly describing the place to be searched and the persons or things to be seized.

Persons may inflict deadly force, on sight, upon anyone who breaks into their home. Trespassers upon land may be subject to force solely if they do not leave upon being warned that they are trespassing. All force should always be avoided if its absence does not put people in peril. However, the primary obligation of citizens is first to protect themselves, their families, their neighbors, and their property, and only then to concern themselves with the civil rights of intruders, burglars, robbers, or attackers. No force used in self-defense shall be considered excessive except upon conviction by two independent Courts and juries.

The laws of the Ethical State must reflect the absolute freedom of any individual to do as he or she wishes with his or her own life, liberty, property, and privacy, so long as the individual does not violate the freedom of another to do the same. When there is a conflict it shall be resolved according to law by two independent Courts and juries.

No one is ever entitled to inflict undeserved harm on another by infringing on a person's life, liberty, property, or privacy. The first obligation of every citizen of the Ethical State, as well as its Government, is never to inflict undeserved harm on anyone. Harm to another is justified solely in necessary self-defense against an aggressor. Furthermore, this harm always has the potential of being unethical, and must be so regarded before the defender takes action. The Ethical State shall never put any prior constraint on the right to life, liberty, property, and privacy, but, after the fact, it may indict, try, and convict anyone who undeservedly harms or recklessly endangers any non-consenting citizen.

2. Right to Self Defense

The right to self-defense against any aggressor is absolute. Toward this end, the right of all citizens not previously convicted of a crime to arm themselves as they see fit, and to organize themselves into independent, free militias for the purpose of self-defense, shall not be infringed by anyone within the Ethical State.

The sole restriction on the right of self-defense shall be limited to not harming or recklessly endangering innocent inhabitants of the Ethical State by acts of self-defense, e.g., by the use of biological, chemical, nuclear, or other weapons of mass destruction. Reckless endangerment of others shall always be regarded as a crime by the Ethical State, to be judged by two independent Courts after the fact. There shall be no prior constraint put on the right to self-defense, but reckless endangerment of others shall always be a crime, and never tolerated.

Harm to an aggressor or anyone who threatens aggression shall be tolerated by all citizens and agents of an Ethical State, so long as the harm inflicted is necessary and appropriate to defend any inhabitant or citizen of the Ethical State. What is appropriate and necessary in any given case shall be determined only after the fact, and according to law, by independent Courts, if charges are made and indictments issued.

3. Right to Fair, Speedy, and Equal Justice

No one shall be indicted for any crime except by the unanimous consensus of a full independent Court and jury. A jury and Court shall be one and the same, and shall consist of exactly four male and four female jurists, unanimously elected as Magistrates by the duly elected representatives of the citizens of the Ethical State. Each Court and jury shall elect, by unanimous consensus, a Representative Pair to speak for it, coordinate and organize its activities, and otherwise interact with all parties to a trial. These elected Representatives of the Courts shall form the higher-level Courts.

All trials, criminal or civil, must be public and open to public scrutiny, but the public may be restricted to a fixed number of spectators if the demand for access to the trial is excessive, or would interfere with the defendant's right to a fair and just trial. When in doubt, greater weight should be given to the need for public scrutiny.

Warrentless arrests shall not be made except during the act, or immediate aftermath, of a crime for which there is clear evidence against the suspect. Otherwise, the arresting authorities must possess a warrant for arrest from a Magistrate, issued upon probable cause or after an indictment. All arrested and/or indicted suspects shall be considered innocent until proven guilty to the unanimous satisfaction of two independent Courts and juries, which shall sit in judgment of the accused simultaneously, but independently of each other.

An arrested suspect must be allowed counsel and a hearing before a Magistrate within twenty-four hours of arrest. All suspects have the right to remain silent, or to provide no information beyond identifying themselves and, if they wish, declaring themselves innocent. The Magistrate shall determine either that the suspect's case be referred to a full Court for indictment, with the suspect remaining under arrest or given the opportunity of bail, or that the suspect shall be set free because of insufficient evidence.

An indictment hearing shall be held before one independent Court and jury, solely upon recommendation of a Magistrate, who shall carefully consider the physical evidence and all sworn testimony and then determine whether there is enough evidence to warrant an indictment hearing.

All indicted suspects shall be regarded as innocent until proven guilty according to law. In criminal trials, or upon arrest, no one may be forced to testify against him or herself, and may remain silent.

A suspect must always be immediately informed of his or her right to remain silent and to seek counsel at the time of arrest. A confession of guilt by the accused may not be used as evidence except after the accused has received, or clearly refused, counsel. The entire burden of proof is upon the prosecuting officers.

The Courts themselves must independently seek the truth in the matter, ask questions, and order independent investigations when necessary. They must not rely solely on the effectiveness of the advocacy system to discover the truth. The objective is truth and justice, not a determination of which side has the most effective advocate.

After arrest, the preliminary case against an unindicted suspect must be quickly sent to a full Court by the Magistrate, if the police authorities have sufficient evidence to convince the Magistrate that the suspect is probably guilty and will probably be indicted by a full Court. The Magistrate shall set or deny bail for the suspect, who shall be freed upon the payment of this bail, pending the indictment hearing before a full Court and jury.

The indictment Court may free the suspect, grant bail if the suspect had previously been denied bail, reduce or increase the bail, revoke the bail, or take other appropriate action, depending on the case against the suspect. If the evidence against the suspect is reasonable and probable, a full trial must be ordered by the indictment Court.

Bail must be offered, or reasonably denied, to a suspect within twenty-four hours of arrest. All suspects are entitled to counsel at the bail hearings before the Magistrate and the full Court. Bail must not be excessive, but must reflect the seriousness of the crime, the danger that the suspect poses to the citizens of the Ethical State, and the probability that the suspect will flee if bail is granted.

While under arrest, the suspect must be treated with respect and kept safe and reasonably comfortable. Unnecessary force may not be used in arresting or restraining the suspect. No suspect may be put in the close company of other suspects, but must be restrained in a place of privacy, safety, dignity, and acceptable human health and comfort.

The Ethical State shall assure that there are sufficient Magistrates, jurors, Courts, and restraining facilities to give all arrested persons quick and prompt bail hearings and trials. The indictment hearing before a full Court must begin within seventy-two hours of the Magistrate's hearing, but the Courts should always give the suspect all the time he or she needs to properly defend him or herself, so long as the suspect remains under arrest and the demands for extra time are not unreasonable. When bail is granted, the trial may take up to thirty days to begin, but, at the request of the suspect, additional time to prepare a defense may be given, solely at the discretion of the Court. Neither the prosecutor nor the complainant in a civil case may demand more time to prepare.

All suspects are entitled to legal representation and counsel from the time of arrest or indictment, whichever comes first. However, the laws and legal procedures must be sufficiently clear and simple that any suspect or civil offender may defend him or herself. The Magistrates and Courts shall never favor either party in a hearing or a trial, but do their best to get at the truth. The advocacy system is never enough for a just trial.

No one shall be convicted of a crime except upon the unanimous, simultaneous determination of guilt by two independent Courts of law consisting solely of two impartial juries unanimously elected by the citizens of the Ethical State, as prescribed by law. It takes solely the unanimous decision of a single Court to acquit a suspect, but conviction can occur solely upon the unanimous decision of guilt by two independent Courts and juries, who shall simultaneously hear the case.

If neither Court can reach a unanimous decision to convict or acquit a suspect, the suspect must be set free without bail; however, at the unanimous request of one of the Courts, two higher Courts must try the suspect once again. If both Courts again fail to reach a unanimous decision to convict, or none of the Courts reaches a unanimous decision to acquit, the suspect must be set free and not tried again, except on the presentation of new evidence, which convinces a new, higher Court that a new trial is warranted by a still higher Court.

There shall be enough Courts and jurists to guarantee that this system can assure each suspect a speedy and fair trial. There shall be no plea bargaining; charges and trials must be based entirely on the true and proper evidence, never on suspicions or plea bargains. If the charges exceed the evidence, then the suspect must be acquitted, even if there is evidence for a lesser crime that was not charged.

All convicted criminals are entitled to appeal to at least two additional, and higher, Courts. After this, there can be no further appeal of the conviction, but the convict may continue to appeal for probation and pardon. Probation or pardon can be given solely upon evidence that the convicted criminal has, with reasonable probability, been rehabilitated, or upon new evidence that the convict might be innocent.

No behavior shall be regarded as a crime unless it deliberately or knowingly imposes undeserved harm upon a victim. There shall be no victimless crimes in the Ethical State. Harm is causing any decrease to a person's intelligence or ethics. Harm is undeserved if it is done against the will of the person harmed for purposes other than self-defense. Possibly harmful but victimless behavior, such as voluntary drug use, voluntary prostitution, and many forms of common, but harmful, educational and religious practices, shall not be considered criminal by the Ethical State, but may lead to charges of dependent abuse if applicable.

However, inducing anyone to harm him or herself unknowingly may be considered a crime, if it is done contrary to law, even if all the parties involved are acting voluntarily. This may include false or misleading advertising, or inducing a dependent to self-harm without the consent of the dependent's parents, though parental consent shall not remove liability for otherwise criminal behavior. Parental consent to induce a dependent to self-harm may lead to charges of abuse against the parent.

Inflicting undeserved harm to another unknowingly shall be a civil offense, remedied solely by just and proper material compensation, as determined by law and two independent Courts.

A civil suit against any party in the Ethical State may solely be brought before the Courts upon the full, unanimous agreement of the Complementary Pair constituting a Magistrate. Such consent shall not be unreasonably delayed or denied, but shall be carefully considered according to the law and the system of justice of the Ethical State.

A Magistrate shall consist of exactly one male and one female citizen of the Ethical State, who have been elected by appropriate

Octets according to law. Any inhabitant may petition any Magistrate anywhere in the Ethical State for a regress of grievances. All Magistrates are required to consider, at least once and both carefully and justly, anyone's petition to sue. The suit may be against anyone within the Ethical State.

When a Magistrate denies a petition, the petitioner may continue to petition Magistrates until one grants the right to sue, or may seek an indictment against anyone upon paying a proper fee. Such fees must be reasonable, just, and not excessive. These fees may increase, as determined by law, as repeated petitions are submitted to and denied by successive Magistrates.

Systematic and reckless behavior by any inhabitant of the Ethical State, if it leads repeatedly to the imposition of undeserved harm upon any of the inhabitants of the Ethical State, may be determined by a Court to be criminal behavior, even if such behavior is not deliberately or knowingly harmful. The reckless endangerment of any inhabitant of the Ethical State shall be considered a crime if it is unanimously judged so by two independent Courts and juries in open public session.

There shall be no punishment for crimes other than exile, fines, and confiscation of property to compensate the victims of the crimes and the citizens of the Ethical State for the true costs and harm of the crime.

At the discretion of the Courts, convicted criminals may be put on probation or sent to temporary exile until they qualify for probation. Probation and exile shall be in accordance with law.

Cruel and unusual punishment is strictly forbidden to be inflicted on anyone by any citizen, dependent, or agent of the Ethical State. Fines, probation, and exile must not be used as a form of punishment, but solely to justly compensate and protect victims or potential victims of convicted criminals. Every form of execution, torture, involuntary servitude, maiming, or excessive restraint shall be regarded as cruel and unusual punishment.

The conditions of probation and exile must allow the convicted criminals a reasonable opportunity to rehabilitate themselves and to qualify once again for full citizenship without prejudice. But the Ethical State's primary obligation to protect the life, liberty, property, and privacy of its citizens must come first. Therefore, the conditions of exile must be adequate to protect its citizens, while giving reasonable opportunities to the criminal for full rehabilitation. This must all be done according to law.

Minor criminals, dependent abusers, and systematic civil offenders may be subject to exile, as a form of probation, to any nation or region that will accept them, after being informed of their conviction. Otherwise, it remains the obligation of the Ethical State to protect humanity from these persons.

At the discretion of the Courts, probation may be granted solely on condition that the convicted criminal becomes the dependent of two parents, one a male and the other a female citizen of the Ethical State, who agree to assume full responsibility for all the civil and criminal acts committed by their new dependent. However, the conditions of probation shall always be at the discretion of the Court granting the probation, so long as they do not constitute cruel and unusual punishment.

The judicial process shall be readily available to all citizens of the Ethical State for the purpose of lodging criminal and civil complaints, and for enforcing contracts. Contracts shall not be legally binding unless they are in writing and signed by all parties to the contract. Contracts shall always be binding if they are notarized by a Magistrate at the time of signing. Otherwise they may be declared valid or invalid by a Magistrate, according to law and after the request of one of the parties to the contract. Solely valid contracts may be brought as evidence in civil trials.

4. Freedom of Communication

All citizens have an absolute right to voluntarily communicate in private any true information among themselves. All inhabitants of the Ethical State have an absolute right to receive any communication from any source, from within or from outside the Ethical State.

Restrictions on communication shall exist solely in regard to the communication of false or undeservedly harmful information, however the voluntary exchange of false information in private may not be infringed. What is false or undeservedly harmful information can be determined solely by independent Courts according to law. There may be no prior constraint on the right to communicate.

Such undeservedly harmful communication shall include false or misleading advertising, threats to impose undeserved harm on anyone, extortion, blackmail, slander, libel, violation of copyright, patent, or privacy laws, child or sadomasochistic pornography whose production imposed undeserved harm on an unwilling participant or any dependent, advertising an unsafe product or service without clearly specifying all the known dangers in using that product or service, offensive noise or odors, and other undeservedly harmful communication, as determined by the laws and Courts of the Ethical State after the fact.

The Ethical State shall have the power to enforce contracts if, and only if, these contracts are in writing. Oral contracts shall not be legally binding, but oral false advertising may be subject to legal sanctions. The violation of a contract is a backward form of fraud, and shall be treated as fraud according to law. Disputes concerning binding contracts should first be resolved, if possible, before a Magistrate with no lawyers present. If they may not be so resolved, the Magistrate, at its discretion, may refer the dispute to two full Courts.

5. Freedom of Assembly

The freedom of peaceful, voluntary assembly on private property is a right which may not be infringed, unless the purpose of the assembly involves a criminal conspiracy or a reckless endangerment of non-consenting parties to the assembly. A criminal conspiracy and the reckless endangerment of non-consenting parties can be established solely by the unanimous consensus of two independent Courts. Arresting officers in the case of criminal conspiracy or reckless endangerment must have clear evidence for these crimes, or they shall be guilty of a crime themselves.

Any form of sexual behavior between mutually consenting citizens which is voluntary and private shall not be infringed by the Ethical State, except when involving dependents, who may not marry or engage in any sexual activity without the consent of their parents. As a consequence, sexual relationships involving dependents may be illegal and may be prosecuted as a crime. For example, statutory rape may be prosecuted at the request of one of the parents, even if the sexual activity was consensual. Dependents may not enter into binding contracts or be given or sold harmful or dangerous substances, no matter what their age.

Marriage implies an ethical, evolutionary contract, even when it is not in writing, and should not be entered into lightly. Marriage, or its absence, shall be a matter of private morality, and shall be of no concern to the Ethical State, but seen as a form of private assembly. However, any written contract of marriage, or of other partnerships, shall be enforced under the contractual laws of the Ethical State if a breach of this contract occurs, and if this breach is proved to the unanimous satisfaction of two independent Courts and juries.

As part of their personal contractual obligations of citizenship, biological and legal adoptive parents of children and other dependents, married or not, must both assume the responsibilities and obligations of parenthood, and provide adequate care, nurturing and education for their dependents, as determined by law, or they shall be guilty of dependent abuse or dependent abandonment. The latter shall be treated as a serious crime. The parents of a dependent may always give their children up for adoption, thereby avoiding all legal responsibility for their former dependents after they are legally adopted.

The formation of private clubs, societies, partnerships, and organizations is an absolute right. The Ethical State may not force any individual, club, society, partnership or other private organizations to accept persons they do not wish to accept. All such organizations may exclude from membership anyone they wish, on any basis they wish.

The Ethical State may demand appropriate restrictions and obligations, according to law, for any assembly that is to be done on public property managed by the Ethical State for the benefit of all its citizens. No permission for any such assemblies shall be given unless the rights of all citizens are respected by the assembly. Permission to assemble on public property shall not be denied except on the basis of criminal behavior or other behavior deemed by law to be destructive or improper.

The use or lease of any natural resources may be similarly restricted according to law, and may be used or leased solely upon the determination, by a Court, that such use or lease does not discriminate against any citizens of the Ethical State. Criteria for the use or lease of resources must be entirely behavioral, and must not involve discrimination against people on the basis of age, national origin, race, gender, belief, religion, ethnicity, social status, or other non-behavioral traits.

These resources must be available to all citizens on an equal basis, or otherwise used or leased with the permission of the authorities responsible for those resources, such permission not to be unreasonably or unjustly denied or delayed.

6. Freedom of Religion

The Ethical State shall neither support nor oppose any religion or ritual, so long as it is private and voluntary. However, the Ethical State and its citizens are obligated to prosecute as criminal activities all religious activities which impose undeserved harm on innocent, unconsenting parties. This shall be done in accordance with the laws governing the communication of undeservedly harmful information and the commission of other crimes.

All religious activities or rituals are unconditionally permitted until they are proved, to the unanimous and full satisfaction of two independent Courts of law, to impose undeserved harm on innocent parties who are not participating voluntarily in these religious activities or rituals. Dependents do not have the right to consent to anything, except with the express permission of their parents, who must be citizens. Otherwise religionists are allowed to harm and destroy themselves voluntarily.

Forcing dependents to participate in religious activities harmful to themselves shall be regarded as a form of dependent abuse, once this is proved to the satisfaction of two independent Courts and juries.

Public resources may not be used to promote any religious beliefs, but may be used to communicate the ethical practices of anyone. A religious belief is any assertion of cause and effect relationships for which there is absolutely no objective evidence for its truth or falsity. Personal opinions for which there is some evidence, but not scientific proof, may be communicated through the use of public resources as personal opinion, but not as fact. In general, the electro-magnetic spectrum may not be used to promote or oppose any religious belief.

Any belief of any kind, even if it is objectively false, may be communicated in private to voluntary listeners. False beliefs may, under some circumstances, be communicated in public, if the information communicated is preceded by the phrase, "I may be wrong, but it seems to me that…"

7. Equal Rights and Obligations Under The Law

All citizens of the Ethical State shall have equal rights and obligations under its Constitution. There shall be no specially privileged classes or individuals. All inhabitants within the territory of the Ethical State shall be entitled to equal rights and protection under its laws. When feasible, the Ethical State shall extend protection to its citizens and their dependents while living or traveling outside of the Ethical State.

Upon receiving a passport, citizens shall be advised by the military of the Ethical State of locales where it is not feasible to protect them, with supporting reasons. The military of the Ethical State shall be responsible for a diplomatic corps under the command of the President. The main function of the Ethical State in regard to foreign relations shall be to protect the life, liberty, property, and privacy of its citizens from foreign invaders at home, and from criminals and foreign governments while traveling abroad. There shall be no foreign treaties nor entanglements, much less alliances, except with other sovereign ethical states. There shall be no foreign aid, loans, or gifts given by the Government of the Ethical State at the expense of any of its citizens.

All citizens of the Ethical State are entitled to a passport to travel wherever they wish and to return at will to the Ethical State. Such a passport shall be easily and speedily granted by a Magistrate upon paying of an appropriate fee, submitting an appropriate photograph, and showing proof of citizenship. All such fees and requirements must be equal for all citizens.

Convicted criminals and persons neither citizens nor dependents of citizens may be excluded from entry into territory of the Ethical State upon the sole and exclusive judgment of any officer of the Ethical State. Anyone with a valid passport, or other proof of citizenship from the Ethical State, shall be deemed to have sufficient proof for entry into the Ethical State.

Once inside the Ethical State, illegal aliens must be given the full protection of the laws regarding any crimes they are alleged to have committed, or before being deported for illegal entry. Illegal aliens shall be treated as foreign invaders, but according to the ethical and legal principles of the Ethical State.

No one shall be denied citizenship or equal protection of the law, nor have their obligations under law abridged, because of age, national origin, place of birth, race, gender, ethnicity, socioeconomic status, or religion. The full rights of citizenship may be suspended temporarily, but solely for persons arrested or indicted for a crime, all such rights being restored upon acquittal. Persons convicted of a crime by the unanimous consensus of two independent juries, as determined by law, may lose their civil rights permanently, and may be exiled outside of the Ethical State, according to law.

The Ethical State shall maintain appropriate places of exile, so that a sentence of exile never becomes a form of cruel and unusual punishment or a form of abuse to citizens of other nations.

8. Right to Limited and Fair Taxation

Taxation must be limited and fair. Solely citizens and partnerships among citizens may be taxed. No citizen or partnership may ever have yearly taxes imposed upon them which are greater than ten percent of their combined gross yearly income, ten percent of the value of all the goods and services they buy or receive during the year, or one percent of the fair market value of all their net assets during the year, whichever is greatest.

At any given time, the Ethical State may levy taxes solely of one kind: on income, on purchases or receipts of goods or services, or on the net, fair-market value of all property owned in any fiscal year. The taxation criteria shall not be changed without unanimous approval by the four highest Levels of Government, allowing at least two years of warning to the public.

All citizens shall pay the same percentage of their gross income, purchases and trades, or their net worth in taxes, which shall be collected from all citizens in a fair and uniform manner.

Any citizen may refuse to pay taxes, and shall no longer be entitled to citizenship in, the protection of, or any services from the Ethical State, but shall not be criminally liable for this refusal, nor owe any future taxes. The sole penalty for refusing to pay taxes shall be non-criminal exile and loss of citizenship. The paying of taxes is part of the contract of citizenship, which is voluntarily chosen.

All taxes, fines, and fees collected by the Ethical State shall be used entirely and exclusively for the defense of the civil rights, life,

liberty, property, and privacy of the citizens and of the public resources, unless there is a unanimous consensus by the five highest
Levels of Government that another activity, such as education or
transportation, should be supported by taxes. This shall be done entirely through the establishment and maintenance of police organizations, military organizations, a system and Courts of justice, a system
of public health and environmental protection, and a representative
system of government, with adequate checks and balances as determined by law.

Taxes may never be used to give advantages, or any kind of benefits, to any group of citizens at the expense of another group of citizens. The activities of Government must be limited entirely to the
equal protection of the civil rights of all its citizens, both inside and
outside the territory of the Ethical State.

Corporations shall pay taxes as if they were partnerships. The
officers and board of directors of the corporation shall be liable for
these taxes and criminally liable for any crimes committed by the
corporation. Stockholders in corporations who are neither officers nor
board members shall not be liable for the debts or crimes of the corporation, but shall be taxed solely on the gross value of all benefits
received from the corporation as part of their personal income for a
given year.

9. Limitations On Corporate Power

A corporation shall be treated as a dependent of its board of directors
and its officers, who shall be personally responsible for any crimes
or civil offenses that the corporation commits, if the corporation cannot otherwise satisfy all fines and compensations legally resulting
from these corporate offenses. Corporations may not own any natural resources or land, but must lease these resources from individual
citizens of the Ethical State. Private citizens are the sole persons or
entities entitled to own land and resources or to lease them directly
from the Ethical State.

The owners of these resources shall remain personally, criminally,
and civilly liable for offenses committed through the use of these resources by a corporation, if the assets of the corporation, its directors,
and/or its officers are not sufficient to cover the costs of the offenses

committed by the corporation. Their criminal liability shall be less than that of the direct controllers of the corporation.

No organizations of any kind may legally exist for the purpose of avoiding taxes. Not-for-profit organizations will have to pay taxes on the basis of their gross income, their purchases, or their net-worth, even if they never pay dividends.

No entity of the Ethical State shall ever have property confiscated for tax evasion except upon conviction by two independent Courts. But they may have liens placed on their property upon indictment. There may be no punishment inflicted upon convicted tax evaders other than non-criminal exile and fair and just confiscation of property to compensate for fraud and back taxes. Those who do not wish to pay taxes should secede from the Ethical State.

10. Right of Secession

Any citizen may, for any reason, secede from the Ethical State upon declaring publicly before a Magistrate his or her true reasons for secession and renouncing his or her citizenship.

Upon secession, the citizen shall have no more obligations or owe any more taxes, but shall keep title to all his or her land and property, as well as retaining all parental rights, if the citizen has no pending legal debts or liens as determined by a Magistrate. If a citizen has such debts or liens, the Courts may, according to law, confiscate some or all of his or her property to pay these debts.

After secession, the ex-citizen and his or her property are no longer part of the Ethical State, and may be disposed of as the ex-citizen wishes, including making them a part of another nation. The ex-citizen and his or her assets shall no longer be under the protection of the Ethical State, and shall no longer be part of the Ethical State.

11. Right to Limited Government

The Government of the Ethical State is strictly limited to protecting the civil rights of its citizens, and may assume no other powers without their unanimous consensus, as determined by law. This is the sole power granted to the Government. The Government of the Ethical State is specifically prohibited from ever using the lives, assets, or taxes of some of its citizens for doing good for anyone else.

12. Right to all Rights Not Granted to the Government

The enumeration in the Constitution of certain rights shall not be construed to disparage others retained by the people. All rights not specifically given to the Government belong exclusively and solely to each citizen of the Ethical State.

STRUCTURE OF GOVERNMENT

The Government shall be structured as a representative republic by consensus hierarchy. All major parts of Government shall consist of men and women, all of whom are citizens of the Ethical State, in groups or committees that work together and make decisions solely by consensus. These groups and committees shall be called "Octets," and shall consist of exactly four men and four women. No part of Government may make a temporary decision unless it has been unanimously approved by an appropriate Representative Pair at an appropriate Level and then quickly confirmed by the entire Octet of which the Representative Pair are members.

Minor parts of Government shall consist of at least one man and one woman, called "Complementary Pairs." All Magistrates and functionaries of Octets must consist of at least one Complementary Pair.

No decision of Government may be made unless it is by agreement of at least one Complementary Pair. Temporary decisions shall continue to be made by unanimous consensus of all the Octets, for increasing periods of time, until there are at least sixteen higher level Octets, at which time decisions shall be permanent unless the law is changed by at least the sixteen highest Octets constituting the full Congress of the Ethical State.

Once there are sixteen higher level Octets, they shall form a Congress of 128 persons who may make permanent decisions on behalf of the entire Ethical State solely by unanimous consensus.

No permanent decision of Government may be made unless it is agreed to by mutual consensus of either all the Octets in the Ethical State or at least the sixteen highest Octets composing the Congress of the Government. Each Octet must always consist of exactly four

Complementary Pairs. If such consensus is not forthcoming, Government should do nothing.

The First Level of Government

The First Level of Government shall exist whenever four Complementary Pairs can reach unanimous consensus on working together for their mutual benefit. This shall be known as a First Level Octet.

Individual members of Complementary Pairs and Octets may choose one another on any basis they wish, and may have special agreements and contracts between them, so long as they do not violate the Constitution and laws of the Ethical State. They need not involve married couples, but must always include equal numbers of men and women.

Citizens at the First Level of Government may choose their Complementary Pairs and Octets as they wish, and change Complementary Pairs and Octets whenever they wish, but once elected to represent an Octet they must keep the same Complement or cease being a representative at all the Levels to which they have been elected. This shall also occur if one member of the Pair resigns, becomes incapacitated, is convicted of a crime, or dies.

Every Octet at every Level shall elect one, and only one, Complementary Pair to represent it at the next Level of Government, until there is a single Complementary Pair representing all the Levels of Government. This last Complementary Pair shall always be designated the President of the Ethical State, no matter how few Octets there are in the Ethical State.

The President of The Ethical State shall be the Commander in Chief of all its armed forces and all other executive functionaries, but shall have no control over any jurists, or any representatives chosen by jurists, except in time of National Emergency, when not more than half the jurists may be temporarily called up to active military duty at the discretion of the President. The President then is their Commander in Chief, but solely in regard to their military duties; their judicial duties shall cease upon call to active military service.

This structure of Government shall exist however small or large the Ethical State may be, but no government shall exist until there is at least one Octet working together by unanimous consensus. One full Octet is the minimum number of persons who can form an Ethical Republic.

All members and affiliated citizens of Level One Octets shall be members of the inactive military reserve, and subject to call to active duty under the direct command of their elected representatives in time of National or Local Emergency, solely at the discretion of their representatives. All Level One Octet members and affiliated citizens must be armed, at their discretion, and ready to defend their families and neighbors at all times from all enemies, foreign and domestic.

At each Level above the First Level, the Complementary Pair representing the Octet at the lower Level shall organize itself with three other Complementary Pairs at the same Level of representation to form a new, higher-level Octet of representation. If there are two or more Complementary Pairs, but not yet a full Octet, at a given Level of representation above the First Level, then the existing Complementary Pairs shall elect a single Complementary Pair to represent them. Until that time they shall work entirely by unanimous consensus, or do nothing.

If there is solely one Octet in the Ethical State, then the entire Government shall consist solely of the single Executive Pair and the Octet that elected the President, and all powers of the Government shall be vested in the President and the one Octet. Consequently, the President may only make temporary decisions; permanent decisions for the full Octet may only be made by reaching full consensus within the entire Octet. No executive decision is binding for more than seven days, unless the full Executive Octet agrees to it by unanimous consensus. No judicial decision is binding unless it is made by two full Courts, or unless it is unanimously approved by all the citizens of the Ethical State when there are not enough citizens for four full Courts, with two to handle appeals.

Each Level One Octet is autonomous and sovereign. The Level One Octets are the units of sovereignty within the Ethical State. The rest of the Government is granted solely the powers enumerated within this Constitution. A Level One Octet may bring onto its own territory in the Ethical State any immigrant it wishes, so long as he or she either qualifies for citizenship or is adopted by unanimous consent of the adoptee and the Octet, sworn before a Magistrate. The Octet may not bring any other person onto the territory of the Ethical State. An Octet may produce, sell, or export any goods and/or services it wishes, so long as this does not cause reckless endangerment to other Octets and their affiliated citizens. It may import any goods, but not persons, that do not cause a reckless endangerment of other Octets and citizens of the Ethical State.

Any Octet may recall any of its representatives at any time, but solely if they have not been elected by a higher Level Octet to a higher Level of Government. Once any representatives are elected to a higher Level of Government, they may be recalled and removed from office solely by consensus among the remaining three Complementary Pairs at the immediately lower Level of Government that elected them, or by the unanimous consensus of the remaining members of the Level One Octet that originally elected this Complementary Pair to represent them. Otherwise, they shall remain in office for a period not to exceed eight years, or until they are elected to a higher Level office, in which case they may remain in that office for a period not to exceed eight years, or until they are elected to a still higher office. This shall hold for all representatives at all Levels of office until they are removed from office by recall, death, incapacitation, retirement, or resignation.

The President of the Ethical State, who cannot be elected to a higher office, cannot remain in office for longer than eight years, or until the Pair is removed by recall, death, incapacitation, or resignation. Once a President has served for eight years, both members of the Pair must retire and never again serve in elected office, although they may return to be members of their original Level One Octet or join any other Level One Octet of their choice that will accept them.

The President may declare a State of National Emergency for a period not to exceed seven days. At that time the State of National Emergency shall cease to exist unless it is unanimously approved by the Octet that elected the President.

Once there are at least two Level One Octets who can agree by consensus to work together as part of the Government of the Ethical State, they may jointly begin electing two sets of Complementary Pairs to represent them, and begin adding to the Second Level of Government.

John David Garcia

The Second Level of Government

The Second Level of Government shall always consist of at least one Complementary Pair, but is not limited in the number of Complementary Pairs, all elected by their respective Level One Octets. Once there are at least four sets of elected Complementary Pairs at the Second Level of Government, they shall, by consensus, form new Octets that agree to work together to elect new Third Level representatives, or work entirely by one hundred percent consensus.

If there are at least two Complementary Pairs, but not yet a full Octet, of representatives at the Second Level, then any Pair they elect by consensus shall be a temporary president until approved by the unanimous consensus of four Complementary Pairs, who shall form the Executive Octet that elects, and includes, the President. Once a Presidential Pair is elected, it can be removed solely by consensus among the remaining Complementary Pairs of the existing Executive Octet, or by the three remaining Complementary Pairs in the Level One Octet that originally elected the President.

The Executive Octet can extend a State of National Emergency by unanimous consensus for a period not to exceed thirty days. Otherwise it shall either work with the President or remove the President by consensus, if the President will not otherwise end the State of National Emergency.

The primary responsibility of the Second Level Octets is to (1) assure that they do not inflict undeserved harm on anyone, and always work within the framework of the Constitution, (2) jointly defend and protect the civil rights of the Level One Octets who elected them, (3) elect new representatives to form the Third Level of Government, and (4) closely supervise the performance of their representatives to make sure that they are properly protecting the civil rights of the Octets they represent, within the constraints of the Constitution.

Second Level Complementary Pairs who cannot form Octets or reach consensus on who shall represent them shall have no representation at the Third Level. They are still obligated to continue doing their best to form such Octets and otherwise to fulfill their obligations to the Octets that elected them.

The lower-level Octets shall focus on their public safety functions, but they shall also be part of the military active reserve and

154

the public health service of the Ethical State. They shall maintain military readiness, and all equipment necessary to perform their obligations. The taxes paid by the citizens of the Ethical State shall be used entirely to maintain the readiness of the Octets at all Levels of Government, through a hierarchical system of tax distribution to be determined by law.

All Octets of representatives at the Second Level of Government shall elect one, and only one, of their Pairs to represent them. If fewer than four Octets are elected to the Third Level, then all the representatives at the Third Level are Executive Pairs of the Ethical State. They shall either elect a Presidential Pair or work entirely by consensus.

The Third Level of Government

The duties and obligations of all the Third Level Octets are similar to those of the lower level Octets, but they shall also do their best to coordinate the activities of the lower-level Octets, with their mutual consent. In times of National Emergency they may, at the direction of the President, assume temporary military command of the lower-level Octets that they represent until the Emergency is over. During a National State of Emergency, the military shall operate as a command hierarchy, according to military law, under the overall command of the President, who shall always be the Commander in Chief.

All Octets of representatives at the Third Level of Government shall elect one, and only one, of their peer Pairs to represent them. If fewer than four Octets are elected to the Fourth Level, then all the representatives at the Fourth Level are Executive Pairs of the Ethical State. They shall either elect a Presidential Pair or work entirely by consensus.

Once there are four Level Three Octets, they shall jointly form a Senate, assume their corresponding duties, and serve to protect and defend all the people of all the Octets that elected them, in conformity with the Constitution. The elected representative Pairs of the four Senatorial Octets shall jointly form the Executive Octet, which may elect a president or work entirely by consensus.

The Fourth Level of Government

All Octets of representatives at the Fourth Level of Government shall elect one, and only one, of their peer Pairs to represent them.

John David Garcia

If fewer than four Octets are elected to the Fourth Level, then all the representatives at the Fourth Level are Executive Pairs of the Ethical State. They shall either elect a Presidential Pair or work entirely by consensus.

Once there are four Level Four Octets, they shall form a Senate and assume their corresponding duties and serve to protect and defend all the people of all the Octets that elected them, in conformity with the Constitution. All their elected Representative Pairs shall jointly form the Executive Octet, which may elect a president or work entirely by consensus.

The Fifth Level of Government

The Fifth Level of Government shall be the highest Level until there are sixteen Octets at the Fifth Level. All these Octets at the Fifth Level shall constitute the Congress of the Ethical State, which, of course, shall also include the entire Senate, the Executive Octet and the President. Solely the full Congress shall be empowered to make permanent decisions, by unanimous consensus, for the entire Ethical State, in passing or revoking laws, or amending the Constitution other than the Bill of Rights. The Bill of Rights may be amended solely by consensus of the entire Ethical State or by consensus of the 512 highest-level representatives, when there are that many representatives. All states of National Emergency shall end within a year unless they are unanimously extended by the entire Congress.

Once a State of National Emergency has been unanimously approved by the entire Congress, it shall remain in effect until it is revoked by either the President, the remaining Executive Octet, or the Senate.

The Sixth Level of Government

The Sixth Level of Government shall be the highest Level until there are at least sixteen Octets at the Sixth Level. The first sixteen Octets at the Sixth Level shall form the entire Congress of the Ethical State. All Octets elected to the Sixth Level, but not elected to the Congress, shall form part of the Judiciary of the Ethical State.

The Judiciary shall consist of at least one Octet, but may include sixty-four or more Octets, at the discretion of the Executive Octet. The

Executive Octet shall balance the defensive needs of the Ethical State against the judicial needs of all persons, including all members of the military, to a fair, speedy, and just trial, and assure that both needs are in proper balance for a period of thirty days.

The size of the Judiciary may be temporarily changed, for a period of one year, by the unanimous consent of the Senate. The size of the Judiciary may be permanently changed solely with the consent of the entire full Congress or by consensus of all the citizens of the Ethical State.

Until determined otherwise according to law, the Judiciary may not exceed a total of 256 Pairs of Magistrates, i.e., 512 individuals, for every 16,384 Level One Octets of the Ethical State, i.e., for every 131,072 citizens. All members of the Judiciary not elected to the Congress form Magistrates jointly with the Complementary Pair that was elected to the Judiciary with them.

The Magistrates form Courts by mutual consensus of four Magistrates. Any Court that wishes may elect its own representatives to a higher Court, which shall exist when there are at least four such elected Complementary Pairs. Therefore, there shall be no more than 256 Magistrate Pairs in the Judiciary for every 16,384 Level One Octets, or one Pair of Magistrates for every 512 citizens, unless it is so determined by higher Levels of Government. The Magistrates elect judges, the judges elect justices, and the justices elect higher justices, forming a consensus hierarchy of Courts, each with four Complementary Pairs.

The 512 representatives on the sixty-four highest Courts shall elect the Congress by the unanimous consent of each Judicial Octet at that Level, one Congressional Pair for each Judicial Octet. The Congress at all Levels has no power over the Judiciary other than to draft some of them and their resources for military service for a limited time, so long as a National Emergency remains in effect. If the Congress confirms the State of Emergency, it may, solely by unanimous consensus, extend the military draft, at random, to not more than seventy-five percent of the Judiciary at the lower Levels. Even in a State of prolonged National Emergency, the highest ranking Octets of the Judiciary shall not be drafted, although their resources may be made available, at their discretion, for use by the military Octets of the Judiciary that have been called to active duty.

Once a Judicial Complementary Pair has been elected at any Level, that Pair cannot be removed from office except by the Octet that elected it or by the six remaining members of the Level One Octet that originally elected it. All the Magistrates at all Levels may be removed by unanimous consensus of the entire Senate, but solely for incompetence or malfeasance. Judicial decisions shall remain in effect even if all the jurists making them are removed from office, unless a higher Court reverses the decision on appeal.

The Higher Levels of Government

In an Ethical State of 524,288 citizens, i.e., with 65,536 Octets at Level One, the Sixth Level of Government described in the previous section is the fifth highest Level.

The fifth highest Level of Government must always consist entirely of jurists. The immediately lower Levels may also consist entirely of jurists, so as to assure that there are a sufficient number of jurists to assure all citizens of the Ethical State fair, just, and speedy trials. Otherwise, the highest four Levels of Government shall be elected by the consensus of the sixteen or fewer Octets of jurists who have reached the fifth highest Level of Government.

In general, when there are not sufficient Octets of jurists at the fifth highest Level of Government, the higher Levels of Government shall adjust to the situation in order to elect a Presidential Pair. The fifth highest Level of Government will decide whether their elected representatives should assume Congressional functions or Judicial functions. Representatives must do one or the other. They cannot carry out both Congressional functions and Judicial functions.

THE JUDICIARY

The Judiciary shall also be organized in a consensus hierarchy of Octets, with the lower Levels assuming the function of Magistrates of the Ethical State, and the higher Levels of the Judiciary forming a hierarchy of Courts to consider appeals of the decisions of the lower Courts. The highest Courts reached in the hierarchy shall administer the lower Courts, in such a way that the civil rights of all citizens of the Ethical State are maximally protected, within the framework of the Constitution.

Courts shall consist entirely of Jurists who agree by consensus to work together as independent Courts and to hear the complaints and appeals that come from the lower-level Octets. Magistrates will always hear a case before it is referred to a full Court. A trial cannot be held until two full Courts agree to hear the case simultaneously to its completion. If the appropriate lower Courts cannot agree on which trials will be heard at the same time, then any higher Court may order the lower Courts under its jurisdiction to hear the case, and the lower Courts must obey.

Jurists have no executive functions, but they are all reserve military officers of the Ethical State; they must participate in military training and maneuvers to retain their military readiness. This shall be done under the direction and guidance of the highest Judicial Octet in the hierarchy to which the reserve officers belong. This direction and guidance shall be given in such a way so as maximally to protect the civil rights of all citizens, while maintaining adequate military readiness. The priority is the judicial process not military readiness, but neither can military readiness be ignored.

The jurists at the highest Judicial Level shall administer all the jurists in their Ascendancy. Their Ascendancy is the set of all Octets who elected them to their current Judicial Octet.

All Octets at the highest Judicial Levels shall elect their representatives. These representatives shall form the Congress of up to sixteen Octets. The Congress in turn shall elect the Senate consisting of four Octets. The Senate shall elect the Executive Octet. The Executive Octet shall elect the Presidential Pair.

THE CONGRESS

The Congress shall consist of all representatives elected to the fourth highest Level of Government by hierarchical consensus. The Congress shall organize itself into four committees of Octets by mutual consensus, to a maximum of four Octets per committee.

These shall be a Committee of the Interior, a Committee of the Exterior, a Committee of Public Health and Disaster Relief, and a

Judiciary Committee. If there are at least sixty-four Judicial Octets at the highest Judicial Level of Government, then each committee shall consist of exactly four Octets. Otherwise, each committee shall consist of at least one Complementary Pair, or that committee shall not exist, and no higher representatives can be elected to that particular function of Government.

The Committees shall be formed by mutual consensus. Once any set of four Congressional Octets agrees on which Committee they will all become, they shall form the permanent Committee for that Governmental function, on a first-come-first-served basis. Each committee shall be Governed by the Senatorial Octet that it elects; otherwise it shall be Governed by mutual consensus.

Each committee shall supervise and investigate the lower functions of Government in its Ascendancy. It shall lodge complaints with the Judicial Octets that elected the representatives, if such action is required, or lodge complaints with the next highest Level of Government, which shall be the Senate.

THE SENATE

Each Octet in each Congressional committee shall elect a Complementary Pair, which shall be a Senator of a corresponding Committee in the Senate. Each Senator shall form an Octet with other Senators elected to the same Congressional Committee, to make laws in the same field of Government as was the responsibility of the Congressional Octet that elected the Senatorial Pair. Therefore, there shall be at least one Senatorial Pair in each area of responsibility which is a legitimate function of Government, but there shall never be more than one full Octet in each area of Senatorial responsibility. Each Senatorial Committee shall elect one Complementary Pair, which, with all the other senatorial representatives, shall form the Executive Octet.

If no one is ever elected to the Executive Octet, then the Senate shall have the powers of the Presidency and the Executive Octet solely by consensus of the entire Senate.

The major responsibility of the Senate is to elect the Executive Octet, supervise it, and approve or disapprove the actions taken by the Executive Octet, which can only be temporary, then communicate their decisions and reasons to the Congressional Octets that elected them.

The Executive Octet

The Executive Octet shall organize itself, by mutual consensus, into four secretariats, each one having exclusive executive responsibility in the areas of Interior, Exterior, Health and Disaster Relief, and the Presidency. The Octets above the highest Judicial Level have no Judicial power or authority, but any Judicial Congressional Octet may supervise, investigate, impeach, and recommend removal of any jurist from office, by unanimous consensus of the entire Senate.

The Executive Octet shall elect the Presidential Pair by unanimous consensus. It shall supervise and approve or disapprove all the policy decisions and official acts of the President, and generally be guided by the President. No action of the President may remain in efect for more than seven days unless it is unanimously approved by the entire Executive Octet. It is the responsibility of the Presidential Pair to convince the Executive Octet to support its policies and acts. Otherwise, the President must cease and desist in those policies and acts.

The Executive Pairs who are not part of the Presidency may, by unanimous consensus, remove the President. But the Executive Pairs who head the other three Executive Secretariats may not be removed except by unanimous consensus of the remaining six Complementary Pairs in the Octets that elected them or by the remaining six members of their original Level One Octet.

The Presidency

The President is the head of state for the entire Ethical State, as well as Commander in Chief of all executive functionaries below the Judiciary Level. The President may order action from any appropriate functionary of the Ethical State, but that action must stop if it is not unanimously approved by the entire Executive Octet within seven days.

The Presidential Pair may declare a State of National Emergency for a period not to exceed seven days, unless it is approved by the entire Executive Octet. At this time it can call up to half of the lower echelons of the Judiciary to active duty, together with all their resources and the resources of the other Jurists. Such drafts of personnel and resources shall be at the discretion of the President.

DELEGATION OF POWERS

Each Level of Government shall have its own budget for implementing its duties to protect and defend the citizens of the Ethical State. The lower Levels will distribute their budget among their three areas of responsibility: the fields of interior (police), exterior (military), and health and disaster protection (both interior and exterior). This distribution shall be done to maximize its benefit to the represented citizens. The proper balance shall be determined by the lower-level Octets, except in case of a National Emergency.

The Judiciary will distribute its budget primarily to serve its Judicial functions, but spending the minimum necessary, as required by the President, to maintain their military readiness.

The President may declare a State of National Emergency, but must suspend the State of National Emergency if it is not unanimously approved by the entire Executive Octet within seven days. During the National Emergency, the President may draft no more than half of the representatives in the lower Levels of the Judiciary. They shall perform their military duties under the command of the President. But the President may not draft any members of the sixteen highest Levels of the Judiciary or the Congress, which, of course, includes all members of the Senate and the Executive Octet.

Every official of the Ethical State, except for members of the Congress, is also an officer in the military, whose rank is commensurate with his or her Level of representation in the Government. Except for service in the Congress, no one shall serve in Government who is not simultaneously part of the military reserve.

Lower ranking officers do not have to follow the commands of their higher ranking officers unless there is a State of National Emergency in effect or a local officer has declared a Local State of Emergency, in which case, all officers of all Octets that elected these higher ranking officers shall come under their direct military command for a period not to exceed seven days, unless this period is further extended in seven-day increments by successively higher ranked officers. But they must listen to the guidance of their representatives, and follow it if it does not conflict with their conscience about how to best serve the citizens that elected them. During any State of Emergency, all lower ranking officers must obey the commands of all the higher ranking officers, and may not remove them from office until the State of Emergency has ended. But the Level One Octets may remove their representatives at any time, no matter how high they are in the hierarchy.

If the entire Executive Octet approves the State of Emergency, then the Emergency shall last for another thirty days, or until it is approved or disapproved by the mutual consensus of the entire Senate. If this consensus is not reached then the State of Emergency shall end.

Once the Senate approves the State of National Emergency, it shall last for no more than one year, at the discretion of the President and the Executive Octet, or until it is unanimously approved by the entire Congress. If the entire Congress does not unanimously approve the State of National Emergency, it shall end within one year.

Once the State of National Emergency is approved by the Congress, it shall remain in effect until either the remaining members of the Senate, the Executive Octet, or the President unanimously declare it over.

Similar processes of consensus shall apply to passing new laws or amending the Constitution. New laws and Constitutional amendments may be introduced by the President, but they shall not become effective unless they are unanimously approved by the entire Executive Octet, the Senate, and the Congress within one year of ratification by the entire Senate. Similarly any representative in Congress may introduce a law or Constitutional Amendment. Such laws shall become effective solely after they are approved by the entire Congress within two years. Amendments to the Bill of Rights must be unanimously approved, within two years after unanimous ratification by the entire Congress, by the sixty-four Judiciary Octets that elected the Congress.

CHECKS AND BALANCES

In order that this system of Government function properly, there shall be mandatory reports in person by each Representative Complementary Pair given once per week to the Octet that elected them, once every two weeks to the Level One Octet from which they come, and once every four weeks to the Octet that elected them to their previous Level of representation. Therefore, the President shall report once per week to the full Executive Octet, once every two weeks to their Level One Octet, and once every four weeks to the Senatorial Octet to which they belonged before being elected to the Executive Octet. Level Two representatives shall simply report once per week to their full Level One Octet. Fourth Level Octet representatives shall report once per week to the Level Three Octet that elected them, once every two weeks to their Level One Octet, and once every four weeks to their Level Two Octet. All such reports must be subject to questioning by the examining Octet and their guests.

SOURCE OF REVENUES

The income of the Government of the Ethical State shall come solely from five sources: limited and fair taxes, fines and judgments in favor of the Ethical State as determined by two independent Courts, leases of the natural resources which are not privatized, gifts from any source, and through control of the money supply. In general the Ethical State shall not participate in the economy. However, as part of its responsibility to protect and defend its citizens, it shall defend their wealth by providing them with a reliable monetary system that shall be protected against both inflation and deflation.

THE CENTRAL BANK

In order to protect the wealth of its citizens, the Ethical State, through the Secretary of the Interior, shall operate a Central Bank which will control the money supply and, at its discretion, lend money to other banks of the Ethical State at interest rates that shall be set jointly by the President and by the Secretary of the Interior. The Ethical State may, through its Central Bank, print paper money, otherwise give credits, and control the money supply, by controlling the interest rates that it charges for the loans that it makes exclusively to the banks of the Ethical State. It shall not otherwise engage in banking activities or issue bonds. The rate of inflation shall be controlled by the money supply and the interest rates, never to rise above five percent. Enough money shall be printed, and/or credit given to the banks and citizens at suitably low interest rates, that there shall never be any significant deflation or depression for the citizens of the Ethical State.

All taxes levied and judgments demanded by the Courts of the Ethical State must be paid by its citizens with money or credits issued by the Central Bank. However, citizens may trade among themselves on any basis they wish, including pure barter. All trades made are subject to taxation on the basis of their value in credits or money of the Ethical State. The accounting on these trades will be used to keep track of the economy in order to control the money supply and to levy limited and fair taxes.

The sole penalty for not paying taxes shall be loss of citizenship and expulsion from the Ethical State; no criminal charges or confiscation of property shall be imposed on the tax evader other than just and proper fines to pay back taxes, debts, and costs incurred for the expulsion of the citizen. Citizens who do not wish to pay taxes may simply renounce their citizenship and secede from the Ethical State.

OTHER POSSIBLE SERVICES

Other aspects of the economy shall be controlled by the Ethical State solely by the unanimous consent of all the citizens of the Ethical State, or by unanimous consent of the sixty-four highest Octets. Such control must be limited to protecting the life, liberty, property, and privacy of each citizen, without ever imposing undeserved harm on any citizen.

Additional fees for any additional protective services shall be imposed on the citizens for these extra services solely with the unanimous consent of all the citizens, or the unanimous consent of the highest 512 representatives in the consensus hierarchy. Otherwise, the Ethical State shall not assume responsibility for these services and shall allow them to be performed entirely by free enterprise or voluntary associations of citizens working by unanimous consensus. Any extra services performed by the Ethical State shall also be allowed to be performed by private citizens, at their discretion and at their risk, but subject to the protection of the Constitution.

John David Garcia

Examples of services which shall be delegated entirely to the private sector, unless these services are demanded by unanimous consensus of all the citizens or their 512 highest representatives, are road construction, maintenance, and policing; air traffic control; mail service; space exploration; oceanography; scientific research and development; education; and other such services.

RESPONSIBILITIES OF THE PRESIDENT AND THE EXECUTIVE OCTET

The President, through the Secretary of the Exterior, shall maintain a diplomatic corps and maintain and command the military and all other executive representatives. The President and the various Secretariats may distribute their budgets, in money, services, or resources, among the lower branches of Government as they see fit, so long as they uphold their basic responsibilities as Executives of the Ethical State.

These responsibilities are to protect and defend the citizens of the Ethical State from criminal activity within the Ethical State and from criminal activity from unethical Governments, terrorists, and pirates while traveling abroad. The objective is to facilitate the citizens' ability to live and travel in safety anywhere they wish, at anytime they wish, for any reasons they wish, and to bring back with them any goods they wish, as well as any persons whom they wish to adopt or who qualify for citizenship in the Ethical State.

The President and the Secretary for Health and Disaster Relief shall also supervise, and, when necessary, finance a public health service that shall protect the public from infectious diseases, pollution from all sources, and from the vagaries of natural disasters. The Ethical State shall not render any systematic medical care, except when demanded unanimously by all its citizens or by the sixty-four highest Octets.

It is the intent of the Ethical State that many services that its citizens initially require from the Ethical State shall eventually be provided entirely by free enterprise and the market or by voluntary associations of citizens. These services shall continue until all the citizens or the sixty-four highest Octets vote by unanimous consensus to end them, but they shall not start without a unanimous demand from the

166

citizenry. Citizens who do not want such services, or who continue to demand them after they are suspended, may secede from the Ethical State, at their discretion.

DISTRIBUTION OF REVENUES

Each Level of Government shall have its own budget to spend on fulfilling its responsibilities as determined by the entire Executive Octet, under the guidance of the President. The revenues from the individual citizens shall be collected by their unanimously elected representatives, from the individual members or affiliated citizens of the Level One Octets, or by the Judiciary.

Individual citizens who are not members of an Octet may remain unaffiliated or affiliate with an Octet, but they must still pay the mutual defense tax to the Government of the Ethical State. Unaffiliated Citizens shall be assigned to nearby Octets at the discretion of the Secretary of the Interior, for the purpose of defending them and their rights while collecting their fair taxes. If they do not wish to pay taxes, they should not be citizens of the Ethical State. All citizens are required to pay taxes in exchange for the police, military, public health, judicial, and executive protection that they receive.

Each Level One Octet shall collect the mutual defense tax from all its members, affiliates, and tax assignees. If any citizen does not pay his or her fair share of taxes, as determined by uniform law for all citizens of the Ethical State, then charges may be brought against that citizen before a Magistrate. If the Magistrate agrees with the charges, the citizen's case will be brought before a full Court for indictment. If the citizen is indicted, then the citizen will be tried for tax evasion before two independent Courts, and may be sentenced to non-criminal exile upon conviction.

Each Complementary Pair representing a Level One Octet shall keep exactly one-half of the taxes that it receives from the Octet. It will use these proceeds to fulfill its police, military, and public health responsibilities. The other half of the revenues shall be given to their Level Two Representative Pair to make the budget of the Level Two Octet to which this Pair belongs. The Level Two Octet shall keep for their own budget one-half of all the revenues that they receive from the Level One Octet that elected them, and then send the other half of this revenue with their Representatives to a Level Three Octet. This process continues all the way to the Presidency.

Therefore, each Octet at each Level of Government has a budget equal to half the revenues that the Representatives from the four lower-level Octets brought with them. Each Octet at each Level of Government has exactly twice the budget of the four budgets of the Octets that elected these representatives. Therefore, the Presidency shall have a budget equal to the nth power of two multiplied by the average budget of all the Octets in the First Level, where n is the number of the Levels of Government that are fully staffed with completed Octets, plus the Presidency.

At each Level, the Octet shall spend its budget implementing the policies of the Executive Octet, and protecting and defending all the citizens in its Ascendancy as best it can. If it has difficulty, it shall petition the Complementary Pair that it has elected to higher office, wherever they may be in the hierarchy, to convince the President, the Executive Octet, the Senate, the rest of the Congress, the Judiciary, and all higher Octets in their Ascendancy to redistribute their revenues among the lower-level Octets as needed. However, each Octet must do the best it can with the budget it has been given; the redistribution of revenues of the higher Octets to lower Octets is always at the discretion of the higher Octet or Octets.

At each Level, the Octets must purchase and maintain the necessary resources to accomplish their responsibilities in response to the guidance they receive from their electors and their representatives. These resources may include contract staff to help them with their work. All such staff serve solely at the discretion of the appropriate Octet, but according to contract. There shall be no permanent civil service. There shall be no bureaucracy.

When there is a conflict, the Octets must first meet the needs of their electors before following the guidance of their representatives. Higher Octets have no power, other than redistributing revenues, over the lower Octets, unless a State of Emergency is in effect. In that case, the entire relevant parts of Government become a military hierarchy, with the highest-ranking representative as Commander in Chief over all non-judicial activities, all according to law, all the way up to the President.

LEGISLATION AND AMENDMENTS

All laws or changes in procedure for better protecting the people of the Ethical State will be implemented for one year through unanimous approval by the Senate and the Executive Octet. If the entire Congress makes any changes in procedure or law, then these changes become a part of the long-term laws of the Ethical State. Amendments to the Constitution require unanimous consensus among the highest 512 representatives of the Ethical State.

The Bill of Rights may be amended solely after any such amendment is unanimously approved by the full Congress, plus all the remaining members of the Octets that elected the Congress, or by the entire citizenry of the Ethical State if there are not at least 384 elected representatives immediately below the Congress in the consensus hierarchy. Otherwise, the Bill of Rights remains in effect, and may not be changed without consensus of all citizens of the Ethical State.

The preceding is the entire Constitution of the Ethical State except for laws and clarifications that shall be made by consensus of all Octets joining and constituting the ever-evolving Government of the Ethical State.

CHAPTER FOUR

BUILDING OUR ETHICAL
FOUNDATIONS

The first thing for people to understand, if they wish to become citizens of any Ethical State, is that an Ethical State is so unlikely ever to occur by any action of government within an existing democracy, that it is not worthwhile even considering the possibility. The best we can hope for is that within the freest democracies, the Ethical State can operate as an educational foundation that seems harmless to the politicians and the bureaucrats.

All democratic majorities are ethically corrupt. They will not give up what they believe is their entitlement to the fruits of the labor of those who are more creative and/or productive than they are themselves. Once majority rule is established, a democracy is on a one-way street toward ever more socialism, and ever more unethical government. Socialism is any system of government that claims that its major responsibility is first to confiscate the fruits of the labor of its most creative minority, and then to redistribute them to its least creative majority in the form of services or subsidies, i.e., through government bureaucracy.

Democratic corruption occurs as follows. First, a majority of the electorate becomes convinced that decisions reached by majorities are *always* ethically superior to those reached by minorities. Second, it accepts that the least creative majority has a *right* to share part of the wealth created by the most creative minority. Third, it believes that the least creative majority has a right to be supported and nurtured forever by the most creative minority. Most democracies are now entering the third, and irreversible, phase of democratic corruption. It usually takes less than two hundred years for majority rule to reach irreversible corruption. This has been the case for Greece, Rome, the United States of America, France, Great Britain, and many other democracies.

Therefore, an Ethical State will not come to be through majority rule. That is why the Libertarian Party in the United States is out of touch with reality. However, imposing an Ethical State on anyone by force is unethical, and self-defeating. Unethical means can never create ethical ends. We can ethically create an Ethical State only for ourselves and those who join us voluntarily in its self-government, which is the only true democracy, solely through one hundred percent consensus. It is still barely possible to do this within the freest democracies. The rest have reached irreversible entropy, along with every other government in the world.

Therefore, the Ethical State begins with us. We cannot teach what we do not know, nor can we lead where we do not go. Our first obligation in life is to ourselves. We cannot love others if we do not know how to love ourselves. The most loving thing we can do for ourselves, as well as for our children, is to live in the freest country we can find.

We love ourselves by following our natural inborn ethics, and becoming as ethical and creative as possible. This is very difficult, but not impossible, if we do not have ethical love and guidance from our parents. It is the primary obligation of our parents to love, nurture, and educate us.

The most important thing parents ever teach their children is how to understand and live up to the fundamental ethical values with which we are all born. It is the tragedy of modern life that almost all parents are incapable of doing this. That is why there are so few Espritals in the world. That is why the world is in moral decay and the *Geistlich* (see Glossary) continue to perpetuate themselves in ever increasing numbers. Ethics are best taught by example, particularly example from parents, teachers, friends, and neighbors.

However, we cannot continue to blame others for our lack of ethics or our lack of creativity. We are all born with the potential to become full Espritals (see Glossary), the *Geistigen.* If we have had the bad fortune to have parents who are *Geistlich*, we should have compassion for them, love them, and never forget that they loved, nurtured, and educated us as best they could. If they failed us, we still owe them love, respect, and honor for the rest of our lives. Otherwise, we shall never learn to love.

Other than through the bad examples of our parents, teachers, and peers, most damage to our natural inborn ethics is done by our animal instincts. These are the instincts with which we are all born. They evolved through natural selection. They co-exist with our purely human, moral nature, which comes exclusively from God. This is what God breathed into Adam, who evolved from matter; this is how God gave humanity a purely human soul *(neshama)* in the metaphor of the Garden of Eden (377, 378). According to Judaism, we also share an animal soul *(nefesh)* with subhuman animals. This is our animal nature, our lower passions.

Our animal nature is the result of over four billion years of evolution. Our Ethical Nature began only about five million years ago, with the first systematically creative hominids. Our Moral Nature began, perhaps, six thousand years ago with the first moral human, "Adam" in the Biblical metaphor (377, 378). God breathed the *Neshama* into him.

As Maslow first observed (237, 238), if we do not adequately satisfy our animal desires when we are young, we may never adequately develop our innate ethical nature and become moral, or, as Maslow mistakenly called moral beings, "self-actualizing." We do not have to be moral or even ethical to be self-actualizing; e.g., Hitler was self-actualizing (117) and he was about as unethical as is possible.

Next to maximizing the creativity of our children, it is our foremost ethical duty and priority, to 1) help our spouse become moral, 2) help ourselves become moral, 3) help our best friends become moral, and 4) help all of our other good friends become moral. We cannot help those who do not share the Evolutionary Ethic with us, and do not have the potential to become our good friends. We shall never be moral if we have never helped another human being become moral at the same time (115).

Morality begins when we have a conscious understanding of our own ethics. It does not mean that we are fully moral beings, and that our ethics are perfect. For a finite being, ethics will always be greater than minus one, but less than plus one, i.e., $-1 < E < 1$ for all finite beings. For those who know some mathematics, remember that C is a vector, I is a matrix, and E is a vector and a random variable. We shall never fully understand all the elements in these vectors and matrix, nor how they interact. Therefore, $C = IE$ is, at best, an approximation.

Ethics shall never be equal to one for us, although we can grow, asymptotically, forever in ethics, intelligence, and creativity. Solely the process that is God is totally ethical, where $E = 1$. As a consequence, solely God is infinitely creative.

By implication, solely a totally moral being is infinitely intelligent. This is what limits the power of evil. All things, other than the process that is God, are finite. God is not a "thing" like our bodies. Solely our souls, which are infinite parts of an infinitely greater order of infinity which is God, are in themselves infinite and eternal.

We live on, and are immortal, solely through the creativity we engender in others. Our souls, but not our egos, live on in the infinite process that is God. God is truth. God is infinite truth. Truth is information that does not require a volume in space, matter, and time. This is the reality of quantum space (33, 34).

A finite being shall always have a finite intelligence with imperfect ethics. Do not expect your friends or your neighbors, or even your best friends or any Esprital, to have the ethics or the intelligence of God. We shall all remain flawed so long as we have imperfect ethics, but our creativity can evolve forever toward infinity, taking us ever closer to God. We never reach perfection. Morality is in the journey, not in the stages of the trip. The universe itself, as we know it, is but one stage in the trip. That is why we do not live in a perfect universe.

The critical threshold of morality for an Ethical State, when ethical evolution becomes irreversible, seems to be the moment when every citizen of the Ethical State is willing to die before diminishing anyone's creativity, including his or her own. This is ethical maturity, when everyone has become an Esprital. This is what can make evolution irreversible and keep us from surrendering to evil through our own fear. This is the beginning of the Moral Society. It may be that none of us have ever reached that degree of ethical development. But even the Moral Society is not perfect; it is possible for any Moral Society to fall from grace, although the Moral Society of all Moral Societies evolves forever.

I believe that Moses, Socrates, Buddha, Confucius, Jesus, Spinoza, and Teilhard de Chardin almost certainly reached the threshold. But perhaps many others, such as Zarathustra, Thales, Pythagoras, the Hebrew Prophets, the Christian Saints, Hypatia, Mohammed, Hildegard von Bingen, Moses Maimonides, Mahatma Gandhi, Rosa Luxemburg, Dieter Bonhoeffer, Albert Schweitzer, Andrei Sakharov, Mother Teresa, and Alexander Solzhenitsyn may have also been Espritals and reached this irreversible degree of ethical maturity.

Others who were highly ethical and creative, but perhaps not quite yet Espritals, were Thomas Jefferson and some of the other Founding Fathers, J.S. Bach, Goethe, Beethoven, Bertrand Russell, Albert Einstein, Constantin Brunner, Madame Curie, Henri Lurié, Barbara McClintock, and Buckminster Fuller. We can learn from all ethical persons. We should not reject the friendship, or the ethics, of those whom we regard as less than perfect in their ethics.

Henri Lurié was not perfect in his ethics, but he was the most committed man I ever met; he was dedicated totally to ethical principles. Buckminster Fuller, father of the geodesic dome and of many other inventions and discoveries involving icosahedral structures, was a loving teacher of all humanity and a great empowerer of the individual. He seems to have been committed to ethical principles during the last two thirds of his life, although he took many wrong turns early in life.

OVERCOMING THE LOWER PASSIONS

The lower passions are the animal instincts and emotions with which we are all born. They are what Spinoza called the "Appetites." Maslow called them the "lower needs." The Jews called them the *Nefesh*.

Our first passion is simply not to be in pain. We cannot develop ethically if we are in constant pain.

Our second passion is not to be in need of sustenance. We cannot develop ethically if we are in constant hunger or thirst.

Our third passion is to feel safe. We cannot develop ethically if we are in constant danger. This is our passion for safety. We never feel safe if we are in pain, lack sustenance, or have no shelter. The mere thought that we may lack these essentials may trigger a feeling of danger, and may fill us with an uncontrollable passion for safety. This is fear, caused by the belief that we cannot create what we most need.

Our fourth passion is to feel loved. If we feel unloved, particularly by our parents, we may not develop ethically. And remember that love is the desire to increase, and the act of increasing, someone's creativity, without ever decreasing creativity for anyone. It is not the desire to make, or the action for making, anyone happy. This is a false love.

If we feel unloved, we will develop a passion for false love and never mature ethically. A false love exists when we value anyone's happiness, including our own, more than anyone's creativity, including our own.

It is the responsibility of our parents, and ourselves as parents, to make sure that children are secure in their basic passions when they are young, or we shall have failed as parents and our children shall not develop as ethical adults, nor become moral, nor reach their full creative potential.

The highest passion we will develop when we are still quite young is the passion to learn. If our parents do not share this higher, non-animal passion with us, we may never develop it and may never become moral adults. However, if we find the love of other good role models while we are still young, and learn the passion for learning from them before the world and our own lower passions have destroyed our ethics, we may still become moral, even if our parents were no more than marginally ethical and loved us minimally when we were young.

Although the passion for learning is inborn and is part of our ethical nature, it is a late evolutionary programming of our brain, and this higher passion is quite fragile. It is intimately tied to our ethics. People will often replace it with a passion for safety, food, false love, or sensual pleasure. All of these lower passions are good, and essential for our survival as a species, but if they are not eventually given a lower priority than our passion for learning, we shall destroy ourselves as a species.

If we follow our innate ethics, we will eventually learn that the true meaning of love is to value the creativity of another as much as we value our own creativity. Then our love will have become a higher passion. We must learn to value creativity more than safety, food, false love, sensual pleasure, and life itself. This can be done.

If it could not be done, Socrates would not have drunk the hemlock, Jesus would not have died on the cross, Spinoza would not have allowed himself to be excommunicated from the Jewish community and to be turned into a pariah for the rest of his life, Rosa Luxemburg would not have been killed mistakenly fighting for socialism, and Sakharov and Solzhenitzsyn would not have individually taken an ethical stance against the entire Soviet System.

When our passion for creativity is greater than all of our other passions combined, then we will truly know the meaning of love. And we will learn to love everyone, including ourselves and our enemies, for their creativity rather than for their happiness.

We must learn to love ethically and to realize that this has nothing to do with anyone's happiness, but that true love, which lasts forever, is concerned solely with the creativity of ourselves first, then of our spouse, then of our children, then of our best friends, then of our good friends, then of all other friends. Once we learn how to truly love, we are empowered forever and shall never again be motivated by fear and the lower passions. We shall guide our life and take all of our actions solely on the basis of ethics.

Fear is the passion that results from believing that we cannot satisfy our basic needs for safety, sustenance, shelter, love, sensual pleasure, and knowledge. Fear is a false belief. This false belief seems to force us to do things that we know in our most innermost being to be unethical. Therefore, we become drug users, sybarites, sexual addicts, criminals, liars, cheaters, greedy hoarders, jealous lovers, philistines, bureaucrats, politicians, and frauds.

The worst frauds are those who seek to convince their peers that they are intellectually superior, doing this in order to feel secure and to receive admiration from others, which is an illusion of love. They become destructive to the ethics and intelligence of others and never do anything creative in their lives again, while possibly destroying the creativity of those more ethical but less intellectually mature than themselves. I have found that these kinds of frauds make up most, *but not all*, of the faculty in most of the universities. Other frauds, if they are a little less clever and less ethical, may become politicians, bureaucrats, predatory capitalists, unscrupulous lawyers, and other kinds of human parasites. These frauds may occasionally even believe that they are ethical, when in fact they may have done nothing creative in their lives since childhood.

Therefore, our obligation is first to educate ourselves until we can understand the true meaning of ethics. Second, we focus on our own ethical development if we do not yet have children. Once we have children, their creativity must always come before ours. Therefore, there is a natural hierarchy in our intellectual and ethical development, which are always correlated. We cannot grow in ethics without growing in intelligence, but we can grow in intelligence without growing in ethics. The universities, courtrooms, and boardrooms of the world are filled with people who have grown in intelligence without growing in ethics.

If we recognize the true meaning of our inborn ethics, nothing can stop us in our moral development, neither torture nor threats of death. If this were not true, we would not have had in the twentieth century people like Albert Schweitzer, Rosa Luxemburg, Mahatma Gandhi, Dieter Bonhoeffer, Bertrand Russell, Teilhard de Chardin, Chaim Weizman, Martin Buber, Mother Teresa, Alexander Solzhenitsyn, and Andrei Sakharov. Why do we not have more people like these?

THE IMPEDIMENTS TO ETHICAL GROWTH

We wish to maximize creativity to the best of our ability in order to grow in ethics, and to become maximally creative human beings, but there is a natural hierarchy that we must follow until we have children of our own. This hierarchy is developed as follows.

1. While we are young, our parents, or other good role models, provide us with at least the minimal amount of safety, nurturing, love, and ethical example to make us clearly ethical and simultaneously to have some passion for learning and not to be neurotically insecure.
2. We educate ourselves, as best we can, within the existing school system.
3. The school system, mostly by luck, is not so destructive that we lose our ethics and all joy in learning. It is the responsibility of parents to choose the least destructive schools that will most contribute to the creativity of their children, but this choice is rarely clear.
4. We begin to read, study, and experiment on our own, outside the regular school system.

5. We begin to develop an interest in the opposite sex, which is healthy and ethical, but distracting from our primary obligations while we are still young.
6. We begin to try to be ever more self-sufficient, and we get an after-school job.
7. We begin to have conflicts among our passions for learning, sex, and autonomy.
8. At this point we need to develop new ethical guidelines about how to deal with the ethical problems we are encountering in school, relationships with the opposite sex, and our desire to be autonomous.

GUIDELINES FOR EDUCATIONAL ETHICS

Our highest ethical priority when we are young is to continue to educate ourselves and grow in ethics. The type of education that is optimal, in terms of maximizing our creativity, is that proposed in the Lifetime Curriculum given in the Epilogue of this book, but this type of education is not yet available at any price anywhere in the world. It is up to our parents and ourselves to obtain this type of education within the regular educational system. This is very difficult.

At the same time that our passion for learning is growing, our passion for sex is taking up more and more of our time and interfering with our studies. Our parents, society, the educational bureaucracy, and our own passion for autonomy are pressuring us to specialize so that we may become employable as soon as possible. The best we can do, it seems, is to go into a secure well-paid profession. The demands of the profession on our studies, and our working time, are such that we can no longer even approach the educational levels of the Lifetime Curriculum. Therefore, in order to survive, we stop being creative, and we regurgitate exactly what we were taught, as we were taught, in order to get good grades and become acceptable to the profession. Our ethics and our creativity are being destroyed by the educational system.

We cannot solve our ethical dilemma in education unless we simultaneously solve the ethical questions posed by our sexual passions and our passion for autonomy. An outline of educational ethics is given in the Epilogue, and in Chapter 6 of *Creative Transformation* (115).

ECONOMIC ETHICS

It is good for children to want to be autonomous and economically self-sufficient, without having to depend on their parents. However, if it is at all possible, it is best for young persons to concentrate on their studies and to remain dependent on their parents until they can continue to educate themselves optimally on their own. This should happen before the age of thirty, which will leave most persons over half of their lifetime to return to the world all that has been given to them. For the most brilliant children, it can happen before the age of eighteen, through scholarships, fellowships, and/or part time work in a field related to their main educational interests.

However it happens that young adults become economically self-sufficient while continuing to educate themselves, they should always bear in mind the following principles of ethical economics.

1. It is, at best, marginally ethical to be an employee or to have employees.

2. It is optimal in ethical economics solely to have partners and to work with those partners.

3. A partner is someone who shares risks as well as profits with other partners, although they do not have to share them equally; an independent contractor is more of a partner than is an employee.

4. An employee is someone who neither shares the risks nor the profits with the employer, but is promised a salary.

5. An employee is a temporary slave who exploits the employer, by working as little as possible for the most possible recompense, and is in turn exploited by the employer, who tries to extract as much work as possible from the employee while paying as little as possible in salary and benefits. It is clear that not all employees and employers are equally exploitive.

6. Every form of exploitation is unethical, whether we are an exploiter or an exploitee.

7. We should always begin the practice of economic ethics within the First Economic Paradigm:

We invest our time in earning the maximum disposable income possible, while assuring that nothing we do to earn our income ever imposes undeserved harm on anyone, and is always in itself a creative, ethical act.

8. We can earn a good living for ourselves and our families within the First Economic Paradigm, but for any person who is growing in ethics, it will eventually lead to great frustration, because we soon discover that those ethical activities which earn the highest income for us are also the least creative activities in which we engage. This leads us logically and inevitably to the Second Economic Paradigm:

We try to maximize creativity for ourselves and others under the constraints that whatever acts we do (a) never impose any undeserved harm on anyone, (b) are always as creative as possible, and (c) produce sufficient resources to support ourselves and provide the necessary security and educational opportunities for our family to become maximally creative.

This all sounds very logical, and more ethical, than the First Economic Paradigm, but it is not effective. I know this from having worked with this paradigm for over fifteen years. If we follow this paradigm, we will not maximize our family's creativity or anyone else's. Furthermore, we will eventually always be on the brink of bankruptcy, no matter how rich we were when we started. If we have not provided adequate security and educational opportunities for our family, they will be ethically damaged. We can provide those opportunities, and security for them, solely within the First Economic Paradigm.

NEVER ATTEMPT TO WORK WITHIN THE SECOND ECONOMIC PARADIGM! We should stay in the First Economic Paradigm until we have provided all the security and educational opportunity our family will ever need. We may then go on with our ethical development.

9. After achieving the goals of the previous steps within the First Economic Paradigm, and avoiding the Second Economic Paradigm, we should leap to the Third Economic Paradigm:

We do our best to utilize the resources in hand, and solely those resources, to maximize creativity, according to the dictates of our conscience alone, while ignoring all economic risk or gain, and making sure that we never impose undeserved harm on anyone. This includes not risking the resources that are essential for our family's security. We never count on any resources that we do not already have in hand, even if they are promised to us by the most reliable people and sources we know. Remember that the most valuable resource we have is our own life. We use and risk solely those resources which are not essential to maintain our own life and the well-being of our family.

This paradigm works perfectly once we have fulfilled our ethical obligations to our family. I know, because I have been working with this paradigm exclusively for the last ten years. It never fails. Use it, and you will maximize creativity for yourself and others, if, and only if, you have first fulfilled your ethical obligations to your family, otherwise you will fail. Nothing must ever come before the maximization of the creativity of your family, including your own survival.

10. Once we have passed through the Third Economic Paradigm, so that we have full confidence in it, we are ready to enter the Fourth Economic Paradigm:

We take all the experience and confidence that we have in the Third Economic Paradigm, as well as all of its ethical principles, and do our best to create an Ethical State before we die. If we believe that we know how best to do this, we do it, and do not just talk about it. An Ethical State is the best legacy that we can leave our children. If we do not have confidence in our own ability, or we believe that someone else has a better strategy, then we become a citizen of their Ethical State, until we can create a better one of our own.

If you understand and follow the economic ethical principles above, you should become economically secure by the time you are thirty, if not much sooner. Economic security comes from having reached a minimum level of practical creativity, not from being independently wealthy. It is at this time that you can ethically begin a family, and then fulfill your obligations to it, before leaving the First Economic Paradigm and leaping to the Third Economic Paradigm, avoiding a fall into The Second Economic Paradigm, which can easily trap us. It trapped me for fifteen years, and it took me another five years to get out of it entirely and to learn to work solely in the Third and Fourth Economic Paradigms.

A more detailed discussion of economic Ethics within the Third Economic Paradigm, without naming it as such, is given in Chapter 7 of *Creative Transformation* (115). It is best to stay in the First Economic Paradigm until you have provided adequate security for your family, although once you understand the Evolutionary Ethic and commit to its principles, it will become increasingly difficult to function in the First Economic Paradigm.

However, what most interferes with our ethical duty to educate ourselves, at least while we are young, is not so much our economic needs or passion for autonomy, but our sexual passions, which can easily trap us in an unwise marriage to someone who is not our complement and does not love us ethically. We can avoid this trap by understanding sexual ethics.

SEXUAL ETHICS

Sexual ethics follow very simply and directly from the Evolutionary Ethic. However, popular mass culture, which has become hedonistic, and our own emotions make it very difficult to understand sexual ethics. In my previous book (115), I thought that sexual ethics were so simple that I left them as an exercise to the reader, with a few hints. I will now go a little deeper into sexual ethics, but my conclusions may not be obvious to the reader. An entire book on sexual ethics may be necessary to make their derivation from the Evolutionary Ethic clear. Do not worry if the following conflicts with your emotions and desires. Follow your own conscience, but remember that your conscience may be driven by fear or lust masked as conscience, and that the more primitive parts of your brain may be fooling the more advanced (ethical) part of your brain when this occurs.

Our sexual passions are natural, and are programmed into the limbic system of the brain by at least two hundred million years of evolution. These passions can easily overcome our ethical needs and judgments if we do not have a good system of ethics to guide us, one which does not conflict with our biology and our true sense of right and wrong. Jewish sexual ethics are much closer to this type of guide than are Christian sexual ethics.

Christian sexual ethics do not come from the teachings of Jesus, but primarily from the teachings of Saint Paul and the bureaucracy that succeeded him. Jesus always claimed to be nothing other than a Jew and also that his teachings were solely for other Jews, saying, "I come to fulfill the law and not to change it. I shall not change a single letter nor jot in the law," and also "Do not throw pearls before swine."

The latter comment of Jesus was in reference to whether his teachings were for non-Jews. All the early Christians had to convert to Judaism before they could become Christians. Saint Paul changed all this by saying that baptized Christians were circumcised in the spirit.

Saint Paul was a high ranking Jew, a Jewish aristocrat and a member of the Sanhedrin. I believe, along with several Biblical scholars, that he was a latent homosexual (176).

Male homosexuality was a capital offense among the Jews of this time. Killing a man for engaging in homosexual acts seems unethical to me, but this was Jewish law. As Jesus, and then Spinoza, noted, neither all Jewish laws as practiced nor the Torah itself are consistent with the true system of ethics taught by Moses (412).

I believe that the true ethical teachings of Moses are best expressed in Genesis and Exodus. Leviticus, Numbers, and Deuteronomy seem to me to represent a corruption of the ethics of Moses, produced by the Hebrew priests as they began to acquire ever more temporal power. Existing copies of the Torah were not produced until hundreds of years after the destruction of the First Temple in the sixth century BCE. Before then, solely the priests had access to the original Torah. Spinoza first made the coherent argument that the original Torah must have been much shorter than the one we now have.

A person in Saint Paul's position could not even think about coming out of the closet and becoming a practicing homosexual. The only feasible alternative for an ethical, Jewish homosexual was to be celibate. (Homosexuality is a congenital condition, not an ethical choice (117). We should have love and compassion for homosexuals, not the fear and contempt taught by some religious fundamentalists.)

Saint Paul's situation produced an anti-sexual neurosis, which manifested itself in the claim that celibacy was the highest moral state for any human being. This is completely contrary to Jewish law and the Evolutionary Ethic, which claim that the married state is the highest moral state for both men and women. As the Bible tells us, "You shall leave your father and mother, and cleave unto your spouse, and you shall become as one flesh."

Homosexuality was probably originally disparaged by the early Jews because it inhibited the natural increase of the Jewish people, which have always been a very small minority among the nations of the world, as are even more so the Espritals. Furthermore, this minority was always on the verge of extinction. It also might be that homo-sexual culture, somehow, decreases the Evolutionary Ethic within a society. The Evolutionary Ethic gives highest ethical priority to children and families. These are values largely absent in most homosexuals. I have never met nor heard of a homosexual who was an Esprital, but there are many ethical homosexuals. This alone precludes the persecution of homosexuals.

In order to give full vent to his neurosis, as well as his considerable ethics and intelligence, Saint Paul built Christianity in his own image and created a basically anti-sexual religion, which sees any form of sexual activity outside of marriage, and many a form within marriage, as an immoral act, and holds that the most ethical life that one can lead is the celibate life. However, in the words of Saint Paul, "It is better to marry, than to burn with lust." This phobia is, of course, contrary to biology, Judaism, the Evolutionary Ethic, and good sense.

The most ethical life that anyone can lead is the most ethical life that everyone should lead. If everyone were celibate, then the human species would become extinct. The extinction of humanity is not an ethical act. Therefore, Christian sexual ethics are false from the point of view of Kant's Categorical Imperative.

The Catholic Church, in demanding that its clergy be celibate, is behaving unethically. This unethical behavior has been used primarily as a form of control over the clergy, so that they will not give first ethical priority to their families, as they should. This will lead to an ever greater concentration of homosexuals and other sexual deviants among the Catholic clergy, which will make the Church ever more out of touch with other Christians. But also a false ethic is the almost universal Christian ethic that all sexual activity outside of marriage is a sin. We need to be guided by the Evolutionary Ethic, which never leads to its own contradiction.

Our sexual passions are among the strongest and most natural passions that we will ever have; it is very difficult not to be dominated by them when we are still young and have not yet developed a love for learning that is greater than our sexual passions. For some, this conflict begins to diminish after the age of about twenty-five, when the sex drive apparently begins to very slowly diminish for most men. For most women, the sex drive does not seem to diminish until after the age of forty or so. For those who will grow ethically all their life and perhaps become Espritals, the Evolutionary Ethic is well established in their minds by the time they are twenty-five, although they may not be consciously aware of it. More important than a diminishing sex drive to the control of these passions is the development of sound sexual ethics to put in their place.

The first thing to understand about true sexual ethics is that although sexual desires are natural and good, not all sexual behavior is good under all circumstances. The most important ethical consideration regarding sexual behavior is that we not produce any children until we are prepared to assume full responsibility for their welfare and to put the welfare of our children ahead of our own. We are usually not prepared to do this until we are well educated, ethically mature, and economically secure. However, the most important aspect of ethical maturity is that we have learned how to love.

If we do not love our spouse and our spouse does not love us in return, we have not provided an adequate family for our children. The greatest love of an ethically mature person is love for children yet unborn, particularly one's own children. Until we are ethically mature, we are not fit to be parents, no matter how intellectually mature and economically secure we have become. We can neither learn to love nor become ethically mature through reason alone. We need to be open to both the mystical paradigm and the scientific paradigm.

Ultimate goals, such as the Evolutionary Ethic, have no basis in logic. They are ends in themselves, not means to an end. We will never choose the Evolutionary Ethic as an ultimate goal if we are closed to mysticism. True ethics come from God. This communication with God is a mystical experience, which people who are totally closed to the mystical paradigm will never have. True love is also a mystical experience coming from God; the experience of true love is even more profound than the Evolutionary Ethic. Anti-mystical people will never have it.

Although both ethics and love can be understood and explained at a purely intellectual level, they cannot be *taught* without love. They must be taught by personal loving example, or we will never learn them. The teachings of Moses gave us the ethical foundation for creating an ethical society, but it is the teachings and example of Jesus that taught us the meaning of true love. That is why Christianity has been much more effective in communicating Jewish Ethics to the world than has been Judaism itself, even though Christianity has been con-taminated by the mistaken teachings of Saint Paul and even though few Christians live up to the teachings of Jesus.

God is truth, but God is also love. True, or ethical, love is based on giving at least as high a priority to the creativity of another as we give to our own creativity. This shall always seem irrational to someone who has not learned to love and who is anti-mystical. In our families, we must love our children and our spouses more than ourselves, or we shall have a dysfunctional family based on false love. A false love for a spouse may be summarized thusly, "I will marry you and love you so long as you make me happy; when you no longer make me happy, I will leave you, and if necessary destroy our family, because nothing in the world is more important than my happiness."

So long as we seek sexual partners on the basis of their ability to make us happy, rather than on the basis of who will be the best pos-sible parent to our yet unborn children, we are still ethically immature, and should have no children. We should have no sexual relations with a partner whom we do not love ethically, and who does not love us eth-ically in return; we owe it to ourselves and to our unborn children.

We know that we are ethically immature so long as we have not learned to love ethically, seeking sexual partners primarily for the pleasure they bring us, rather for the love we give them. If we love someone, we will never knowingly do anything to harm that person, even if he or she desires it. If we have a sexual relationship with some-one whom we do not love, we will almost certainly eventually harm her or him in some way, particularly if we have children together. The highest manifestation of our love for another is to wish to have children together. We can do this ethically if, and only if, the desire is reciprocated, and we are both sufficiently mature ethically, intel-lectually, and economically to have children, and if both will give the children's creativity the highest priority in life. Next to this, our own happiness is trivial.

Therefore, ethical sexuality requires more than intellectual ma-turity and an ethical nature. It takes these things together with the capacity to love. The capacity to love truly and deeply takes an open-ness to mysticism. We will never learn to love without the example of someone who has loved us. What we learn from this example is what cannot be learned from books or in school. We learn to have empathy, compassion, patience, and trust, based not on reason, but on love. Without this kind of a capacity to love, we shall never understand nor follow the sexual ethics that come from the Evolutionary Ethic.

Sexual ethics as herein developed are intended primarily for young heterosexuals, although in great part they also apply to homosexuals. The entire concept of the Ethical State is optimized for heterosexuals who are committed to the Evolutionary Ethic and what is best for their children. It is not intended always to accommodate the needs of homosexuals, or anyone who is not committed to the Evolutionary Ethic. Those who cannot fit into the Ethical State should form their own societies and not seek citizenship in the Ethical State, although they should all be tolerated within the Ethical State, so long as they obey its laws. No one who has not yet learned to love shall ever understand well the Evolutionary Ethic, or the sexual ethics that follow from it.

All this leads to the following summary of true sexual ethics, which maximize creativity; I hope that it is of some practical value.

1. Have no children until you are ethically mature, well educated, and sufficiently secure economically to support a family entirely by yourself; this applies equally to both men and women; the most important gift we give our children is an ethical home, with an ethical mother and an ethical father; it is unethical, and irresponsible, to have children unless we can provide all these things for them.

2. Never have sexual relations with any person unless you love that person.

3. The minimum amount of love that should exist between people who have sexual relations is that they love the other at least as much as they love themselves.

4. If you cannot commit eventually to giving first priority to the creativity of your sexual partners over your own, then you do not have enough love for them to have sexual relationships with them. A spouse is a sexual partner whom you love more than yourself.

5. If you would never have a sexual relationship that would lead to a child exactly like your partner, you do not have enough love for him or her to have sexual relations ethically, even if you believe that your sexual relations will never lead to children because of age, health, or birth control. Remember that it is unethical to be certain.

6. If neither of you can give all your children's creativity first priority over your own, then you do not love each other sufficiently to have children or sexual relations together, even if you believe that you can never have children together, or that you are using the most fool-proof method of birth control in the world.

7. You should avoid all coital activity, but not necessarily all sexual activity, until you are sufficiently educated, ethically developed, and economically secure to care adequately for any children you might have. Until that time arrives, practice solely safe sex, or better still remain celibate.

8. If it is biologically or psychologically impossible to keep your sexual desires from interfering with your education, then limit yourself to sexual activity that will not lead to children, i.e., practice solely safe sex. Recognize that you can easily lose control and end up with children, whom you must then give first priority in life for the rest of their lives, thereby possibly failing to develop full creative potential for yourself, your spouse, and your children.

9. Never use abortion as a form of birth control; accidental pregnancies should be handled by adoption, never abortion, unless the life or health of the mother is threatened. Abortion solely for convenience is almost always an unethical act, but it is a private act that should always be at the discretion of a woman and her doctor. It is her body, not the fetus', much less some fundamentalist busybody's. It is up to a man to choose a sexual partner who will not abort his children and who will be a good mother to them; this is his ethical obligation.

10. Women who engage in any kind of coital activity will almost always eventually become pregnant, if their health and age are adequate, no matter what form of birth control is used. A couple I have heard of, where the divorced woman had a tubal ligation to make sure she had no more children and the divorced man she had recently married had a vasectomy to make sure that he had no more children, much to their amazement had a baby boy within a year of their marriage. They named him "Houdini."

11. Be very careful not to contract or spread any of the sexually transmitted diseases which are now ubiquitous. It is an unethical act to contract, or spread, any sexually transmitted disease. We are

ethically responsible for making sure this does not happen, which means we must never surrender to casual sexual passion. If we cannot control our sexual passions before marriage, we must practice solely safe sex with someone we love enough to marry gladly if he or she were to become accidentally pregnant. We must not be promiscuous.

12. Sexual activity without adequate precautions and love between the participants can be very harmful emotionally, spiritually, and physically to our partners and ourselves; any such harm is an unethical act.

13. Whatever your gender, sexual orientation, or age, do your best to be celibate until you find a person of the opposite sex who is truly your complement.

14. Always seek out as many complements as you can find for the rest of your life, but try to keep your relationships platonic until you are both ready to commit to each other and to your children first.

15. Solely marry and commit exclusively to someone who is your complement if there is mutual sexual attraction between you. After this you must do your best to assure that the love between you and all your other complements is purely platonic, and is in no way sexually based. Never try to make a mate or a spouse out of someone you are not attracted to sexually; keep him or her exclusively as a platonic complement. Sexual attraction is a way nature tells us that we are genetically compatible with another, although sexual attraction can occur without ethical compatibility, and the latter is what is most important.

16. Never engage in any sexual activity which seems wrong to you, particularly if you do not like it or if it has any significant potential for inflicting harm on anyone, including yourself.

Hopefully, these ethical guidelines, although not logically derived here in detail from the Evolutionary Ethic, are sufficient for avoiding the traps of unethical sexual relationships and premature marriage, which can easily destroy our creative potential for the rest of our life. It is our responsibility as ethical beings to be guided by ethics in everything we do, and not by our animal passions. When we reach this degree of ethical maturity, we can begin an Ethical Republic. However, not all citizens of an Ethical State need be this ethically mature.

Ethically committed, loving heterosexual monogamy is the most creative form of sexuality, but other types of sexuality are not necessarily unethical; they may, however, border on the trivial if they have no purpose beyond mutually desirable pleasure. Sex without ever any possibility of reproduction may at best be trivial and at worst destructive. Happiness that does not affect creativity is the essence of triviality. Trivial behavior always increases entropy in the short run, and decreases creativity in the long run.

Polygamy may seem ethically optimal for some people, but it is almost always harmful to our children and spouses. If we love our spouse and children ethically, we will have a monogamous relationship with our spouse, no matter what the opportunities for having sexual relationships with other very willing, attractive, and maybe even uniformly superior partners. The commitment of love that we make for the sake of a spouse and our children is to be monogamous, no matter what the temptations. Our first ethical obligation is not to inflict harm on anyone, ever, for any reason. We should not leave a spouse unless he or she is irreversibly destructive to us or to our children.

Every polygamous society in the world seems uniformly inferior in its collective creativity to every monogamous society. The greater the social, economic, and political equality between men and women, the more creative will be the society, and our primary ethical obligation is to maximize creativity, not to maximize pleasant sexual experiences, even if they *seem* more creative than the one we have with our spouse. Our ethical obligations are first to our children, then to our spouse, then to ourselves, then to the rest of the world. We cannot ethically maximize creativity for others and ourselves while decreasing creativity for our spouse and children. Unethical means can never produce ethical ends.

The sexual passions are very difficult to supersede. We should be patient, loving, and compassionate with those who cannot overcome them. As Jesus said, "Let him who is without sin cast the first stone."

There is, however, one last lower passion that we must overcome in order to reach our full ethical development and our maximum creative potential. This passion is our fear of death.

John David Garcia

THE ETHICS OF DEATH

Fortunately, when we are young, we have little fear or thought of death; this is why the young make the best soldiers. The main fear of the young is the fear of pain, and secondarily of permanent damage to their bodies. But eventually all these fears come together in the passion for life, and a fear of death.

Fear is based upon the belief that we cannot create. We must learn not to fear death, and to know that our major ethical responsibility in life is not to stay alive, but never to decrease the creativity of anyone, including our own. At the same time, we inevitably come to the logical conclusion that we cannot create once we die, and that we all die eventually.

The major focus of almost all organized religion is to counter this fear with a fantasy for which there is no objective proof at all. The belief that the ego is a part of the soul, and that the soul, as the immortal part of us, lives on and continues to be creative, either in heaven or in a newly reincarnated body, is wishful thinking induced by fear. It is completely contrary to all scientific evidence, and it is unnecessary.

These beliefs in the continued creativity of the soul or the ego after death are, in my opinion, false beliefs. However, false or true, they are irrelevant to our ethical obligations, which are (1) never to decrease anyone's creativity, including our own, (2) to maximize creativity while we are alive, (3) to go on living so long as we are creative, and (4) to die when we are no longer creative. That is how we maximize creativity in general.

When our creativity has sunk to the level where we can no longer create the resources that we need to stay alive, then the only creative act left for us to do is to die, and not to be a parasite on those who love us and may choose to adopt us as their dependent. We should certainly not expect those who do not even know us to tax themselves to keep us alive as an uncreative parasite. However, this does not mean that the essence of what we are dies with our body.

We are immortal in our souls, which live forever in the creativity that we have engendered in others during our life, and through our creations perhaps long after our deaths. We are also immortal in that every creative act that we ever do becomes an eternal part of the infinite mind of God, i.e., part of quantum space, the implicate order

(33, 34, 410–412). But our ego is a product of our body, and it dies with our body.

Therefore, part of our ethical development is to overcome our attachment to ego and the consequent fear of death, and to replace this entirely with the highest passion, which is to maximize the creativity of the universe. If we are not willing to die before decreasing the creativity of our neighbor, or of ourselves, then we are not yet moral. If we are not yet an Esprital, then our contributions to the creation of an Ethical State may not be as great as possible, but they will not be irrelevant. We can always help those we recognize as Espritals in creating the Ethical State. One does not have to be an Esprital to be a citizen of the Ethical State, merely understanding and doing one's best to live up to the Evolutionary Ethic is enough.

If we have become Espritals, we are ethical warriors and follow the code of the warrior, which is never to surrender. Part of our ethical obligation in life is never to surrender to evil, allowing another to control or destroy our creativity. This must be resisted to the death. But most of us are not there yet, and enough pain and/or threats of death can force us to surrender to evil, which turns us into a destructive force. All we can do is the best we can, and try to adopt the ethics, courage, and warrior's code of an Esprital, and that is enough to create an Ethical State.

Espritals never see themselves as Espritals; they are too well aware of their own imperfections. But they recognize other Espritals, and do their best to love them and serve them by spreading their ethical message and their wisdom. However, sometimes the followers of Espritals forget that they were flawed humans, and turn them into mythical, imagined paragons of virtue. This happened to Moses, whose fundamentalist followers believe to have been the recipient of the entire Torah dictated directly by God, letter by letter. It also happened to Zoroaster, Buddha, Confucius, Lao-Tse, Socrates, and Jesus. The latter was conceived by his followers to be a literal, biological Son of God who was resurrected from the dead and rose directly into heaven. The teachings of Mohammed were also distorted by his followers, who conceived him to be the last and greatest of all the Prophets of God, also rising directly into heaven. This has happened to the teachings of many others who have become anointed as saints and prophets.

This would have happened to Spinoza, had he not been so reviled by virtually all the Jews and Christians of the world, and had he not himself recorded his greatest thoughts, leaving them for us exactly as he had them, and not as his followers would have distorted them. Distortions of Spinoza's teaching did in fact occur, and led to the teachings of Jefferson (most ethical), Hegel, Marx, and Lenin (least ethical). Most of their followers did not know that they were following a distortion of the teachings of Spinoza.

Spinoza is my Rabbi, and I am his devoted follower, according to my own interpretations of his teachings. He was also the Rabbi of Constantin Brunner and Henri Lurié. Henri accepted Constantin Brunner as the greatest Esprital he ever knew. And I accept Henri as the greatest Esprital I have ever known, and he had many, many ethical flaws, as did Constantin Brunner.

Although I encountered Teilhard de Chardin in person shortly before he died, I never knew him except through his books. He is the Rabbi who first raised my ethical level to the point that I was willing to risk my life greatly, but not yet quite willing to die, for ethical principle. It was the love and the implicit evolutionary ethics in Teilhard's writings that so moved me, not his greatness as a scientist. Teilhard de Chardin was a Jesuit priest.

Today, Moses, Jesus, Spinoza, Jefferson, and Teilhard are jointly my Rabbis, and I have done my best to bring all their ethical teachings together in my books, and to teach and disseminate the common ethical message that they all brought to the world. This common message is something worth dying for.

Judaism says that we should do anything to stay alive, short of idolatry, murder, and destructive sexual practices. I go a little further, and say that we should die before decreasing anyone's creativity, including our own. Once we accept this Ethical State for our own mind, we shall never again fear death, torture, or surrendering to our own fear. It is a liberating experience that comes from simply understanding and following the imperatives of the Evolutionary Ethic.

It is unethical ever to nurture a parasite. A human who is never able again to create at least as many resources as he or she will consume has become a parasite, and he or she should accept death gladly, without expecting or wanting anyone to nurture him or her. However, this is sometimes difficult for those who love us, who will often try to keep us alive even after we have become parasites. If those who love us nurture us after we have become parasites, they are diminishing their creativity, as well as the collective creativity of humanity, and doing us no favor. However, it is highly ethical to comfort and in every possible way to communicate love to dying friends, and to all those we love. Communicating love to those we love is among the most creative things that we can do to enhance our own creativity.

We shall all become parasites if we live long enough. Fortunately, many of us die before becoming parasites. I would rather die than become a parasite. And I ask all those who love me to allow me to die when I can no longer nurture and/or care for myself.

I recognize that suicide is unethical if it has no purpose but to end suffering. However, I respect anyone's right to commit suicide, with or without another's help. However, no one ever has the right, except in necessary self-defense, to end anyone's life without his or her clear consent, given before impartial witnesses, even to end their suffering. Suicide, as with any form of self-harm, is, at best, a private unethical act.

I shall finish this section by reproducing a copy of my own living will, which I left for my family in case I become incapacitated and can no longer make decisions concerning my medical treatment.

THE LIVING WILL
OF JOHN DAVID GARCIA

I wish to live as comfortably and simply as possible so long as I remain creative. My major creativity is in writing and teaching. If I become so ill that it is no longer likely that I will ever be able to write or teach again, then I wish to die as soon as possible.

While I was in Mexico in December 1999, I became incapacitated for a period of four days. If I ever become incapacitated again, so that I cannot make decisions for myself, I do not wish any heroic or invasive medical procedures to be used to keep me alive, unless there is a good chance that I will fully recover my creativity. Therefore, unless I am likely to recover my creativity, I do not wish any life support, surgery, invasive procedures, or anything to prolong my life performed on me.

If I am ever in a condition where I am not likely to recover my creativity, I wish to be allowed to die as quickly, painlessly, and peacefully as possible. I give full authority to my wife Bernice and/or my daughter Karen, who is a physician, to act for me under this circumstance, with my other daughters, Miriam, Jackie, and Laura, in that order, acting individually in their place if Bernice and/or Karen are unable to assume this responsibility.

Witnessed and Testified to on February 13, 2000 by,

John David Garcia

DEATH AS A CREATIVE ACT

Death is essential to life. Without death there can be no evolution by natural selection, since then higher life forms could never replace the less evolved life forms. It is inevitable that as we grow older, we eventually begin to decline in creativity, until maintaining our life costs more in the creative efforts of others than the value of our total creative output for the rest of our life. At this point the most creative thing we can do is to die and allow someone else to take our place in the ongoing experiment that is evolution.

The sole value and meaning of our life lies in the creativity that we engender in others. Each human life is an experiment in evolution. It will have been a successful experiment if we leave the biosphere a little more creative than we found it. If we have had a good life, someone will be able to build on the reflection of our soul that we left behind, and to help humanity take one more step along the road that leads to the Ethical State, the Moral Society, and ever closer to union in God. Solely moral beings achieve true union with God; solely they can continue to grow in creativity forever. Solely morality can engender immortality.

There can be no evolution by natural selection without death. Only highly ethical moral beings can continue to evolve forever and contribute to the evolution of the universe without having to die. Until then, we have an ethical obligation to die and make room for another experiment in evolution.

Dying is the last creative act of our life; we need not fear it.

Therefore, we learn to ignore death, and focus on maximizing creativity without any expectation of reward or fear of punishment, knowing that we are contributing to the creativity of the universe by dying, and that we have done the best we can. That is all we can expect from life, knowing that we did the best we could, that we refused to surrender to evil, that our creativity has come to an end, and that it is time to die.

Our soul will continue to live forever in the creativity that we have engendered in others. This seems to me to be the only heaven there is. We should expect no other reward, nor fear any punishment. Even if there were a hell, in which I do not believe, all suffering is trivial if we can no longer create. At this time we should welcome oblivion, and the final annihilation of our ego. It is the end of pain.

If we succeed as a species in creating a Moral Society, then our descendants may become sufficiently moral to grow in creativity forever, without having to die, but we are not there yet. Our death is the last gift we leave for our children and all our future descendants, as well as all the descendants of those we love. It's not such a bad deal. In any case, it is the only deal that God offers us. The rest is a fantasy engendered by, and for, those who fear death.

HOW TO BEGIN AN ETHICAL REPUBLIC

An Ethical State begins with us, and must evolve into an Ethical Republic over time. An Ethical Republic cannot exist without a Constitution. I have given you one example in the previous chapter. I gave another inadequate, and I now know impossible, example in my first book (116). But you should write your own constitution if you find mine inadequate. When you have written what seems to you, according to your own conscience alone, the best constitution you can think of, then you can begin creating an Ethical Government, but not yet a Republic, by creating an octet for yourself.

Do not consider political expediency at all. Do what is most ethical and creative, not what will sell politically. This was Saint Paul's ethical mistake; he distorted the teachings of Jesus so that they were more salable to the Greco-Roman world. Every ethical compromise you ever make for political expediency will fail, and will lead instead to the destruction of what you are trying to create. This is also what happened to Jefferson and the Founding Fathers. They should have been prepared to lose the Revolution, and to be hanged, before compromising on the issue of slavery.

Stand alone all your life if you must. But always seek citizens for the Ethical Republic you are trying to create, listening to their feedback, but not compromising on what you believe is ethically necessary. If you cannot create for yourself a single ethical octet with four men and four women, you will never be able to create an Ethical Republic.

Compromise is not what is needed. What is needed is a totally ethical political structure, and a totally ethical political plan and strategy, whether or not it may seem feasible within the current political realities in which you live. Listen to others. They can help you correct your errors, but be guided solely by your own conscience alone. Unethical means can never produce ethical ends.

Therefore, your first task is to develop enough ethically and intellectually to create an octet. I have been trying to create an Ethical State for thirty years. I have created over a thousand octets in several countries over the last twenty years. Almost all of them were failed experiments, which gradually taught me what not to do, and to understand the fragility of people's ethics. People can easily sink into fear, particularly into the fear of not being loved, the fear of being an outcast among their social and religious community, the economic fear of not having the bare essentials of security, the fear of being persecuted by the current political system under which they live, and finally the fear of death, which leads them to accept the comforting lies of the popular religions.

The most important thing to learn is how to work in octets by unanimous consensus. The particular form of creative synergy which I call "autopoiesis" appears to be very effective for achieving creative consensus, but it needs further experimentation under more highly controlled conditions (115). Anyone who can come up with a more ethical and creative technique for achieving creative consensus within ethical octets is ethically obligated to do so and then communicate it to others.

Here is the outline of a strategy for creating ethical octets.

1. Form as many complementary pairs as you can, investing a minimum of time in interacting with persons who do not share the Evolutionary Ethic with you and avoiding those who are systematically destructive.

2. Begin working with your best complement in an octet as soon as possible. Try never to have more men than women in the octet, but it is all right to have more women than men, so long as the maximum number of persons does not exceed ten, and so long as there is at least one man in the octet. A single complementary pair can also engage in autopoiesis (115). Meet as an octet at least once per month, but not more often than once per week. Be extremely scrupulous about keeping your commitments to one another within the octet; come when you say you are going to come, and arrive on time or slightly early. Try never to be late; it decreases creativity for those on time; it is an unethical act.

3. Focus at least the first eight to ten autopoietic sessions on solving whatever personal problems are put forth by each member of the octet, until each member of the octet has posed his or her most pressing problem of the moment to the octet at least once and has confidence in the joint power of the octet. All octet transactions should be held in highest confidence and never discussed outside the octet without unanimous permission of the entire octet. Constantly review and keep the Contract for Creative Transformation (115).

First brainstorm all problems classically without autopoiesis before addressing them autopoietically. Record the brainstorming and the autopoietic sessions regarding how to solve each problem, then transcribe and make a book out of them. Remember that everything is done by unanimous consensus, including giving a classical interpretation to the autopoiesis.

5. Study *Creative Transformation* (115) and *The Ethical State* individually, and collectively as an octet, striving for consensus on what everything in the books mean. Correct whatever errors you find, and expect to find them. Recall that the only time we know that we know is when our alleged knowledge enables us to predict and control something in objective reality without diminishing anyone's ability to predict and control anything else.

6. When you have all finished studying *Creative Transformation* and *The Ethical State*, and you have all had at least one brainstorming

session and one autopoietic session on a pressing problem of your own, then you may have completed this first phase of autopoiesis, which is called the "Social Phase." When, by consensus, you are all satisfied, you may, by consensus, go on to the second phase, which is called the "Common Interest Phase."

7. In the second phase you all choose by unanimous consensus a project which is an end in itself for all of you, and can readily be implemented by all of you with the resources you have on hand. The project must be solely and entirely in the Third or Fourth Economic Paradigm. The resources should primarily be your own creative labor, with minimal material resources, the expenses of which should be equally borne by each person. No one should ever receive resources, subsidies, or charity of any kind, including loans, from anyone else in the octet, but all should try to equalize their contributions to those of the greatest contributor. In phase two, try to avoid material contributions. All may trade equitably among themselves, by consensus, for their time and resources, but I recommend avoiding all commercial transactions among yourselves until you have become an economic octet.

When you have all by consensus finished the project of common interest, you may all decide, again by consensus, to go to phase three, or to stay in phase two for one or more projects of common interest until everybody is ready to go on to phase three. Good, ongoing phase two projects might develop the curriculum and educational ideas leading to the Lifetime Curriculum (see Epilogue). This can be done one level at a time, to meet the needs of your children or of yourselves within the environment in which you live.

Remember that all important decisions of the octet affecting the whole octet are always made by unanimous consensus; never let the need for expediency impede your working by unanimous consensus. No one should ever be forced to act contrary his or her conscience.

8. In phase three you become an "economic octet," and you begin investing, in an equitable way, your time and resources in projects that might require more than creative talent and may consume considerable resources. All phase three projects should be done solely within the Third or the Fourth Economic Paradigms. Use the First Economic Paradigm solely to fulfill your obligations to yourself and your family. Never enter into any economic project with persons who do not share the Evolutionary Ethic with you. If necessary stay in the First

Paradigm entirely by yourself until you find ethical partners who are qualified to participate with you in an economic octet.

It is possible to work simultaneously in the First, Third, and Fourth Economic Paradigms. But be sure to avoid the Second Economic Paradigm. Balance your activities so that you are providing adequate security for your family until you are ready to move to the higher paradigms.

In the economic octet, you share any profits from economic projects in proportion to the value of your investment in time and resources, all agreed to by unanimous consensus before the project is begun. Yet you should expect no profit, nor consider any material risk, in the Third or Fourth Economic Paradigm projects, but simply do what you all agree is the most creative thing you can do with the resources you have at hand. The sole risk, which must always be considered, is that you may inflict undeserved harm on someone, including yourselves.

Also have a plan so that anyone who wishes may withdraw from the project, at will, and have an equitable distribution of the resources he or she invested and of any profits made in the project. This formula should also be agreed to before the project begins. Put all your agreements in writing, and make sure you all agree in advance on what each agreement means. Write and keep your consensus agreements by yourselves, without involving lawyers or the courts.

Remember always that these are Third and Fourth Paradigm activities, where you consider neither economic risks nor profits, but solely choose, by one hundred percent consensus, to do maximally creative projects for which you have on hand all the resources, human and material, necessary to finish the project. But you may still engage, individually and collectively, in First Paradigm activities, where your objective is to maximize your income under the ethical constraints of solely engaging in at least minimally creative activities, and totally excluding unethical, destructive activities. Keep completely separate the activities in the different paradigms, or you may easily fall into the Second Economic Paradigm.

It is best to separate your First Paradigm activities from your higher paradigm activities as much as possible, and to do no First Paradigm activities with your octet.

The most important higher paradigm activity is to become as fully self-sufficient as soon as possible in every aspect of existence, in this order of priority: a) education, b) economics, c) food, d) clothing and housing, e) research and development, f) every form of manufacturing for which your octet is a major consumer, g) energy and transportation, h) health, i) defense, and j) everything else.

The best laboratory for maximizing creativity for any octet is total self-sufficiency. You should expect to invest several years of your life in the Creative Transformation process, before you are ready to begin Phase Three.

All octets may begin with a single complementary pair and may at first include individual members who are not yet in a complementary pair. Complementary pairs or other gender-balanced subgroups from the octet can form new first phase octets to incorporate new persons into an octet, after the new candidates have understood *Creative Transformation* and *The Ethical State*, and made the Contract for Creative Transformation, quantum and classical, among themselves (115). Try never to have more men than women in an octet or subgroup at any time, and make sure that there are no all-woman octets.

OBSERVATIONS AND SUGGESTIONS: BEWARE OF FALSE PROPHETS

All the persons likely to read this are probably ethical persons of high creative potential, or they would not have gotten this far. However, you must all generalize in areas outside of your specialties, never forgetting to seek more depth in every area while generalizing. Again, a start in this is reading and understanding my earlier books, particularly *Creative Transformation (115)*. If you have difficulty understanding *Creative Transformation*, then try reading *Psychofraud and Ethical Therapy* (117), which is my simplest book.

It may be that we are all vulnerable to psychofraud while we are intellectually and ethically immature, because of an ignorance of scientific method and its rigorous applications to every aspect of human existence, which requires a good knowledge of probability and statistics.

Learn to be skeptical, including of what I say. Remember that science does not create new knowledge; it merely tells us whether any information is possibly true or probably false. In order to be maximally creative, we must be scientific and generalized in our mysticism, as well as mystical and generalized in our science; alone, each paradigm is entropic.

The purest scientific study, which I recommend to all of you, is that equivalent to getting at least a Bachelor's degree in physics. The mathematics learned in this process is necessary, and a good start, but it is not sufficient in the long run if you wish to master the Lifetime Curriculum (see Epilogue). In any case, do the best you can in this direction, even if you might not finish studying the equivalent of a Bachelor's in physics during the rest of your life. If you cannot handle physics, try chemistry or another physical science first, and if you cannot handle that, try biology, but keep coming back to the physical sciences for the rest of your life, if necessary, until you have the equivalent of at least a Bachelor's in physics. You can then go on with the rest of the Lifetime Curriculum, as best you can. Getting any degree in the social sciences is mostly a waste of time. I know, because I have one of my degrees in psychology. One survey course in each of the social sciences is probably enough to teach you how to read and study these things on your own.

It is difficult, but not impossible, to learn mathematics and natural science on your own. Focus on physics, chemistry, biology, and mathematics in your formal studies, until you are sufficiently mature to tackle the Lifetime Curriculum on your own. We learn a subject best by teaching it, and by using the knowledge to develop practical technology in the business world.

There seem to be only two widespread ultimate goals: creativity and happiness. Solely the goal to maximize creativity does not lead to its own contradiction. This is the only criterion of optimization by which the social sciences and their techniques can be ethically evaluated and compared. The objective increase of creativity is the sole criterion for good, and the objective diminution of creativity is the sole criterion for evil. This is the only irreversible judgment that I have ever made.

The moral structure of the universe is such that good will always triumph over evil in the long run, because evil will always destroy itself. However, evil can also destroy much that is good before it destroys itself; recall the examples of Hitler, Stalin, and Pol Pot. The worst evil is an evil which masquerades as ethical principle, e.g., Nazism and Communism.

Humanity can destroy itself by surrendering to evil, i.e., to its own fear, and yet other parts of the universe can continue to evolve into the Moral Society. However, becoming a negative example to the universe is not what maximizes creativity. Our ethical responsibility is to evolve forever, by maximizing creativity to the very last breath of our life, thereby paving the way for our descendants. Each destructive act by a human being diminishes the probability that humanity will ever be part of the Cosmic Moral Society. Only morality can engender immortality.

There are certain unethical behavioral characteristics of which we should all become aware. You should go into a purely ethical exchange mode, with no scientific, technical, or otherwise objective information given, whenever you perceive these traits in anyone, including me; I am not immune. Beware of false prophets, and keep in mind the following caveats.

1. Beware of people who are method-oriented rather than goal-oriented. If we have no ethical goals, our methods can at best achieve solely trivial ends, and, while never creating, can at worst destroy. Combining ethical methods with ethical goals is the only true course. Those who tell you otherwise are false prophets.

2. Beware of people who constantly repeat the same solution to every single problem, and who believe that they have found a method that solves all problems. These people may be destructive. They are false prophets.

3. Never accept notions or do things which violate your innate sense of ethics, your sense of right and wrong, your conscience. If you do, you will fail in creating an Ethical State, at even the octet level. You may be following false prophets. Remember that all paradigms are, at best, incomplete, and at worst false. Always do what your conscience tells you is right; never do what seems wrong, no matter how persuasive the arguments or rigorous the "scientific" evidence to the contrary; then establish scientifically whether you have acted wisely.

4. Some false models offer what seems to be an attractive premise to many people: that one may rightly obtain power without ethical commitment or development. This belief is abhorrent to me, and,

again, it probably violates the ethical constraints of the universe. The Satanic myths are metaphors for such a model. Any paradigm which exalts the maximization of power will always be a false paradigm. A related paradigm, also invalid, places greatest value on maximizing intelligence by maximizing the amount of true information at our disposal, without considering ethics. This is the foundation of the academic bureaucracy. Increasing intelligence without increasing ethics is suicidal. Remember that ethics are always more important than intelligence. Never get trapped by the appeal of power without ethics. If you do, you will have surrendered to evil, the "dark side of the Force." At best you will be an academic bureaucrat; at worst you will be a politician, and in either case you will be following false prophets.

5. Our ability to receive and utilize negative feedback is an essential indicator of our ethical development. Recall that it is unethical to be certain about any cause-and-effect relationship. We can be certain solely about the existence of our thoughts and perceptions, never about their causes. Ultimate goals also have no basis in logic. We can be certain about the validity of an ultimate goal solely if it does not lead to its own contradiction, as have all forms of ritual, superstition, majority rule, and socialism. Persons who are closed to negative feedback are always false prophets.

6. Finally, there is something wrong with a person who cannot imagine, even at the metaphorical level, an alternative to his or her paradigm. This is true of all religious fundamentalists, and of such contemporary counterparts as Marxists, socialists, cultists, existentialists, hedonists, and other like ideologues. These persons will always be false prophets and will probably be highly unethical. But we should never judge anyone absolutely to be unethical. We merely try to avoid systematically destructive people and to give them a minimum of our time. The best way to avoid destructive people is to be as self-sufficient as possible.

We avoid bureaucrats and politicians by never cooperating with them, within the limits of the law. We have an ethical duty to live in the nation which has the fewest unethical laws and politicians. All existing nations are far from perfect in this respect, but some are much worse than others. We do the best we can.

We use creativity as the sole criterion by which we evaluate all social science. Increases or decreases in creativity must be evaluated scientifically. If we have decreased a single person's creativity, then we have done an unethical act, damaging that person, his or her descendants, and many of the people with whom they interact. We should always avoid such acts. This is impossible, to the best of my knowledge, without the full use of scientific method, which is based on experimental validations of the predictions made by paradigms and theories

Remember that it may not be a creative act to ameliorate any disease, physical or psychosocial, in a person who is not ethical. We begin by maximizing ethics, not intelligence or well-being. However, as we can never know with certainty who is ethical or unethical, we must treat everyone as if they were ethical, but limit our exchange solely to ethical information until we know that a person is not systematically destructive in his or her behavior. We judge acts, not people.

The crucial thing is not to substitute one set of symptoms for another, such as by turning a socially-unacceptable psychopath into a socially-acceptable bureaucratic parasite. That is not Creative Transformation. Ask yourselves, "What have I or my teacher done to discover scientific laws, invent machines, create great works of art, *or help others do these things.*" If you answer "nothing," then you have solely learned, or taught, pure psychofraud.

Creativity is its own reward; we need do nothing other than maximize creativity in order to have on hand all the resources necessary for continuing to maximize creativity. Beware of anyone who needs someone else to provide the resources needed to maximize creativity. If we are creative, the least we can do is to be creative with what we have at hand, and not depend on others to nurture us or our projects.

Weak ethics can mask our fear as conscience, and lead us to accept falsehood as truth. We do not have to believe anything. We should be guided solely by goals, never by methods alone. We can always improve our methods. We cannot improve on the Evolutionary Ethic. Every other ethic will lead to its own contradiction.

Many paradigms are popular because they are both original and good. However, in popular paradigms usually what is good is not original, and what is original is not good. What is best in all modern paradigms is often what comes from the implicate-order, holographic model of David Bohm (32–35). Many new paradigms incorporate this model as a form of mysticism, and that is what makes many people believe that their models have a lot in common with the Evolutionary Ethic, when in fact there is no shared ethical base.

In order to be maximally creative we must be completely scientific in our mysticism as well as completely mystical in our science. Placebos can make us happy, and may even cure disease, but they cannot increase creativity, as I showed in *Psychofraud and Ethical Therapy* (117).

My emphasis on science notwithstanding, the essence of my system lies in my original concept that **C=IE**. It is more important to become maximally ethical than to become maximally intelligent, because creativity is negative when ethics are negative. This is so even if David Bohm's model is totally wrong.

Everything I have said or written may be error. Only the ultimate goal and choice of maximizing creativity, the Evolutionary Ethic, cannot be error, because it is an ultimate end beyond logic which leads to no contradictions, as do other ultimate goals. Clarify your ultimate goals and concentrate on achieving them without ever being married to any method or paradigm, my own or anyone else's. It is ethical to doubt. Be skeptical; avoid certainty. Avoid false prophets.

EPILOGUE

Method and Curriculum

I have developed an educational program that not only maximizes creativity while strengthening a student's ethics, but also enables the student, child or adult, to acquire all the traditional educational information many times faster and more coherently. This is done by teaching the student through a process of rediscovery, where all subjects are taught in the same order and context as the human race learned these things.

Instead of merely regurgitating information, the student is encouraged to use his or her imagination and creativity to reinvent the accumulated knowledge of humanity, in the same order and context as humanity invented and discovered this information. This takes patience and creativity on the part of the teacher. Traditional methods of teacher training seem to destroy creativity for both the teachers and their subsequent students. Therefore we do things in new ways, never before tried.

Students, particularly if they are children, should never be punished in any way, or forced to do what they do not wish to do. Instead they are given ever growing creative opportunities specifically tailored to their individual abilities and inclinations. These opportunities are both the intrinsic rewards for their creative actions, as well as more attractive, interesting alternatives to their destructive actions.

Many of these objectives will be accomplished simultaneously by organizing the students into voluntary, cooperative octets of four males and four females, who learn as a group and decide by consensus what they should focus on next. Students should join the octet whose pace and inclination for learning is most compatible with their own. Students may change octets any time they cannot reach consensus in their octet, or if they find a better octet for themselves.

Students who wish to work individually, or in other-sized groups, should also be able to do so, and should be encouraged to change their organizational structure to whatever structure is most creative for them. It may be that the available octets are not optimal for all students at all times during their lives. Students should have an opportunity, not an obligation, to work and study in voluntary, cooperative octets. The prediction is that those who choose to work in these octets will maximize their ethics, their creativity, and their intelligence. If not, our educational methods can be changed.

Given this background, we now focus on a curriculum which maximizes creativity. What follows is an outline of a thirteen-year curriculum arranged in three subject areas—physical, biological, and psychological—and a fourth track which attempts to integrate the three. Students will of course move at their own pace; this approach can well provide material for a lifetime of learning.

John David Garcia

Avg. Level	Avg. Age	Physical		Biological	
		Physical Theory		Biological Theory	
1.00	3.00	Cause and effect	The lever	The human body	Body care
1.25	3.25	Clubs and poles	Modifying trees and branches	Animal bodies; small domestic animals	How to care for a pet
1.50	3.50	Different stones and their properties	Using stones	Edible plants and their properties	Gathering edible plants and mushrooms
1.75	3.75	Shaping stone	Building simple stone tools	Edible animals and fish	Hunting and fishing
2.00	4.00	Shaping wood with stone	Using stone tools to modify poles and clubs	Food preparation and preservation	Cleaning and preparing small game and fish using bone, wood, and stone
2.25	4.25	Handling fire	Use of stone and wood to control fire, use of fire to harden spear points	Advanced food preparation	Cooking vegetables, fish, and meat on open fires
2.50	4.50	Advanced fire handling and control combining wood and stone tools, theory and design	Hafted axes and choppers are made; stone fire carriers, simple weaving and knotting of vines and leather	Elementary tanning and use of bone, vines, and vegetable fiber	Skinning animals and fish, preserving leather, advanced cooking; preparing vines and vegetable fiber
2.75	4.75	The bow and fire-making	Making bows and starting fires	Advanced food preparation; advanced tanning and bone work	Advanced cooking; clothes from animal hides; use of sinew and thongs; hunting with dogs
3.00	5.00	The use of clay and the bow and arrow; design of simple rafts	Making and baking clay pots on an open fire; making and using simple bows and arrows	Advanced food preparation including drying, smoking, and curing; health care	Cooking, drying, and smoking with clay pots; preparing and using medicinal herbs and poultices
3.25	5.25	Advanced paleolithic stone work of knives and axes; advanced bow making; advanced clay work without wheel; large rafts	Making stone tools to make other stone tools; making advanced bows and arrows; bellows and advanced pottery.	Gathering seeds and planting edible plants; basic first aid	Gardening; preparing soil and cultivation; practice of first aid
3.50	5.50	Neolithic tools; construction of shelters; advanced counting; how to make a small dugout canoe and paddle	Construction of simple neolithic tools; the use of tally marks and stored pebbles; building a small dugout canoe.	The biological need for shelter; building of lean-tos and simple teepees; clothes for extreme cold; simple agriculture	Construction of lean-tos and teepees; more advanced gardening; making bone needles and a parka
3.75	5.75	How to construct advanced neolithic tools and work stone and wood; more advanced counting and Arabic numbers to 10; how to build a large dugout canoe	Building advanced neolithic tools; working wood, simple carpentry, building semi-permanent structures; advanced tallying systems; building a large dugout canoe	How to make boots and moccasins from leather and plant fiber; how to know when to plant and when to harvest; taking care of goats and sheep	Construction of complete wardrobes of leather, plant, and animal fiber; more advanced gardening and animal husbandry

212

The Ethical State

Avg. Level	Avg. Age	Psychosocial		Integration	
		Psychosocial Theory	Pyschosocial Practice	Integrative Theory	Integrative Practice
1.00	3.00	How to communicate	Exchange of information	Ethics of personal obligation	Free-form drawing and painting, simple songs
1.25	3.25	Verification of information	Repeat same message from different source	Truth and lying, paleolithic stories	Free-form drawing and painting; paleolithic stories; drums
1.50	3.50	Games of information	Teams for sending and receiving messages	Advantages of cooperating vs competing.	Songs, dancing, drawing, painting, telling stories
1.75	3.75	Making pictures to communicate information	Drawing picture stories	Obligations of making oneself understood	Free-form art, stick-figure drawing for stories
2.00	4.00	Advanced picture stories	Making up stories with pictures	Ethics of separating fact from fiction; paleolithic stories	Wood carving and free-form painting; paleolithic stories created and drawn
2.25	4.25	Picture symbols which stand for complex events	Team communications games and "charades" using picture symbols	The difference between a symbol and the thing it symbolizes; paleolithic stories	Charcoal drawing on stone; universal religious symbols; creating stories
2.50	4.50	Advanced picture symbols and counting	Making up stories by stringing together picture symbols	Creation myths of paleolithic people	Making up creation myths
2.75	4.75	Rebus writing combined with picture writing	Making up stories with rebus and picture writing	Advanced creation myths of Native Americans and some religious beliefs; symbols.	Native American art; free-form art for what students value
3.00	5.00	The notion of an alphabet and sound symbols	Stringing sound symbols together to make a word	The religions of native Americans and the evolutionary ethic	Percussion instruments, carving, dance, and art to express religious feelings
3.25	5.25	Reading advanced paleolithic stories with evolutionary ethical theme	Writing simple stories and accounts using alphabet, rebus writing, or pictures as desired	The importance of separating truth from fiction in our writing to avoid misleading others	Late paleolithic art and religion; students' expression of their own feelings about them
3.50	5.50	Reading stories and history of early neolithic life with evolutionary ethics theme	More writing of stories using alphabet, rebus writing, and pictures as desired	Simple analysis of neolithic culture and religions in light of the evolutionary ethic	Neolithic art and stone carving; self-expression of students
3.75	5.75	Reading more complex stories of neolithic life about religion and creativity in ancient Jericho and Mesopotamia	More writing of stories and accounts using alphabet and rebus writing, but no pictures; show difficulty of communicating numerical concepts over 10	Analysis of why neolithic culture advanced so slowly before the beginning of Sumer; the energy that went into religious ritual and the corrupt priestly bureaucracy	The flute and harp and the neolithic music possible with them; advanced neolithic art and religion; self-expression in all art media

Avg. Level	Avg. Age	Physical		Biological	
		Physical Theory	Physical Practice	Biological Theory	Biological Practice
4.00	6.00	The concept of the wheel; smelting metal from ore; making a simple calendar from astronomical observations; counting and use of Arabic numbers to 1,000 for calendar making, time-keeping, and other uses	Making a potter's wheel and using it; making an advanced bellows driven by a pedaled wheel to heat a charcoal, earth, and clay oven; making a spinning wheel, a sundial, a simple loom	Advanced gardening; the making of cloth from plant and animal fiber; advanced care and management of sheep and goats; gourmet cooking with spices and herbs using ovens; making more advanced permanent shelters of wood and stone	Spinning fiber; simple weaving of cloth with no loom; wheat and corn cultivation; making bread with and without yeast; breeding sheep and goats with seasons; training dogs; constructing small stone and wood huts
4.25	6.25	More advanced metallurgy; the saw and how to use it; how to cast bronze tools, nails, the chisel, and metal hammer; advanced use of wheels; simple arithmetic; adding and subtraction with Arabic numbers; simple geometry	Construction of wheeled push carts; construct bronze tools and show how inferior they are to steel tools; use steel tools in all construction; use pick and shovel and push cart to build small irrigation system and buildings; show how arithmetic and simple geometry help construct these projects	Group design of large irrigated garden suitable for self-sufficiency of 16 persons; advanced looms and weaving; advanced animal husbandry and selective breeding of sheep and goats; care of chickens and cattle	Construct and plant garden; advanced cooking and preserving of food; fermentation to produce alcohol, distillation of alcohol with copper still
4.50	6.50	Advanced bronze-based metallurgy and smelting of other similar metals; identify related ores and other rocks; simple glass technology; building an oxcart from wood, leather, and bronze; simple multiplication with Arabic numbers; more simple geometry, right triangles, and the circle; advanced calendar-making and time-keeping; how to make a simple boat.	Smelt and cast advanced bronzes and similar metals; make and cast glass sheets; make mirrors of metal and glass; build an oxcart; show how arithmetic and geometry are useful; use detailed astronomical observations to make a better calendar, and show how arithmetic and geometry help; build a small sailing and rowing boat	Show how to use a simple plow and fertilizer to prepare land; show how to make fertilizer from minerals and organic substances; show how to cross-pollinate and hybridize plants and trees; show how to use advanced fermentation techniques to produce wine and alcohol; discuss effects of alcohol as drug and preservative; storage and preservation of grain	Advanced agriculture and gardening projects; make fertilizers, crossbreed and hybridize plants; grow grain and grapes, ferment to alcohol, distill alcohol, and use as a fuel, preservative, and disinfectant; cultivation of yeasts and advanced baking
4.75	6.75	More advanced arithmetic and geometry, division of numbers, simple fractions; creation of more advanced sailing craft, the ideas behind a horse-drawn war chariot, the compound bow with metal-tipped arrows, how to construct the two-person war chariot and its relationship to the oxcart; the Babylonian abacus theory	Show how arithmetic and geometry contribute to following group projects: build a more advanced sailing craft; build a war chariot using steel, wood, and leather; show how much more difficult it was with only bronze; build compound bow with bronze-tipped arrows; practice with bow until expert, practice with war chariot	Domestication and use of the horse as a biological machine, special care and breeding required by horse, horse behavior and anatomy, equipment for controlling horse and how to make it	Horse training and use for farming and pulling chariots, speed comparisons, training horse for chariots and bareback riding

The Ethical State

Avg. Level	Avg. Age	Psychosocial		Integration	
		Psychosocial Theory	**Pyschosocial Practice**	**Integrative Theory**	**Integrative Practice**
4.00	6.00	Reading stories in personal terms about the possible prehistory of the Sumerian people; vocabulary development and the practical use of grammar	Write stories of fiction and personal activity us r g only alphabet; show how convenient it is to know when a sentence starts and ends, and how punctuation prevents misunderstanding	The ethics of larger groups; how it is possible for several octets to cooperate if they have common rules and objectives; how ancient civilizations were slave-based and ruled by priestly bureaucracies	Students construct rules and goals of cooperative behavior in order to build large-scale projects, buildings, irrigation systems to benefit hundreds of persons
4.25	6.25	Realistic but fictionalized history of the founding of Sumer and they created their culture up to the invention of writing; show how the religion and its ritual became overwhelmingly important, and how by controlling food the priests controlled people, warriors, and kings	Write stories of fiction and personal activity; write essays on behavioral ethics; use proper punctuation for carity of ideas and teach correct punctuation for students; have students ethically analyze in writing the history of Sumer and discuss what might be wrong	The ethics of individual rights; show that taking rights away from individuals for a larger group damages the group it is supposed to help; show how creativity is important to progress and how liberty is important for creativity	Students study Sumerian art and try to express their own feelings about Sumer in ceramic figurines similar to the Sumerians'; stone sculpture project; reproduction of Sumerian relics and artifacts
4.50	6.50	Read a simple non-fictional history of Sumer; show their writing and accounting systems and note their defects; show how clay as prime resource led to cuneiform; read full accounts of Sumerian myths, including Garden of Eden, Gilgamesh, and Noah	Write an analysis of Sumerians' history and their collapse; write an analysis of their myths and what they mean; write your own myths to communicate the same ideas as the Sumerian myths; write a creative story of your own choosing	Ethical analysis of the rise and fall of Sumer, the ethical nature of the conquerors of Sumer, their strengths and weaknesses, the weakness of theocracy and hereditary aristocracy, why these entropic systems went on for so long	Creative synthesis; high Sumerian art compared to art of conquerors; artistic group project to communicate the rise and fall of Sumer through music, painting, sculpture, and dance
4.75	6.75	Read a simple world history of the Ecumene from the fall of Sumer to 600 BC; show how little progress and creativity there was until then; show how Aryans spread Sumerian civilization to the entire old world and possibly to the Americas; read literary examples of each major culture	Write an ethical analysis of each major culture and why they could not significantly improve on Sumerian civilization; write an analysis and interpretation of their literary works; write your own story to express what you feel about this period of history	An ethical analysis of the Sumerian religion and those that followed; show how ethical vitality in primitive cultures can lead to conquest of advanced civilizations; show how religions that seek reward for ethical behavior is destructive; why it was necessary to invent morality	The art forms of Babylon, Egypt, Crete, pre-Confucianist China, and India; make your own version of these art styles; improvise music on the instruments of these times; do a group art project on this period of history

Avg. Level	Avg. Age	Physical		Biological	
		Physical Theory	**Physical Practice**	**Biological Theory**	**Biological Practice**
5.00	7.00	The smelting of iron and simple steels, forging iron and blacksmithing; simple astronomy and navigation, advanced sailing ships that might have crossed the Atlantic; the iron forging necessary for controlling a horse in battle; pre-Greek geometry and arithmetic using Arabic numbers, advanced theory of the Babylonian abacus	Smelt ore, forge from iron a complete set of tack for a horse, plus horseshoes; forge and make iron sword and spear; make large clay jars for storing grain, oils, and wine; begin one-year sailing ship construction project for group; show how geometry and arithmetic help in the above projects, build a Babylonian abacus	Advanced study of equestrianship for war, shooting a compound bow while riding horseback, the use of the lance and the sword from horseback; mammalian reproduction in detail, nursing and care of young mammals; processing milk into cheese and yogurt	Horse handling, training, and riding; grooming and care of horses, shodding and equipping the horse, the use of different bits, saddles, and stirrups; mammalian reproduction and breeding; comparisons of dogs, cats, sheep, goats, cows, and horses; cheese and yogurt from cow's milk; extract oil from fruits and nuts; make and store wine; optimal physical training of the human body
5.25	7.25	Continue with projects begun previous quarter	Continue with projects begun previous quarter	Continue with projects begun previous quarter	Continue with projects begun previous quarter
5.50	7.50	Advanced metallurgy, casting bronze sculptures through lost wax process; making of hard steel alloys, nails, bolts, and screws; making advanced presses and catapults; fractions and decimals, empirical basis of Pythagorean Theorem, right triangles, circles, spheres, and parallelopipeds	Continue work on sailing ship; do precision bronze castings; make knives using hard steel alloys; make nails, bolts, screws, presses, and catapults; show applications of mathematics and geometry to the above	Human reproduction, comparative male and female anatomy, hormonal cycles, fertility cycles, puberty and emotions, lactation and nursing, care of infants, normal patterns of growth for young boys and girls	Advanced breeding of animals and plants; extraction of fats and oils from vegetables, fruits, and seeds; extraction of animal fats from carcasses and meat; nursery work caring for small children 1–2 years old
5.75	7.75	The geometry and mathematics of Pythagoras, several proofs of his theorem, the Pythagorean solids, the harmonics of vibrating strings and the physical basis of music; geometry applied to navigation, astronomy, building and surveying; the technology of glass, glass blowing	Construct the Pythagorean solids, use several approaches to making dodecahedron and icosahedron; construct navigational computer, advanced abacus; construct glass bottles, mirrors, parabolic mirror; finish sailing ship	Human health and the Greek medical tradition, Aesculapius and Hippocrates; a healthy mind in a healthy body; physical culture and optimal health; diet, exercise, and health	Gardening and preparation of food for optimal health; an exercise plan for lifetime health, strength, and energy; construction of a glass still; care of young infants

The Ethical State

Avg. Level	Avg. Age	Psychosocial		Integration	
		Psychosocial Theory	Pyschosocial Practice	Integrative Theory	Integrative Practice
5.00	7.00	The story of Zarathustra; how he changed the Persian people and how they went on to create the world's greatest empire until conquered by Alexander; the Zoroastrian religion and myths in detail	Analysis of ancient Persian history and religion; write a story of how Persian history might have been different if the religion had been different	Ethical analysis of Zoroastrian religion and ethical system, strengths and weaknesses, and how it was doomed to failure	Ancient Persian art, architecture, music; analyze and reproduce style according to your own feeling about this culture; do a group project expressing ancient Persian civilization
5.25	7.25	The story of Confucius and his teachings and how they changed China; the books of Confucius are read, discussed, and compared to the philosophy of Lao Tse; the interaction of Taoism and Confucianism in Chinese history is discussed	Written analysis of each of the books of Confucius and stories about Confucius; a study of Lao Tse; writing of imaginative stories about life in China; essay on how you personally feel about Confucius and Lao Tse	Ethical analysis of Confucianism and Taoism as ethical systems and as ways to knowledge, and of the civilization they produced; what was right and what was wrong	Ancient Chinese art to Tang dynasty, analyze and reproduce style in sculpture, painting, and music; use Chinese style to express your feelings about classical Chinese culture in group art project
5.50	7.50	The story of Buddha and his teachings and how they changed India and the East; emphasize the basic ethical nature of Buddhism and its tolerant compassion toward others; show how Buddhists became psychosocial specialists and stopped innovating in the natural world; compare to Hinduism	Write essays on the meaning of Hinduism and Buddhism and how they relate to you; how Buddhism and Hinduism relate to each other, how you would feel and act if you were suddenly put into a Buddhist or Hindu society; give evidence for and against reincarnation, what impact these societies have on the world, predictions	Hinduism and Buddhism in light of the evolutionary ethic and the eight Ethical Principles; the historical impact and consequences of those religions; the ethics of the caste system; why Buddhism is more successful as an export; common Aryan origins of Hinduism, Buddhism and Zoroastrianism	Experience directly Buddhist and Hindu meditation and its comparison to autopoiesis; Buddhist and Hindu art; draw mandalas of your own, sculpt in Buddhist and Hindu style, make up mandalas, learn to play Buddhist and Hindu music; do art works expressing how you feel about Buddhism and/or Hinduism
5.75	7.75	Early Greek history to Thales; the Iliad and the Odyssey; the story of Thales and Pythagoras and how they laid part of the foundations of Western civilization; the rational and mystical as reflected in those two men; Thales and ethics; Pythagoras and religion	Write an essay on the ethics of the characters in the Iliad and Odyssey, the ethics of the mythical characters and gods, the attitudes toward women and their role in Greece; make up a Greek-style myth of your own	The warlike Aryan tradition and how it led to Greek culture, the obsession with domination and personal freedom, the oppressiveness of a slave-based culture, the extreme military specialization of Sparta; why a love of truth and intelligence is not enough if there is no love for others.	Geometric art using Pythagorean and Greek principles, composition of music using Pythagorean theory of harmonic scales; begin a sculpture project in the Greek style; Greek music and dances including those of Sparta

John David Garcia

Avg. Level	Avg. Age	Physical		Biological	
		Physical Theory	Physical Practice	Biological Theory	Biological Practice
6.00	8.00	The geometry of Euclid using modern algebraic notation, introduction to algebra as it applies to geometry, use of geometry and vectors to sail against the wind; give many examples of the practical applications of geometry in many fields; the Atomic Theory of matter of Democritus; other Greek theories of water, earth, air, and fire	Use geometry to calculate size of the earth, distance to the sun, size of the sun; use geometry to construct and use a large catapult; build a bridge by geometric design; work with glass making lenses and mirrors; begin design of ship that can sail against the wind; practice sailing the ship built last year	Internal anatomy of vertebrates, fish, frog, rat, and pig; the true role of each organ and what Aristotle and Galen thought they were for; Greek theories of evolution compared to modern theory; point out how dangerous it is for authorities to be wrong; the value of doubt	Dissection of fish, frog, rat, and pig; identification of all major organs and bones; practice in meat processing, packaging, and preservation without refrigeration; continue practice in caring for young infants in first year
6.25	8.25	Continue the previous work and continue with the geometry and science of Archimedes; use modern algebraic notation and point out how difficult the work of Archimedes was because of notation; theory of pullies and parabolic mirrors; show how abacus answers the notational problem	Construct a system of pulleys and a block and tackle; construct parabolic mirrors to collect solar energy by heating water, and work out schedule for how mirrors should be aligned as function of time of year and day; finish design of ship	Detailed survey of Greco-Roman medicine and the modern versions of these beliefs; guide to the use of herbs and medicines for curing and preventing illnesses; taxonomy of herbs; review Greco-Roman theories of biology	Plant a garden of medicinal herbs, take field trips to collect medicinal herbs, prepare poultices and medicines that have been validated by time and modern usage
6.50	8.50	The works of Archimedes continued, the school of Alexandria, and the continuation of Greek mathematics, science, and technology; full development of algebra and trigonometry using modern notation; solid geometry and trigonometry, applications to navigation, the construction of lenses	The design and construction of water pumps; the design and construction of steam turbines; practical lens making continued; begin modification of ship made in fif year to sail against the wind; glass blowing continued	Study of preventive medicine; germ theory of infection and how hygiene can prevent it (although Greeks had lenses, no one discovered germs for 2000 years), parasites and their life cycles, the danger of eating meat, the importance of cooking and cleanliness	Use lenses to study small organisms, examine parasites in intestines of animals, show how maggots hatch from fly's eggs; basic entomology observed; use microscope to study basic parasitology
6.75	8.75	Continuation of the study of the science, technology, and mathematics of the School of Alexandria	Continuation of the above; make crude telescope and microscopes	The study of microscopic life; how lack of scientific method inhibited medical practice for 2000 years; how to prevent the spread of disease; viruses as submicroscopic organisms not to be discovered for 2000 years	Study of amoebas and major human parasites; animals as sources of infection for humans; the parasitic worms

218

The Ethical State

Avg. Level	Avg. Age	Psychosocial		Integration	
		Psychosocial Theory	Pyschosocial Practice	Integrative Theory	Integrative Practice
6.00	8.00	Greek history from Thales to the Roman conquest, the Dialogues of Plato, a survey of Aristotle, a survey of the Greek plays and the fables of Aesop, the ethical teaching of Socrates, the Macedonian interlude and Alexander	Perform one play by Sophocles and one by Euripides; write a critique of Greek culture and why it failed; write a critique of Socrates' life considering whether Socrates should have drunk the hemlock; write an epic poem on Greece	Ethical analysis of the teachings of Socrates, Plato, and Aristotle; show how the lack of love and the will to power forced Greece to destroy itself; consider that the great thinkers of Greece never had power nor were they free of tyrants except at first	Write a play in the Greek style on Greek themes, critique one another's plays; finish sculpture in the Greek style; do a group art project on the meaning of Greece
6.25	8.25	Greco-Roman history from the start of Rome to the time of Jesus; analysis of the works of Lucretius; what the Romans had of their own and what they learned from the Greeks; Roman ethics and theories of government; how tyranny can always replace a Majority Rule by promising to take from the rich and give to the poor	Learn Greek and Latin roots to English and scientific and technical terms, emphasis on nouns; the Greek alphabet, brief survey of Greek and Roman grammar and its complexity, showing how English grammar more practical; show how as vocabulary expands grammar can be simplified; write essay comparing Greek and Roman culture	Sexual ethics and how the Greeks and Romans related to them; pleasure as an end in itself; the exploitation of women, exclusion of women from all important decision making, women as sexual objects, the absolute authority of the father; Roman law and evolutionary ethics, subservience to the state and ethical principles	Design a domed and vaulted building made of wood and masonry, calculate stresses, and show the use of the arch and dome; play Roman music and practice sports; do a group art project on the meaning of Rome under Augustus
6.50	8.50	The history of the Jews; read the Old Testament, the ethical principles derivable from it, the mixing of ethics, techniques, and ritual; the Jewish interaction with the Aryans after the Babylonian captivity, the resistance to Hellenization, the conquest by Rome, the Jewish bureaucracy, sampling of the Talmud	Essay analyzing Old Testament as a historical account and as a myth; compare to Iliad and Odyssey; Jewish laws are analyzed in terms of their ethical value and their political implication; essay on Judaism as an ethical system	Ethical analysis of the Old Testament, personal ethics, health implications of many of the Jewish laws; show how the means became the ends and how ritual destroys ethics; the destructiveness of becoming specialized in one's own religion	Jewish abstract art in the form of the Menorah and the Star of David; paint an art work using Jewish symbols to express a Jewish theme without including the human form or animals; Jewish music and Passover songs
6.75	8.75	The New Testament and the life of Jesus, the ethical teaching of Jesus, Jesus as a Jewish reformer and rabbi, the deification of Jesus, the teachings of Jesus in relationship to the Greco-Roman religion, St. Paul and Christianity as a synthesis of Judaism, Jesus, and Greco-Roman religion and philosophy	Write an essay on Jesus and the meaning of his life and death, essay on the criticisms of Jesus against traditions and the Jewish bureaucracy, essay on whether Jesus could have studied in India and/or Tibet, essay on Jesus' teaching and the school of Alexandria	Ethical analysis of the New Testament, the high ethical content in the teachings of Jesus compared to their corruption by St. Paul, the mythification and deification of Jesus in the Roman tradition by those who did not know him, analysis of synoptic gospels showing how they were all derived from a simpler, common source	Draw and paint art showing the unification of Judaism, the teachings of Jesus, and the Greco-Roman religion (Michelangelo's Sistine Chapel is best model); write a poem expressing this synthesis; do a group art project expressing the essence of Christianity

219

John David Garcia

		Physical		Biological	
Avg. Level	Avg. Age	Physical Theory	Physical Practice	Biological Theory	Biological Practice
7.00	9.00	Consolidation of Greek mathematics and geometry using modern notation; practical chemistry in purifying common elements from their ores and making chemical compounds such as sulphuric acid, nitric acid, hydrochloric acid, aqua regia, and gun powder	Use geometry and mathematics to design a cathedral using Roman arches, vaults, and buttresses; isolate elements from their ores; make acids and simple compounds, gun powder, and paints; make mortars and cements; continue modification of sailing ship	Further study of microscopic life, protozoa, mites, worms, and other microorganisms that live on and in mammals; diseases they cause and symbiosis they provide	Microscopic observation of microorganisms, classification in modern terms; observe sea plankton, sponges, and hydra, and observation of their life cycles
7.25	9.25	Mathematical modeling of nature through advanced algebra, geometry, and trigonometry; derive solutions to quadratic and cubic equations; advanced navigation, the compass and the theory of the sextant; advanced geometry, trigonometry of arches, domes and vaults	Masonry work, making stone arches and vaults; begin construction of small wooden house with some masonry; continue to work with lenses and practical optics, make reflecting telescope; make better microscope; make additional chemical compounds, acids and paints, dyes and cements; construction of an astrolabe; finish modifications on sailing ship	Animal systematics; invertebrate zoology; comparative organ systems; organ structure and function; cell theory of animal structures	Laboratory dissection and study of the invertebrate phyla in an evolutionary context; detailed experimentation for function of organ systems and microhistology
7.50	9.50	Mathematical modeling of nature continued; quartic equations; heliocentric model of solar system compared to Ptolemaic; comparison of Viking ships as fast raiders to more seaworthy sailing ships; prepare for two-week ocean trip; theory of alchemy	Continue work with wood and masonry; begin construction of accurate water and weighted clock; begin construction of astronomical telescope with instruments; alchemical preparation for isolating elements and making compounds; the alchemical symbols as archetypes	Continue classification of invertebrates for all remaining major phyla, specifying organ functions and histology; show how all metazoa have same types of cells and all start as single cell, simple embryo egg	Laboratory dissection and microscopic observation of major invertebrate phyla; tissue and embryology; transition species to vertebrates: tunicates and amphioxus
7.75	9.75	Begin study of conics and analytical geometry; begin study of the dynamics of falling bodies and the pendulum; continue study of alchemy, showing how acceptance of wrong hypotheses impeded progress; consider measurements of time, temperature, and position	Finish wooden house; using telescope and clocks, begin observations of movements of planets and earth relative to sun, and deduce Kepler's laws; take a two-week ocean trip; begin construction of sextant	Continue classification of invertebrates; compare with anatomy of simpler vertebrates; study all organs and their physiology and function; identify cells common to vertebrates and invertebrates	Microscopic observations and dissection of simple vertebrates and their organs; observation of simple embryology and comparison to invertebrate embryology; full dissection of shark

220

The Ethical State

		Psychosocial		Integration	
Avg. Level	Avg. Age	Psychosocial Theory	Pyschosocial Practice	Integrative Theory	Integrative Practice
7.00	9.00	The Roman Empire and its interaction with Christianity, the Greco-Roman disdain for manual labor, the Christian disdain for the natural world; the Gnostic Christians; the stagnation and disintegration of the Roman Empire until the rise of Islam	Write speculative essay on how Roman Empire might have endured and what the world would be like if it had; write speculative essay on how Christianity would have developed if the Gnostics had not been persecuted	The ethical decay of Rome; Roman bureaucracy; how the Catholic bureaucracy established itself; Catholic intolerance of deviant views; persecution of heretics; inferiority complex about pagan knowledge; the destruction of Alexandrian library; Hypatia	Finish design of cathedral; paint Christian symbols that express what is best in Christianity; sing Gregorian chants in Latin after studying translations; do an art project expressing the meaning of the Catholic church
7.25	9.25	The rise of Islam; read the Koran; early history of Arabia to 7th century; relationship of Islam to Zoroastrianism, Judaism, Christianity, and surrounding cultures; the political vacuum in the Middle East	Essay on why so many Jews rejected Islam; essay on why Islam was able to grow and expand so rapidly; essay on the ethical contradictions within Islam compared to Judaism and Christianity	Islam as a closed system; how Islam induces fanaticism; its comparison to Christianity; why Christianity is more open in spite of church bureaucracy; Islam and creativity; the reason for Islam declining as Christianity rose	Islamic abstract art; how lack of representational art diminishes creativity; draw abstract designs in the Islamic style; Islamic mandalas; paint representational art of Islam; compare to Persian and Mogul art forms
7.50	9.50	The great theologians, St. Augustine, St. Gregory, Averroes, Avicena, Maimonides, St. Anselm, Abelard; show their depth and breadth of vision; the weakness of having orthodoxy to defend; the Holy Roman Empire and its relationship to Islam, India, and China; Charlemagne and his successors	Essays on the "proofs" of the existence of God and the ontological arguments; essay on the humanizing role of the Church while it bureaucratically decayed; essay on priestly celibacy and its implications; write your own ideas about God	The dominance of ideology and bureaucracy over ethics and truth, the preservation and distortion of the teachings of Jesus, the fundamental power of the teachings of Jesus in spite of the negative elements	Compare Byzantine with Western religious art and paint a synthesis of the two; paint a synthesis of Christian, Chinese, Hindu, and Muslim art of the period; begin study of the organ
7.75	9.75	St. Thomas Aquinas and the rise of the Holy Roman Empire; the feedback produced by the great schism; the decline of Byzantium relative to the newly emerging West; Roger Bacon and the rise of science; the apparent cultural superiority of Islam, India, China, and Byzantium	Write essay on the theology of St. Thomas Aquinas, indicating the holes in his arguments; essay on Thomistic ethics; the schism analyzed in theological and bureaucratic terms; why schism was so important to Western progress	The relationship of rational theology to mathematics; the church as an arbiter of power between barbarian states; the moral authority of the church in a world of brute force; the cathedral as the synthesis of Western technology, art, and religion	Study and do detailed drawings of major cathedrals; plan to implement construction of cathedral design; begin construction of scale model in stone

Avg. Level	Avg. Age	Physical		Biological	
		Physical Theory	Physical Practice	Biological Theory	Biological Practice
8.00	10.00	Continue with study of analytical geometry; begin solid analytical geometry using Cartesian notation; study the design of clocks, thermometers, and astronomical instruments; a study of Kepler and his ideas about nature and the music of the spheres	Continue with mini-cathedral building project; build full-fledged observatory with telescopes, but in spirit of Tycho Brahe make observations to deduce Kepler's laws; take two-week ocean voyage on sailing ship; discuss how Europe extended itself throughout the 16th century	Continue vertebrate comparative anatomy through higher mammals and relate to human anatomy; show how embryology of all vertebrates overlaps at stages; relate to Greek evolutionary theories	Dissect and study vertebrate anatomy, tissues, and organs; go through modern systematics for all major mammalian orders; study embryology of related groups with microscope; the fetal pig and its full dissection
8.25	10.25	The early basis of the scientific revolution, Francis Bacon's Novum Organum, Boyle's studies, Galileo, the inventions of Leonardo da Vinci, the notion of experimental "proof"; finish analytical geometry and learn elementary, the concept of limit, and early concepts of calculus to explain Kepler's laws	Continue observation project, build improved clocks, finish sextant, finish mini-cathedral, study map making and various forms of map projections; set up experiments to test Boyle's laws, simple gas laws, and circulation of the blood	Human anatomy in detail; all organs, tissues and bones, gross structure of the brain; embryology using the fetal pig; anatomical drawings of da Vinci and Vesalius, plus Gray's Anatomy (these integrated studies will last a year)	Dissect human cadavers, male and female; observe tissues, and relate to other mammals; show similarity of all organs for all mammals; note how different human brain is
8.50	10.50	The Newtonian synthesis; full study using modern notation of Principia Mathematica and the Opticks; derive Newton's laws from Kepler's observations; derive calculus from the need to mathematically describe the laws of motion and gravity	Begin making windmill and waterwheel; predict the orbits of the planets using Newton's laws; predict the eclipses of the sun by the moon at different spots of interest on the earth; repeat Newton's experiments showing that light is a system of particles, and that white light contains the spectrum	Continue studies of human anatomy and embryology	Continue anatomical dissection and microscopic studies; learn micro-techniques and make your own slides
8.75	10.75	Derive the calculus up to the use of simple differential equations; derive the formulas for optics and the creation of compound lenses; compare Newton's and Leibnitz' approach	Continue work on windmill and waterwheel; build a Newtonian reflecting telescope; build a chromatically-corrected set of compound lenses for the telescope already constructed; make an improved microscope	Continue studies of human anatomy and embryology	Continue work of previous quarter

The Ethical State

Avg. Level	Avg. Age	Psychosocial		Integration	
		Psychosocial Theory	Pyschosocial Practice	Integrative Theory	Integrative Practice
8.00	10.00	The rise of humanism leading to the Renaissance and the Reformation; the writings of Erasmus, Luther, and Calvin; the Council of Trent and the rise of the Jesuit order; Giordano Bruno; the philosophy of Descartes, and a review of his contemporaries	Essay on the ethical implications of the Reformation; were the Protestants any less bureaucratic? mutual discussion of essays among the octets; essay on the ethical implications of the scientific method and the new philosophy	The literary synthesis, Dante's *Divina Comedia*, Cervantes' *Don Quixote*, Marlowe's *Dr. Faustus*; the music of Monteverde and Palestrina; the art of Bosch, Leonardo da Vinci, and Michelangelo	Write an epic poem about the Christian view of Hell; write a play about a modern Don Quixote; continue study of organ and harpsichord; compose and perform music in the style of Monteverde and Palestrina
8.25	10.25	Hobbes, Montaigne, and Spinoza; read Spinoza's Ethics without analyzing proofs and note how this is a huge leap over the philosophy of Descartes and is the first totally rational treatment of ethics in history	Apply Spinoza's ethics to solving problems in practical ethics, politics, and religion; relate Spinoza's ethics to Christianity, Islam, and Judaism; apply Spinoza's model to formulating a model of the universe and evolution; write an essay on the meaning of Spinoza	The literary synthesis continues: Shakespeare's *Romeo and Juliet*, *Othello*, and *Hamlet*; the music of Handel; advanced musical theory and composition	Continue study of organ and harpsichord; build a harpsichord as a group project; write a last act to *Hamlet* in which Hamlet lives; play the music of Handel
8.50	10.50	The philosophical contemporaries of Spinoza; Leibnitz, Locke, and Hume on improving the understanding; world history from 1000 AD to 1775	Essay on the hostility to Spinoza; an ethical analysis of the lives of Spinoza and Leibnitz; essay on why Europe embraced the scientific method and modern philosophy while the rest of the world did not	Spinoza's ethics, Christianity, Judaism, and respect for human rights; the rise of democratic ideology; Islam becomes totally entropic; conservative belief systems in the rest of the world; European predation	Group project to perform *St. Matthew* or *St. John Passion* of Bach; all learn to play *The Musical Offering* and *The Art of the Fugue* in an octet; each octet does its own orchestration for *The Art of the Fugue*
8.75	10.75	Human rights and 18th century philosophy; Voltaire, Rousseau, Diderot, and the Encyclopedists; the American Revolution; the philosophy and writings of Thomas Jefferson, the social contract, and *The Federalist Papers*	Essay on Rousseau and irrationalism; essay on the libertarian ideal and the democratic compromise; essay on the U.S. founding fathers allowing slavery to continue: was losing the revolution and hanging a better alternative? Write scenario on what would have happened if there had not been tolerance of slavery	The artistic synthesis continues; further study of *The Art of the Fugue* and the music of Mozart; the pessimistic writings of Jonathan Swift, a tragic interpretation of the democratic experiment	Compose and perform a conclusion to *The Art of the Fugue*; perform as a group project one Mozart opera of students' choice

John David Garcia

Avg. Level	Avg. Age	Physical		Biological	
		Physical Theory	Physical Practice	Biological Theory	Biological Practice
9.00	11.00	Begin advanced calculus and partial differential equations; detailed study of the work of Lagrange and Euler, the calculus of variations from Newton to Lagrange, elementary probability theory from Pascal to Cauchy and LaPlace; applications in optics, astronomy, theory of heat	Begin construction of simple steam engine, making from scratch, doing all machining of parts by treddle-driven lathes and water and windmill power; check the detailed mathematical models against astronomical observations	Conclusion of the study of human anatomy and embryology	Conclusion of dissections and microscopic observations; the general functioning of the human body
9.25	11.25	Continue work of previous quarter; detailed theory of steam engine, the work of Lavoisier, Priestley, and Dalton	Continue above project, switching to electrical machinery; do early experiments in electricity by Gauss, Coulomb, Ampère, and Volta; the atomic model of chemistry and experiments	Begin study of animal physiology and describe biochemistry through mid 19th century; repeat experiments of Helmholtz in biophysics	Experiments in basic physiology showing how human body consumes oxygen and produces carbon dioxide; human body as a heat engine
9.50	11.50	Continue work in chemistry; the work of LaPlace and Carnot, the laws of thermodynamics, the experiments of Faraday; advanced studies in partial differential equations; wave mechanics in optics; begin study of the works of Gauss	Continue chemistry experiments; finish work on steam engine; test efficiency using Carnot's concepts; begin repeating the experiments of Faraday and empirically derive the basic laws of electricity and magnetism, including Ohm's law	Animal physiology and biochemistry continued; the work and life of Pasteur	Experiments in animal physiology and biochemistry continued
9.75	11.75	Maxwell's work on the wave theory of light and the derivation of Maxwell's equations and their applications; continue study of Gauss' mathematics and physics	Electromagnetic motors and generators; construction of batteries; transmission of electromagnetic waves; early work of Tesla; the telegraph and the wireless constructed	A course in botany and plant physiology; begin experiments in plant genetics after Gregor Mendel	Study and dissection of major plant species; field studies, microscopic dissection, plant breeding per Gregor Mendel

224

Avg. Level	Avg. Age	Psychosocial		Integration	
		Psychosocial Theory	Pyschosocial Practice	Integrative Theory	Integrative Practice
9.00	11.00	Detailed analysis of the American and French Revolutions; detailed analysis of the writings of Jefferson and his correspondence; comparisons between Jefferson, Washington, and Napoleon; how Napoleon betrayed the French Revolution in the pursuit of personal power; how the U.S. government betrayed the Libertarian ethic	Write essays comparing the ethical course of the American and French Revolution; relate the ethics of Spinoza to these revolutions; relate to evolutionary ethics and show where they went wrong	Artistic synthesis in the early work of Goethe and the music of Beethoven; ethical synthesis in the philosophy of Lessing, Goethe, and Moses Mendelssohn and their interpretations of Spinoza	Reorchestrate and perform Beethoven's *Grosse Fugue* for octet; read Goethe's prophetic poetry
9.25	11.25	The life and philosophy of Kant, *The Critique of Pure Reason* and *The Critique of Practical Reason*; compare to Spinoza; Kant's cosmology compared to LaPlace; explain Catholic hostility	Write essays on the scientific and ethical implications of Kant's philosophy; analyze in terms of the evolutionary ethic	Artistic synthesis continued in the work of Goethe and Beethoven; Goethe's *Sorcerer's Apprentice* and pessimism; the romantic hope and self-delusion	Produce as a group project Goethe's *Faust* and performance of Beethoven's *Ninth Symphony* for several octets; write a sequel to the *Sorcerer's Apprentice*
9.50	11.50	The philosophy of Hegel: how he could be so wrong and so influential; Hegel and the misinterpretation of Spinoza; Hegel's theory of history and ethics; Hegel as the father of Marxism and Nazism; de Tocqueville as a visionary and prophetic historian	Essay explaining Hegel's influence through present times; a comparison of Spinoza and Hegel: how Hegel could so misunderstand Spinoza and deceive himself and others; why de Tocqueville was so accurate in his predictions	The romantic poets, Byron, Shelley, and Wordsworth; the art of Watteau, Houdon, David, and Degas; the music of Berlioz and Liszt; Wagner as the musical equivalent of Hegel	Write epic poetry on a hopeful future from a romantic perspective; do a musical satire on a Wagner opera; paint a heroic romantic painting
9.75	11.75	A history of the world from 1775 to 1910; development of major ideas and philosophies, with particular attention to USA, Britain, France, Germany, Japan, and Russia; basic economics from Adam Smith to Marx and Engels	An essay explaining the Newtonian model and its influence on the intellectual history of the world; why Islam, India, and China were so far behind, why Japan was able to catch up	An ethical analysis of European and American imperialism; libertarian and socialistic ethics; the ethical turmoil of the age of liberty and social obligation; read *War and Peace* by Tolstoy; the paintings of Turner and the Impressionists	Read and analyze Pushkin, Melville, Dickens, Hugo, Balzac, Dostoyevski, Tolstoy, George Eliot; study the music of Mahler and perform *Das Lied von der Erde*

John David Garcia

Avg. Level	Avg. Age	Physical		Biological	
		Physical Theory	**Physical Practice**	**Biological Theory**	**Biological Practice**
10.00	12.00	Gauss' mathematics and physics continued; general thermodynamics, the work of Boltzman, Clausius, and Gibbs; Maxwell's demon, the inventions of Edison and Tesla; the work of Mendeleev and the beginning of organic chemistry; probability theory as understood by Gauss and Galton	Construction of AC generators and regulators, simple radios, light bulbs, and recording devices; begin design and construction of simple internal combustion engine; experiments in organic chemistry and synthesis of organic compounds	The life and work of Charles Darwin and Alfred Wallace, the evolution of evolutionary ideas, the theory of natural selection, and the three laws of thermodynamics; the work of Pasteur	Each student gathers evidence for and against Darwinian evolution, taking into account basic genetic knowledge and probability
10.25	12.25	Non-Euclidean geometry and statistical mechanics; introduction to systematic probability theory and statistics; continue work in thermodynamics and organic chemistry; the work of W.R. Hamilton and Henri Poincare is studied	Construct interferometers and repeat the Michelson/Morley experiments; repeat experiments of Planck to derive Planck's constant; develop and derive the special theory of relativity; begin construction of automobile; continue internal combustion engine project	Neo-Darwinian theories of evolution and evolutionary genetics up to R.A. Fisher's *The Genetical Theory of Evolution*; explain disease and parasites in evolution	Do genetic experiments with fruit flies and molds, giving evidence for and against neo-Darwinism, theories of evolution, bacteriology; systematic study and laboratory work in bacteriology
10.50	12.50	The physics of the 20th century, including the General Theory of Relativity up to the discovery of quantum mechanics, presented as a year course in modern physics as it might have been given at Harvard, Cambridge, or Gottingen in 1925; physical and organic chemistry, also a year survey course; finish study of Henri Poincare	Continue work on automobile; repeat experiments leading up to Bohr atom; handmade basic tubes for radio and oscilloscope; construct a more advanced radio and oscilloscope using tubes; make photocells; synthesize organic compounds	Introduction to cell biochemistry and advanced genetics; begin chromatography and electrophoresis for separating common biochemical constituents of mammals	The chemical structure of the constituents of life; isolating nucleic acids and proteins, determining their properties through chemical and spectrographic analysis; create genetic mosaics
10.75	12.75	Continuation of previous quarter; relate physical chemistry and organic chemistry to biochemistry; theory of x-ray machines and electron microscopes	Continuation of previous quarter; finish automobile; study of x-ray machines and electron microscopes; organic chemistry laboratory; motion pictures	Continuation of previous quarter; introduction to x-ray crystallography and electron microscopy for the study of large molecules and viruses	Continuation of previous quarter; use of x-ray crystallography to determine chemical structure; electron microscopy of viruses and large molecules

The Ethical State

Avg. Level	Avg. Age	Psychosocial		Integration	
		Psychosocial Theory	Psychosocial Practice	Integrative Theory	Integrative Practice
10.00	12.00	The theories of Marx and Engels in detail, *Das Kapital* and *Dialectics of Nature*; the ideas of August LeComte and social science in general; the psychology of William James	Critical essay on Marxism and dialectic materialism; what is wrong and what is right about theory, what scientific evidence exists for and against the theory; why social science is so full of nonsense	Ethical analysis of Marxist philosophy and ethics; how and why Marxism violates the evolutionary ethic; read *The Brothers Karamazov* by Dostoyevsky	The music of Arnold Schoenberg, the plays of Frank Wedekind, the early paintings of Picasso and the Cubists; the opera Lulu by Alban Berg is performed
10.25	12.25	The philosophy of Nietzsche and Spencer; evolutionary ethics as propounded by Spencer; ethical Darwinism; an introduction to the life and ideas of Sigmund Freud; the rise of racist fascism in Europe	Essay comparing the neo-Darwinian ethics with Marxism; the incipient Lamarckianism in Marxism compared to its ethics; essay on European racism and fascism growing out of social Darwinism	Ethical analysis of neo-Darwinian philosophy and of social Darwinism; how and why social Darwinism and fascism violate the evolutionary ethic; Freud as a Newtonian psychologist looking for mechanistic explanations which may not exist; ethical implications of the unconscious	The music of Richard Strauss, *Ein Heldenleben*, *Also Sprach Zarathustra*, and the opera *Elektra*; *Man and Superman* by G.B. Shaw is also performed
10.50	12.50	World history from 1910 to 1925; the basic writings of Lenin and a study of his life; World War I and the Russian Revolution, the world fear of communism, Leon Trotsky as an idealized communist; Freud's later works	Essay or the origins and consequences of World War I; essay on the origins and consequences of communism in Russia; essay on how the brilliant, ethical Trotsky went wrong and helped create a Frankenstein	An ethical analysis of how the Soviet Union betrayed its own revolution and turned into a monster; how the centralization of power makes corruption inevitable; read *Darkness at Noon* by Koestler and *Animal Farm* by Orwell	The music of Prokofiev and Shostakovich; the films of Sergei Eisenstein, including *Ivan the Terrible*; perform the Shostakovich opera *Lady Macbeth of Murmansk* and Mussorgsky's *Boris Gudenov*
10.75	12.75	World history 1925 to 1939; the basic writings of Mussolini, Hitler, fascism, Stalin, and Soviet communism; a study of Hitler and Stalin as complementary personalities who changed history; early works of Pavlov and Jung	Essay comparing the conflicting ideologies and economic factors leading to World War II; what could have been done to prevent World War II; why the United States was so immune to both communism and fascism	An ethical anlysis of how capitalist greed and the political cowardice and vindictiveness of the European democracies made World War II inevitable; read *Winds of War* by Wouk	The music of Stravinsky, the early art of Dali, the films of Chaplin, Bunuel, Lang, and Pabst, plus Academy Award winners; perform Hindemith's opera *Mathis der Mahler* and Brecht's *Mahagonny*

227

Avg. Level	Avg. Age	Physical		Biological	
		Physical Theory	Physical Practice	Biological Theory	Biological Practice
11.00	13.00	Continuation of previous quarter; begin to focus chemical studies on biochemical processes and molecules; theory of ultracentrifuges and mass spectrographs	Continuation of previous quarter; begin construction of small airplane; begin design and construction of black & white television; continue experiments in atomic and nuclear physics; study of ultracentrifuges and mass spectrographs	Continuation of previous quarter; use of mass spectrograph and ultracentrifuge	Continuation of previous quarter; use of advanced techniques to determine gross structure of RNA, DNA, and proteins
11.25	13.25	Continuation of previous quarter; begin an introduction to quantum mechanics and how it explained and enabled us to predict and control the facts that were causing paradoxes; study Pauling's work on the chemical bond	Finish small airplane and learn to fly it; complete construction of black & white television; begin practice flying airplane; experiment with microwaves; build simple radar transmitters and receivers	Continue work of previous quarter; analysis of biochemical molecules and their reactions	Continue work of previous quarter; experimental physiological chemistry
11.50	13.50	The formal study of quantum mechanics continued; work of Bohr, de Broglie, Schroedinger, Heisenberg, and Bohm; critical experiments analyzed; Von Neumann's formalization of quantum mechanics into operators in Hilbert space; the predictive power of quantum mechanics; advanced theory of probability and statistics	Perform experiments to show that photons, electrons, and other quantum entities are both waves and particles; construct transistor, laser, and hologram; begin design and construction of color TV; begin design and construction of analog and digital computers	Biochemical analysis of DNA and RNA; how their structure was derived and how heredity and biological information is encoded in these molecules; relate to Pauling's work on the chemical bond	Biochemical isolation of DNA and RNA; prepare crystals for x-ray diffraction, determine their structure with exactitude; determine exact structure of insulin molecule
11.75	13.75	Continuation of previous works; Einstein's objections to quantum mechanics, including the EPRB paradox, and how these objections were resolved; quantum mechanics and chemistry	Continuation of previous experiments and constructions; experiments in superfluidity and superconductivity as macro quantum events	Molecular biology of the gene; how to read the genetic code; quantum processes in DNA	Experiments in gene splicing and working with recombinant DNA in bacteria; genetically engineer bacteria to produce human interferon

228

Avg. Level	Avg. Age	Psychosocial		Integration	
		Psychosocial Theory	Pyschosocial Practice	Integrative Theory	Integrative Practice
11.00	13.00	World history 1939 to 1949; the later theories of C.G. Jung and I. Pavlov; the philosophy of existentialism	Write essay on the role of the United States in World War I and how it erred in its ethical obligations and thereby lost the peace; write essay on what the world and the United States would be like if the United States and England had united to prevent other nations from acquiring nuclear weapons	An ethical analysis of the factors leading to WWII and how democratic ideology is used to combat communism; the communist views of democratic capitalism, the democratic view of totalitarian communism; Read *War and Remembrance* by Wouk	Nazi films of Leni Riefenstahl; a study of *Citizen Kane*; students write script, score, produce, and direct film of their own as group project using TV camera; study films of the Holocaust and World War II
11.25	13.25	The basic writings of Jean Paul Sartre, Camus and other modern existentialists; the philosophy of Teilhard de Chardin; an introduction to behaviorism starting with work of Watson	Write essay contrasting the ethical consequences of existential pessimism with evolutionary optimism, analyzing the social implications of a society that produces both; do simple conditioning experiments with rats	Ethical analysis of existentialism as the national philosophy of France and how that led to French defeat and collaboration in WWII; the creativity of the French	The films of Jean Renoir, Cocteau, and Clement; the music of "Les Six"; the paintings of Matisse and late Picasso; make a film in the French style
11.50	13.50	The writings of E.F. Skinner on behaviorism; study of the school of behavior therapy; animal and human comparisons; compare to the psychotherapy schools spun off from Freud	Conditioning experiments with rats, cats, and dogs; biofeedback experiments with humans; use of conditioning to break bad habits, compulsions, and phobias	Ethical analysis of the implications of behaviorism; show how this is a classical model of a quantum process; show how ethics can overcome conditioning and how ethics can also be destroyed by conditioning	Study of psychological films from *Spellbound*, *The 7th Veil*, and *The Cobweb* to *A Clockwork Orange* and *The Prisoner*; as a group project make a B&W film satire of *Walden II*
11.75	13.75	A survey of 20th century philosophy after Bertrand Russell; start with G.E. Moore's writings on ethics; study Wittgenstein's *Tractactus Logicus Philosophicus* and *Philosophical Investigations*, Schlick's and Hare's work on ethics, Russell's analysis of matter and analysis of mind, Schroedinger's *What Is Life?* The Vienna Circle, and Logical Positivism	Write essay on the relationship between science and the school of rational analysis; write essay on how the academic study of ethics is becoming trivial and unscientific; how ethics can be made scientific by following Spinoza's approach	Ethical implications of quantum mechanics for human behavior; relationship between determinism and free will; chance and necessity in evolution and human choice; read *Chance and Necessity* by Monod	Study the paintings of Dali and other surrealists; study Dali's films with Bunuel and Bunuel's later films; as group project make a film expressing surrealism and ethics

John David Garcia

Avg. Level	Avg. Age	Physical		Biological	
		Physical Theory	Physical Practice	Biological Theory	Biological Practice
12.00	14.00	A one-year synthetic study in cosmology uniting field theory, particle physics, and the Big Bang theory; show the evolution of matter, space, and time from the instant of the Big Bang to the present; discuss alternative explanation such as the steady-state theory	Astronomical observations of astrophysics, quasars, and possible black holes; the different types of galaxies are observed; the red shift and radio astronomy are studied and observed; results of experiments in high-energy particle physics are analyzed	A year study of chemical evolution after Blum, Calvin, and Manfred Eigen; show possible deterministic origins for DNA and protein and how autopoiesis might start as a quantum process; relate information and entropy, information theory and thermodynamics	Laboratory simulations of chemical evolution leading to protein and DNA through many different pathways; show how RNA encodes information to DNA
12.25	14.25	Continuation of previous quarter	Continuation of previous quarter	Continuation of previous quarter	Continuation of previous quarter
12.50	14.50	Continuation of previous two quarters	Continuation of previous two quarters	Continuation of previous two quarters	Continuation of previous two quarters
12.75	14.75	Continuation of previous three quarters; the latest cosmological models of Guth, Hawking, and Hoyle; their successors	Continuation of previous three quarters; observation of possible primordial strings as indicated by large gravitational lenses	Continuation of previous three quarters; trace a possible pathway to RNA, protein, DNA, cells	Continuation of previous three quarters; try creating simple proteins which when combined with RNA produce DNA through autopoiesis

		Psychosocial		Integration	
Avg. Level	Avg. Age	Psychosocial Theory	Pyschosocial Practice	Integrative Theory	Integrative Practice
12.00	14.00	A survey of the leading theories of psychotherapy and humanistic and transpersonal psychology during the 20th century; show that they are transitory fads which almost never last and that they do not have a scientific base even though they produce millions of true believers	An analysis and essay on psychofraud as a human phenomenon; why persons resist scientific explanation to behavior; why clearly untrue fads with no scientific basis are so popular; an essay on the human-potential movement	The psychology of self-deception and its relationship to ethics; why it is possible to eliminate most self-deception from physical and biological science but not from social science	The art of self-deception and quantum vision, the drawings of M.C. Escher, self-reference based drawings and paintings; study of the films of Stanley Kubrick, particularly 2001 and A Clockwork Orange
12.25	14.25	A survey of late 20th century economics beginning with Keynes' General Theory, covering the ideas of Paul Samuelson and Milton Friedman; supply-side economics and non-zero sum games.	Essay on the inability of the leading economists to deal with creativity as the central factor in economic growth; the ethical obligations of the rich toward the poor	The economic implications of evolutionary ethics; the ethical implications of genetic engineering and eternal life; is it ever wrong to share knowledge? is it ever right to impede the flow of knowledge?	The music of Penderecki as a manifestation of 20th century entropy and ethical obligation; performance of Penderecki's Dies Irae, The Devils of Loudon, and Requiem
12.50	14.50	A world history from 1950 to the present showing that no combination of socialism or capitalism is likely to work; show that Islam and all other societies alienated from western civilization are evolutionary deadends; the need for an alternative	Write essay showing how in their structure and in their actions both socialism and capitalism repeatedly violate the evolutionary ethic; essay on an alternative political socio-economic system to both capitalism and/or socialism	Art as a medium of protest; read Koestler, Pasternak, and Solzhenitsyn; read the latter's criticisms of the West; read the anticapitalistic writings from Clifford Odets to Arthur Miller's Death of a Salesman and The Crucible	Study the films of Costas Gavras as indictments of both socialism and capitalism; Z, The Confession, State of Siege; Apocalypse Now, and The Godfather series; begin a TV film as a group project expressing hope in the world of entropic world order
12.75	14.75	An introduction to a general theory of evolution unifying ethics, evolutionary theory and science; show the place for mysticism in the scheme of things and how mysticism inadequately balanced by science always leads to self-delusion; develop a thermodynamic, information-theoretic model of evolution and creativity	Write essay showing how to implement the general theory of evolution and the evolutionary ethic as an alternative socio-economic and political system to that of any country, taking into account practical constraints of scale and of culture; do a mathematical prediction of possible futures for evolution and creativity	Study the recent writings of ethical Christians within and without the Catholic church; see how Christianity and Judaism are evolving a more humanistic ethic more in harmony with the evolutionary ethic; relate to other major religions	Finish the film; write an essay on how persons who practice the evolutionary ethic can best communicate with adherents of each of the major religions, using art and common ethical values

Avg. Level	Avg. Age	Physical		Biological	
		Physical Theory	Physical Practice	Biological Theory	Biological Practice
13.00	15.00	Seminar on cosmology covering latest findings, theories, and alternative ideas, usually will cover the most important findings and breakthroughs of the last year; unify field theory, quantum mechanics, particle physics, and astronomy	Observations and computer simulations of cosmological models; derivation of original models	Seminar on genetic engineering and recombinant DNA; latest findings, ideas and theories	Experiments in engineering new life forms and correcting genetic defects in mammals
13.25	15.25	Seminar on chemical evolution leading to living cells; latest findings, theories, and ideas; how can autopoiesis be induced at the precellular level?	Experimental attempts to recreate the chemical evolution that led to the first cells in the laboratory; any form of chemical autopoiesis will be evaluated	Seminar on brain physiology and function; how the brain contributes to our intelligence and our mind; the brain as a classical device and the brain as a quantum device are emphasized	Experiments in understanding and enhancing brain function; life-style and the brain; EEG and brain physiology during autopoiesis
13.50	15.50	Seminar on the latest findings and discoveries in solid-state electronic devices, memory chips, microprocessors, pico-circuits, etc.; discuss performance, manufacturing techniques, and areas for new research; solid-state physics and chemistry appropriate to these devices	Laboratory and experiments on how to create micro- and pico-circuits; developing the crystals and modifying them; design and construction of advanced computers	Seminar on human health; how to prevent and cure diseases; focus on viral infections, degenerative diseases, and the aging process	Laboratory and clinic on preventive medicine and health maintenance for maximization of creativity
13.75	15.75	Seminar on latest discoveries in macro quantum physics, lasers, holography, super-conductivity; developments of other important technologies like quantum computers, artificial intelligence, and any technological breakthrough in any field; also, extensions of EPR and nonlocal interactions	Laboratory and experiments with important new technologies and processes covered in or related to the accompanying seminar; quantum technologies and advanced energy systems are experimentally treated	Seminar on the latest findings in biological evolutionary theory, particularly scientifically plausible deviations from orthodox Darwinian paleontology, genetic distance, and other findings relevant to evolutionary biology	Laboratory and field studies in paleontology, evolutionary genetics, and computer modelings of the evolutionary process, particularly relating to rates of evolution, punctuated equilibrium, and quantum evolutionary processes in evolution

Avg. Level	Avg. Age	Psychosocial		Integration	
		Psychosocial Theory	Pyschosocial Practice	Integrative Theory	Integrative Practice
13.00	15.00	Seminars in evolutionary ethics and the general theory of evolution as an integrating theory in the social sciences; correct theory where it seems wrong and extend where it seems right	Use the general theory of evolution to integrate the social sciences and other sciences when possible into a unified whole using mathematical models and emphasizing information theory and thermodynamics	Seminar on the latest developments in art which express a synthesis of ethics, humanities, and technology	Experimental creation of films, study of original films and their techniques; other techniques that integrate ethics, humanities, art, and technology
13.25	15.25	Seminar on human creativity and how to maximize it; show relationship between ethics and intelligence and how to maximize their interactions; study the interaction of ethics, science, technology, mysticism, and human organization; show both negative and positive findings	Experiments in how to maximize creativity for different persons in different environments; test the limits of what can be done for persons driven by fear who have not been able to make a commitment to the evolutionary ethic; test to see what can be done environmentally to maximize intelligence for those who are committed	Seminars on musical theory and composition; development of notation and expressive media for dance and opera; discuss latest work with high ethical content	Original composition of music, dance, and opera; performances of new works and interactions with latest technologies.
13.50	15.50	Seminar on the economics of creativity and how best to organize the creative economic output of individuals; compare to work in economics and the latest findings in these fields; test and improve the theory of creative transformation, octet formation, and autopoiesis	Laboratories in alternative forms of human organization for maximizing economically relevant creativity; kinds and numbers of persons and how to communicate and assure creative feedback; are there creative alternatives to self-screening and selection into octets?	Seminars on the latest developments in the plastic arts, drawing, painting, sculpture, carving, ceramics; new forms, styles, and techniques are discussed; emphasis is on art with an ethical content	Workshops in the plastic arts; individual and group projects in any combination of plastic arts
13.75	15.75	Seminar on the prediction of historical and social events using the general theory of evolution and other techniques that made correct predictions in the past	Laboratory on how to organize octets into larger systems without losing creative output; how to delegate power within systems of octets without producing corruption and a loss of liberty	Seminar on world literature and philosophy, what is being expressed and how, how it relates to the general theory of evolution, what can be incorporated into the general theory, and what is detrimental to its development	Critical readings and group discussions of important literary, philosophical, and religious writings; write alternatives to rejected ideas

GLOSSARY

Aberrant   Pertaining to actions or things which deviate from what is considered normal and proper by the person(s) applying the term.

Amoral   Lacking morality. Only sub-human beings are amoral. To be amoral is to be unaware of the Game of Life at both the unconscious and conscious levels. Amoral beings are only pieces, never players, in the Game of Life. An amoral species is doomed to extinction. Only a moral species can continue to evolve without mutating physically.

Art   A process which uses entertainment to expand creativity. This is usually done symbolically through unconscious stimulation of the mind. Art is similar in its social function to dreaming. Art reflects the creativity of a culture.

Asymptotically   In a manner wherein something is always getting closer to something else but never reaches it. Our ethical evolution is an asymptotic process by which we become ever more ethical and moral, but our ethics are never perfect, and we are never totally moral.

Autopoiesis   The process within living cells by which protein catalyzes the reproduction of DNA while DNA catalyzes or creates the reproduction of proteins. Neither can create itself by itself, but together both can create each other. This term was first coined by Francisco J. Varela and Humberto R. Maturana in 1974. Its meaning is broadened in the theory of Creative Transformation to include any creative exchange of complementary information such that a new epiphenomenon arises. DNA and Protein exchange chemical information, and are complements.

Bacteria   The set of all free-living cells without a well-defined nucleus, where the DNA may be diffused throughout the cytoplasm.

Behavior Divided into subjective and objective behavior. Subjective behavior is action observable only by the person behaving, e.g., thinking. Objective behavior is action observable by more than one person, e.g., speaking.

Behaviorism A system of psychology and psychotherapy which states that all models of behavior must be based entirely on measurable objective criteria. Behaviorism has been effective in predicting and controlling simple animal and human behavior. It has not been shown to increase creativity in any way. Conditioning desirable human behavior through external rewards and punishments can destroy the creativity of anyone.

Belief A state of mind in which someone is certain that something is true. In science there are no beliefs, only probabilities of certain relationships holding under certain circumstances. In science there is never certainty. Only ideologies propound certainties about nature.

Biomass The total mass of all living creatures which inhabit a specific environment at any given instant. The percentage of the total biomass taken up by a given species is a measure of the biological success of that species in that environment at that instant.

Biosphere The envelope of life which surrounds the Earth. It includes all life forms on water, land, or in the air. According to Teilhard de Chardin, the biosphere is the precursor to the Noosphere. The Biosphere includes the biomass of the Earth.

Bureaucracy An organization which destroys truth by seeking to destroy all means of detecting its errors and shortcomings. A bureaucracy operates without utilizing feedback and self-correction. Whatever its *de jure* purposes, a bureaucracy's *de facto* purpose is limited to enhancing the security of its members. Bureaucracies control their members by convincing them that they are uncreative and can only survive as parasites. A bureaucracy is always threatened by anyone's creativity. All bureaucracies ultimately wish to destroy all creativity and live in a totally classical world. Their first step is to force everyone to ask permission of the bureaucracy in order to do anything creative in the bureaucracy's *de jure* area of authority and responsibility.

Certainty   A state of mind in which no doubt exists about one or more cause-and-effect relationships. It is unethical to be certain about anything except the existence of our own thoughts and perceptions, which are not cause-and-effect relationships. The need for certainty may be the fatal flaw in human nature. Through Creative Transformation, humanity can learn to cope with the insecurity of uncertainty. One cannot learn when one is certain.

Chaos   Total disorder, where nothing has meaning or purpose and all is random. The lowest level of awareness and creativity. A patternless nothingness. A state of maximum entropy. It is postulated that the quantum field always brings order out of chaos in our universe. This is the creativity of God.

Child   A transitory being bridging the gap between amorality and morality. Children are always ethical for at least a while. When children become unethical, they may become immoral adults. Immoral adults can only have power by controlling children. Children are pliable and can just as easily become moral or immoral adults. An unethical society turns most of its children into immoral adults. An immoral society turns all of its children into immoral adults. The converse is true for moral and ethical societies. Humans have been children for most of their existence. *Homo sapiens* seems to be the first species of human with the capacity to produce ethical adults. Ethical adults are moral beings who are aware and have intelligence about their true ethics. "Child" as here used is an ethical descriptor and not a chronological indicator. "Young child" is used to describe "children" in the more conventional sense. Young children are almost always "children" in the ethical sense. The converse is not necessarily true, i.e., not all biological adults are ethical adults.

Civilization   The culture of civilized people. A civilized people may be defined as a group of persons tied together by a common ethical code, who systematically predict and control their collective ability to predict and control. The essential difference between civilized and uncivilized people is that among the uncivilized peoples there is no systematic group effort to create machines for the benefit of the group as a whole. Such machines may require several persons to operate and perhaps may not be used for several months or even several years after construction is begun on them. It is this notion of long-range planning and concern for the creativity of future generations which distinguishes the civilized person from the barbarian, who typically never has any vision beyond tomorrow, or the savage who lives entirely in the present. The longer into the future the planning is projected, the more civilized is the society. Therefore, a civilization never comes into being, or survives, unless it is guided by a cooperative group of persons who have a vision of and concern for the generations yet unborn. This vision of the future is always tied to an ethical code.

Communism   A socialist system with a rigid, unscientific, bureaucratic foundation derived from Marxist and Leninist ideology. It propounds the materialistic ethic. The *de facto* ethic is to maximize the power of the Communist Party and its leaders. *glasnost* and *perestroika* were tolerated by some of the Communist bureaucracies only because it was argued by some that these reforms were essential to reverse the obvious decay in Communist society. Marx was merely a well-intentioned propounder of a false ideology. Lenin and Stalin were the implementers of one of the most evil tyrannies in history.

Complement   One member of a complementary pair (see).

Complementary Pair   A pair of entities naturally occurring together, e.g., a proton and an electron, or two people of the opposite sex who love each other, at least, as much as themselves, and help one another in their creative and ethical development so that at least one of them will eventually love the other more than him or herself, forever. That person will have become a moral adult.

Connectors   Channels through which information flows from one component of intelligence to another. In our bodies connectors are represented by nerves and hormones.

Conscience   Our inner sense of right and wrong, truth and falsehood, which unconsciously guides us through our intuition. Our conscience is apparently always correct, and never fools us. We apparently only fool ourselves by substituting fear for conscience, and equating the two. Our conscience is produced by the interaction of our brain with the infinite-enfolded truth of quantum reality.

Conscious   Pertaining to that state of mind in which we can predict and control our own thoughts and perceptions. The conscious mind is the set of all our predictable and controllable thoughts and perceptions. Solely ethical beings can become fully conscious. See **Unconscious**.

Conservative   A person who is intolerant of innovation. This characteristic exists on a continuum, with adamant opposition to any innovation at one extreme and complete tolerance for any innovation at the other. See **Liberal**.

Control   The deliberate, causal formation of a predicted set of events. Control is essential to intelligence. Without control an entity is deprived of feedback, and becomes incapable of correct prediction. Control is ethically neutral. It may be used creatively or destructively.

Cosmic Force   The collective operation of all natural laws. The cosmic force has two major components: evolution and entropy. All is an effect of the cosmic force. Some call the cosmic force "God."

Cosmic Moral Society   The Moral Society which results from the joining of two or more distinct Moral Societies with independent origins on different planets.

Creation   The deliberate organization of energy, matter, life, and/or mind into new patterns which increase intelligence. The patterns may only be new to the creator; they are not necessarily original. Creation is the joint result of intelligence and ethics. All ethical persons are to some degree creative. Moral persons are extremely creative; they are the ones who create new, coherent models of the universe and engender new societies. Immoral persons can never create; they only destroy.

Creativity   The ability to organize the total environment–physical, biological and psychosocial–into new patterns which increase truth for at least one person, while not decreasing truth for any person. Creativity is a direct function of intelligence and ethics: $C = IE$, where, C equals creativity in quanta of new knowledge generated per unit time. It ranges from infinity to negative infinity,

I equals intelligence in quanta of old knowledge controlled per unit time. It ranges from zero to infinity, and

E equals ethics, a dimensionless quantity between -1 and +1 representing the fraction of our total energy spent decreasing truth (negative) or increasing truth (positive).

This equation is an approximation. **C** is a vector, **I** is a matrix, and **E** is a vector. Each component in each vector and each matrix is infinitely complex, and may never be fully understood by any finite being.

Critical Mass   The point at which the density and quantity of a substance is such that completely new effects take place. For example, a critical mass of ethical persons (four men and four women) is necessary to create an Ethical State. A critical mass of moral persons is sufficient to engender a Moral Society and make evolution irreversible. It seems that the critical mass of moral adults necessary to create an embryonic Moral Society is equal to 131,072 or twice four raised to the eighth power. This is the minimum number of persons necessary to create the Government for a full Ethical Republic.

Culture   The total sum of extra-genetic information possessed by a people or by a civilization.

Cyborg (cybernetic organism)   An entity which incorporates a machine as an integral part of its structure. May be pictured as a robot with a person inside it who completely controls the robot and uses it to amplify and simulate his individual powers. Humanity is becoming a cyborg.

Death   The state of maximum entropy for life. It is the state where the intelligence produced by life sinks to the level of matter. The preponderance of scientific evidence indicates that for all life forms death represents the total extinction of the ego. More generally, "death" is a decomposition of a system into its components, e.g., a molecule into atoms, an atom into elementary particles, or a society into disorganized individuals. Death is essential to evolution by natural selection.

Decency   The refusal to deliberately enhance one's welfare at the expense of another person's welfare. Decent persons are ethical if, and only if, they interpret "welfare" as synonymous with creativity. Decent persons are unethical if, and only if, they interpret "welfare" as synonymous with happiness. Decent unethical persons increase entropy by destroying negative feedback for themselves and others. Indecent persons are always unethical, and increase entropy by destroying other persons' creativity, as well as their own, as a means of increasing their own happiness.

Decline (decay)   A process by which total collective creativity continuously decreases, while entropy increases until the capacity to evolve disappears.

Democracy   A system of representative government in which the representatives are chosen by majorities in free elections. Elections are assumed to be free if and only if all persons are guaranteed personal freedom. It is assumed, ideologically, that freedom is a necessary and sufficient condition for progress. All democracies eventually are controlled by unethical demogogues who tell the masses the lies they wish to hear. "Democratic ethical government" is an oxymoron.

Democratic Ethic   The belief that the greatest good is that which makes for the greatest welfare for the greatest number, that the rights of large majorities are absolute over small minorities. This is a false ethic.

DNA (deoxyribonucleic acid)   A complex polymeric organic molecule in the form of a double helix. DNA molecules carry all the information for structuring all known life forms. All the information for structuring the body of a human being is contained in the DNA molecules of a single cell. The DNA molecules are the blueprint from which all life can be structured. DNA is built on templates of RNA, although information transfer appears normally to go the other way.

Destruction   The diminution of creativity by decreasing truth. This may be done by generating false information or degrading true information. Unethical persons destroy more than they create. Children may create or destroy. The more intelligent an unethical person is, the greater will be his or her capacity to destroy. Destruction is negative creativity.

Destructiveness   The disorganization of the total environment into patterns which decrease the ability of any or all ethical persons to predict and control their total environment-physical, biological and psychosocial. Negative creativity. The decrease in ethics, truth, or creativity for any person.

Direct Perception   The clear realization of a pattern in nature, analogous to the perception of our own thoughts. Illusions of certainty are sometimes mistaken for direct perception. Direct perception is valid only insofar as it enables us to predict and control in the objective world. Direct perception is usually considered a mystical experience by the perceiver. All mystical experience is transformed into self-deception, unless our direct perception is combined with scientific method.

Disease   Any condition of an organism acquired through heredity or environment which decreases its intelligence, i.e., ability to predict its total environment—physical, biological and/or psychosocial.

Ecosphere   The region around a star in which it is possible for a planet with liquid water to exist. The sun's ecosphere extends from just inside the orbit of Earth to just outside the orbit of Mars.

Education   Any process which increases the creativity of those exposed to it, or any process which increases any organism's ability to predict and control by increasing or altering the information content of the organism without damaging ethics. In modern society, many alleged forms of "education" are destructive because they destroy ethics, although they may increase intelligence. External rewards and punishments in the educational process can destroy ethics.

Effectors   Those components of intelligence which generate events in the total environment. Within the body, effectors are represented by our bones, muscles and connective tissues in general. Effectors directly alter the environment.

Ego   That part of us that takes its identity from our memory and experience. The ego is driven by fear and the desire to be happy, as opposed to the soul, which is driven by love and the desire to maximize creativity. The ego dies with our body; the soul lives on in the creativity we engender in others. See **Soul**.

Emotion   A pre-programmed pattern of behavior which is primarily instinctual, i.e., genetic, in origin. All emotions, except love, are becoming increasingly destructive, i.e., they serve only to decrease creativity in biological adults instead of to expand it. All emotions are useful for survival in a primitive, Darwinian environment, where there is little knowledge at hand. This applies to most children in the world as of the year 2000. Love is always a constructive emotion because it catalyzes the creative transfer of information, thereby inducing a higher order autopoiesis. When we substitute fear for creative action we become ever less creative. All emotions are combinations and permutations of love and fear.

Entertainment   Any process which increases the happiness of some persons without necessarily increasing the creativity of any person. Entertainment which increases creativity is called "art."

Entropy   A condition of chaos as well as a force which increases the chaos in the universe. The entropic force drives mind toward matter and matter toward chaotic energy. Entropy manifests itself in mind by decreased intelligence and/or ethics. In humanity, entropy is measured by the amount of illusionary information and by the effectiveness of the mechanisms for limiting feedback. Entropy feeds upon itself and is negatively correlated with creativity. Creativity is sometimes called "negentropy." The evil in the universe is limited by the laws of entropy. This leads evil to always, eventually, destroy itself and its message, although sometimes this may take a very long time. Evolution and entropy are a complementary pair.

Epiphenomenon   A phenomenon which arises as a not-readily predictable effect of many complex underlying phenomena. An epiphenomenon can in turn affect the effects which caused it. For example, life is an epiphenomenon of the infinitely tangled hierarchy of protein creating DNA as DNA creates protein. Life in turn affects both protein and DNA. Similarly, consciousness is an epiphenomenon of the infinitely tangled hierarchy of the brain modifying its field effect, the mind, as the mind modifies the brain, and both becoming increasingly receptive to the infinite, true information in the implicate order through the potential of the quantum field.

243

Esprital   A word coined by Henri Lurié to mean "true spirituality," which is ethically based, or a person who has achieved this.

Ethical (good)   Behavior is ethical if, and only if, it is a strategy in the Game of Life. Therefore, only behavior which increases creativity is ethical. Persons are ethical if, and only if, they are increasing creativity. In other words, persons are ethical if, and only if, they play the Game of Life more often than they play the Game of Pleasure. To be ethical is to create. Ethical behavior is, therefore, synonymous with creativity; it is the highest form of intelligence. Only humanity has clearly and systematically exhibited ethical behavior, because only humanity has increased creativity as a species. Almost all other species only increase intelligence by mutating into new species. Virtually all human beings are ethical during their early childhood. Persons only become unethical by being subjected to random entropy and to the pressures of an unethical society, which manipulates and controls them through fear. The other higher primates, cetaceans, and elephants also have ethical elements in their behavior, but they do not seem to create systematically.

Ethical Intelligence   The ability to predict and control the total environment creatively.

Ethical Principles   Logically derived principles that follow directly from the evolutionary ethic. ("We should do our best to maximize creativity, without ever decreasing anyone's creativity.") The evolutionary ethic cannot be in logical error since it is an ultimate goal, not a means to any other end. The derived ethical principles may be in logical error; we should follow them only if they lead to no ethical contradictions according to the dictates of our conscience and objective evidence. These principles lead to other intuitively proper maxims of conduct such as the Ten Commandments and other Biblical imperatives, Buddha's Eight-Fold Way, the Sermon on the Mount, and the American Bill of Rights. The eight ethical principles: 1. Only actions or persons which increase creativity are ethical. 2. Any action or person which decreases anyone's creativity is unethical. 3. Unethical means can never achieve ethical ends. 4. Means which are not ends are never ethical. 5. It is unethical to tolerate destructiveness. 6. It is unethical to be certain. 7. It is ethical to doubt. 8. Inaction is unethical.

Ethics   Rules of optimal behavior. It may be shown logically that behavior is optimal if, and only if, it is a strategy in the Game of Life. The rules of the Game of Life are, therefore, the ethics of life, and are the only true ethics. All other forms of behavior are unethical or trivial. Ethics occur in life when an entity has intelligence about its own intelligence, and it can predict and control its own ability to predict and control. Ethics are the highest form of intelligence. Morality is the highest form of ethics. See **Good** and **Morality**.

Evil (unethical)   Any action or thing which decreases creativity for anyone, including oneself.

Evolution   A condition of intelligence as well as a force which pulls everything in the universe toward greater intelligence and complexity. Evolution is the complement of entropy. The evolutionary force pulls matter toward life, life toward mind, and mind toward ever greater intelligence. A level of evolution is measured by its degree of intelligence. The greater the intelligence of a being, the higher it is on the evolutionary scale. Evolution is a law of nature, and not a coherent plan. Evolution has a direction of ever greater intelligence, and certain properties; however, it is basically a random process because it always coexists with entropy, and uses entropy to correct the random errors. The higher a being is on the evolutionary scale, the less subject it is to entropy, if it behaves ethically. Therefore, evolution catalyzes and derandomizes itself through intellectual development in general, and ethics in particular. See **Entropy**.

Evolutionary Ethic   "We should do our best to maximize creativity, without ever decreasing anyone's creativity, including our own."

Evolutionary Pressure   The propensity of natural selection to favor some mutations over others because of the current environmental opportunities that exist for those mutations. This has nothing to do with an outside directed force, conscious or otherwise. Evolutionary opportunities are the biological response to environmental factors which favor certain types of mutations. The "pressure" pulls the species toward these opportunities. It does not push them forward. The pressure can be seen as a pull from the future.

Extended Family   Any family not an immediate family. See **Family** and **Immediate Family**.

Falsehood   Information that decreases our ability to predict and/or control any part of the total environment when we believe it, or have been conditioned to accept it.

Family   A group of beings tied together by mutual love. See **Extended Family** and **Immediate Family**.

Fear   A function of the belief that we cannot create. Fear originates as an emotional pre-programming of the R-complex, that predisposes us to fight or flee in the face of danger. See **Emotion**.

Feedback   The perception of the consequences of our actions. Positive feedback results in perception of success, when the relevant part of the environment was in fact predicted and controlled. Negative feedback results in the perception of error, i.e., when attempts at prediction and control have failed.

Freedom (liberty)   A state in which we can do and say as we please, so long as we do not in the process interfere with the right of another person to do and say as he or she pleases. When there is a conflict, a compromise can be reached which maximizes creativity for both persons. In general, free persons can do as they please so long as they do not impose undeserved harm on others. Freedom gives us the right to destroy our own creativity, but never the right to destroy anyone else's creativity, without their consent. Freedom is a necessary, but not a sufficient, condition for ethical evolution.

Game   A set of rules of how to behave in order to win a specified stake. The stake may be symbolic or tangible. A game has no purpose beyond itself. All persons play games either consciously or unconsciously. Every game is either a variation on the Game of Life or a variation on the Game of Pleasure. For any given person, the same game may be a variation on the Game of Life at one time and a variation on the Game of Pleasure at another time.

Game of Life   A game in which the stakes are ever expanding creativity. The Game of Life is the pivotal point between good and evil, life and death. The Game of Life is the basis of all evolution. To play the Game of Life is to increase creativity. To deliberately play the Game of Life is to increase creativity as much as we can for the rest of our life.

Game of Pleasure   A game which serves solely to increase happiness, never creativity. Persons who play the Game of Pleasure are the major source of entropy for the human race. Players of the Game of Pleasure make themselves and others increasingly unethical until they become immoral. All players of the Game of Pleasure unconsciously long for death.

Geistig   A German word used by Constantin Brunner to mean "ethically spiritual."

Geistlich   A German word used by Constantin Brunner to mean "superstitious" or "falsely spiritual."

Generalist   A person who is aware of the total environment—physical, biological, and psychosocial—in approximately equal degrees. Generalists try to learn, in approximately equal amounts, all of human knowledge. They attempt to maintain sphericity (116) by not developing great depth in one area while still ignorant of another area. It is possible for a generalist to have more depth in all areas than a specialist has in only one area. We generalize by learning what we know least. We specialize by learning more about what we know most, increasingly ignoring what we know least. See **Specialist**

Genotype   The genetic make-up of an organism which interacts with the external environment to produce the overt appearance and behavior of the organism. See **Phenotype**.

Good (ethical)   Any action or thing which increases creativity, for at least one person without decreasing creativity for any person. See **Evil**.

Great   That which significantly affects the creativity of others. This applies to art, science, or persons. Greatness implies extremely important social morality, or immorality.

Guru   A teacher whom we revere and trust to the point of surrendering our conscience to him or her, thereby letting the guru determine for us what is right or wrong. This is destructive for both the guru and the disciple. We should always follow the dictates of our own conscience alone and not abdicate our conscience to anyone, nor allow anyone to abdicate his or her conscience to us. However, we should always listen to ethical criticism of our behavior, and check it out scientifically.

Happiness   The state of mind which results from being in the process of fulfilling our desires. The intensity of happiness is directly proportional to the strength of our desires and the rate at which we fulfill them. In the absence of desire there is neither happiness nor unhappiness; the more ethical a person is, the more that person's happiness comes from maximizing creativity. Happiness and creativity are not mutually exclusive; neither are they synonymous.

Health   The physical and mental condition conducive to predicting and controlling the total environment. Whatever diminishes our ability to predict and control the total environment diminishes our health. When this occurs through physiological change, such as a broken leg, then it is our physical health that is diminished. When this occurs through a change in the information content of mind, then it is mental health that has been diminished, resulting in neurosis. When there is a combination of deleterious physiological and information changes in the nervous system, psychosis may result. The best objective indicator of health is creativity. Unethical persons are neither healthy nor creative.

Hedonism   A sense of values which gives the highest value to pleasure and happiness. Hedonism represents the pursuit of happiness to the exclusion of creativity. A hedonist seeks to maximize happiness above all else. The pursuit of happiness without creativity leads solely to death.

Heritability   A statistical notion based on the theory of analysis of variance. It is expressed by a number between zero and one. A heritability of zero indicates that the phenotypic differences between statistically differentiable groups are not due to genotypic differences, but are solely determined by the environment of the organism. A heritability of one indicates that the environmental differences between the groups in question produce no significant differences with respect to a specified trait; all differences concerning the trait are assumed to be due to genetic differences.

Homo moralensis   Moral man. The latest development in *Homo sapiens* represented by persons who deliberately play the Game of Life. The successor to Teilhard de Chardin's *Homo progressivus*. Every *Homo moralensis* is living in an Ethical State.

Homo progressivus   Progressive man. A term used by Teilhard de Chardin to connote persons who perceive and value human progress and have faith in mankind's future. The successor to *Homo sapiens*. Persons capable of entering the Ethical State, with the potential to become moral adults.

Homo sapiens   The species of humans which has been dominant for about 50,000 years. Cro-Magnon was a *Homo sapiens*; Neanderthal was not. The two species could probably interbreed, as can lions and tigers.

Ideology   An interdependent set of ideological beliefs. An ideological belief is a belief in a cause and effect relationship which is not based on scientific evidence. All superstitions are ideological beliefs. All religions are ideologies. Marxism and most of what is called "social science" are ideologies. Ideologies are not necessarily wrong, merely unscientific.

Ignorance   A lack of important true information within the nervous system of an organism.

Illusionary Information   Information which has no basis in reality. It can occur by imagining a model of cause and effect relationships which cannot be substantiated scientifically. Most illusionary information results from accepting the imagined model of someone else as true, when it is in fact false. Skepticism is the best defense against illusionary information. Systematic, creative skepticism is the basis of the scientific method. It is unethical to be certain. It is ethical to doubt.

Imagination   That component of intelligence which generates information independently of the sensors. Imagined events are used to complete the pattern of sensed events so that there are no inconsistencies. The effectors test the validity of the completed pattern by generating new events until all the sensed events are consistent. This is how creativity grows. Imagination has never been localized as have other components of intelligence. It seems to be associated with the neocortex in general, and the frontal lobes in particular. The more ethical a person is, the more imaginative he or she seems to be. It may be that Imagination is produced in part by the moral field of the Cosmic Moral Society, and that receptivity to this field depends on ethics. The moral field and the quantum field may be synonymous.

Immediate (Nuclear) Family A family limited to our parents, children, spouse, and siblings. See **Family** and **Extended Family**.

Immoral A person is immoral if and only if he deliberately declines the challenge of the Game of Life and consciously chooses to play the Game of Pleasure. Immoral persons consciously reject the Evolutionary Ethic, and consciously choose to play the Game of Pleasure as often as possible. Persons become immoral by becoming increasingly unethical until all their actions are strategies in the Game of Pleasure. Immoral persons choose never to play the Game of Life again; they have irreversible entropy. Persons are made immoral by an unethical society. Only highly intelligent persons can become immoral. Most unethical persons are children, not immoral adults.

Immoral Community That group of persons who seek power without creativity. When these persons are decent, they seek to make others happy. When they are indecent, they seek only to make themselves happy. The immoral community is represented by the "establishment" in every country. The immoral community serves solely to increase the total entropy of the human race.

Important Significantly affecting creativity, either positively or negatively. "Unimportant" is synonymous with "trivial."

Industry Any effort which serves to produce goods or services other than artistic entertainment and ethical education.

Information The symbolic representation of events and their relationships. Information is an essential component in the structure of intelligence. An entity devoid of all information would have no intelligence. All the information in our bodies, except instinct, is produced by the sensors or by the imagination. Instinct is produced by the biological information we inherit through our genes.

Innovation   The production of any new information or behavior. If it is a creative innovation, it is an invention; if not, it is a merely trivial or even deleterious innovation. Humanity has the capacity to produce more creative than non-creative innovations. All other existing species seem to produce creative and non-creative innovations equally.

Intelligence   The ability to predict and control the total environment—physical, biological, and psychosocial. Intelligence is a structure with discrete components, namely, will, memory, logic, imagination, sensors, effectors, connectors, and information. Each of the components is essential to intelligence. All the components, except for information, seem to have a largely hereditary basis. The components themselves are infinitely complex, and are tied to the implicate order of the quantum field; they are infinite parts of the infinite process which is God.

Invention   The creation of a new machine, new information, or new behavior which decreases the entropy of the biosphere. A new machine or behavior which increases entropy is called a deleterious innovation, not an invention. An innovation must increase the net creativity of the universe to be a true invention. Not all innovation is creative. For example, Hitler was highly innovative, but not very creative.

Investigator   Any person who systematically seeks new knowledge on any subject(s).

Joy   A condition of extreme happiness. Joy is happiness without anxiety; it is a happiness which we have no fear of ever losing. It seems that solely the deliberate expansion of creativity for ourselves and others produces true joy.

Knowledge   A critical mass of true information which enables us to predict and control something. Our knowledge is a function of our innate intelligence and our environment. The geometry of our knowledge (i.e., a spherical or an ellipsoidal surface) is dependent on ethics; the depth (volume of the ellipsoid) depends on our intelligence. True information becomes knowledge solely when it is a component of intelligence. Knowledge comes from creativity.

Leftist   A person who believes that behavior is determined primarily by environment and not heredity. This belief exists on a continuum.

The extreme leftist believes that heredity plays no role in shaping behavior, and that environment is all important. The extreme rightist believes the opposite. See **Rightist**.

Liberal   A person tolerant of innovation. This characteristic exists on a continuum with the extreme conservative—intolerant of all innovations—at one extreme and the extreme liberal—tolerant of all innovations—at the other. In modern American society, socialists are mistakenly called "liberals", but they are often conservative socialists. See **Conservative**.

Liberty   See **Freedom**.

Life   That effect of matter which produces an intelligence of non-self and causes intelligence to expand and grow, until it produces intelligence about intelligence. At this juncture, mind begins to develop rapidly, until it ceases to be an effect of life and becomes an effect of itself. Living creatures all have the capacity to make choices. The more intelligent they are, the more options they have. The more ethical the mind, the more it becomes an effect of itself, ever less dependent on space, time, matter, or life. The mind of God does not depend on life. Matter cannot make choices. Its behavior is entirely predetermined, although not precisely predictable, because of the uncertainty principle with respect to the quantum field. See **Mind**.

Logic   That component of intelligence which determines when different quanta of information and/or knowledge are inconsistent. Logic is a filter which tells the Will which events are inconsistent, in order that new events may be generated until all events are consistent. All events are consistent if, and only if, a person is infinitely intelligent. Therefore, all events are never consistent. A person who sees inconsistent events as consistent is either psychotic, ideological, or both. Logic appears to be a function of parts of the neocortex, although other levels in the brain seem to have their own logic.

Love   A type of behavior, as well as an emotion. As an emotion it is a pre-programmed state of mind which predisposes us to behave in such a way as to enhance the welfare of another, even at the cost of our own welfare. When welfare is seen as synonymous with happiness, then the love is perverse and unethical. When welfare is seen as synonymous with creativity, then the love is natural and ethical. Ethical love is the only antidote to fear. No one can ever lose anything of value by loving or being loved ethically. Ethical or true love is the desire to increase, and the act of increasing, the creativity of another.

Machine   An invented device which converts one form of energy into another. Language, clothing, computers, houses, tools, and organizations are examples of machines. The machine is an essential component in human evolution. Since the advent of *Homo sapiens*, human evolution has depended almost entirely on the development of ever better machines and on our increase in ethics.

Materialistic Ethic   "That which makes for the greatest material security for the greatest number is the greatest good." From each according to his ability, to each according to his need.

Measure Zero   A concept from set theory which says, very loosely speaking, that a point set has measure zero if there exists a finite or a countably infinite set of open or closed intervals of length l or smaller that cover all the points in the set, and the total length L of the sum of these intervals. Therefore, all finite or countably infinite subsets have measure zero because we can multiply the preceding sum by any arbitrarily small positive number to get a sum of intervals that is arbitrarily small. There are also non-countably infinite sets of measure zero, such as the mathematically well-known Cantor set. Measure zero for a set means that it almost never occurs relative to its complement. Trivia is a set of measure zero, because in the long run almost all acts either increase or decrease creativity. An act which never decreases anyone's knowledge, but imparts zero knowledge forever, will decrease creativity by wasting the energy and time of those committing the act. Therefore, trivia is at best a set of measure zero in the short run and an empty set in the long run.

Memory   That component of intelligence which stores information in retrievable addressable units. The address is determined in part by the nature of the information and its relationship to other information. In our bodies, memory seems to be a process by which molecules are altered in the brain by sensed or imagined information, and the brain is thereby physiologically altered. It may be that memory is holographic, so that all the information of the brain is stored in each brain cell (280).

Metazoa Multicellular animals as opposed to protozoa, which are unicellular. Sponges, insects, fish, and humans are all metazoa.

Military Any organization which serves to impose the will of any authority by force. This force is ethical when it is used for defense, and unethical when it is used for aggression.

Mind The set of all our thoughts and perceptions. Insofar as thoughts and perceptions are predictable and controllable, the mind is conscious. Insofar as thoughts and perceptions are unpredictable and uncontrollable, the mind is unconscious. We know with certainty only the existence of our own minds. We infer from the behavior of other organisms, and our own behavior and mind, that other organisms have minds similar to our own insofar as they behave similarly to us. From this inference we can develop a mind model of behavior which can objectively be shown to enable us to predict and control behavior. The mind model is analogous to the model of gravity. We cannot perceive directly the existence of gravity, but it is a model which enables us to predict and control. Gravity is an effect of mass as mind is an effect of the brain. Gravity affects mass just as mind affects the brain. Any mind may be an interactive effect of a living body and the quantum field.

Minimax Strategy A plan for minimizing our risks by obtaining the best of the worst in a game. In the Game of Life the worst is entropy; therefore, in this case, the minimax strategy is also the uniformly optimal strategy which maximizes our creativity while minimizing our entropy. In the Game of Pleasure the worst is unhappiness, and the best of the worst is extinction. Death is, therefore, the minimax strategy in the Game of Pleasure. Following the rules of the Game of Life is a uniformly optimal strategy in both the Game of Life and the Game of Pleasure. Following exclusively minimax strategies leads to death; this is a strategy followed solely by those who are driven by fear. See **Uniformly Optimal Strategy.**

Moral Having the quality of actions which either increase objective truth or are trivial. Persons become moral if, and only if, they see the maximal expansion of creativity as the only purpose of life, and are indifferent to anyone's happiness, including their own. Persons become moral solely after their intelligence is sufficiently great that they can predict and control their own ethics. Persons become moral when their ethics have reached the point that they will die before they knowingly perform an unethical act. This does not mean that they are ethically perfect. The more intelligent moral persons are, the more creative they will be. Moral persons never knowingly behave unethically again after becoming moral. Moral persons are devoid of fear. They always behave lovingly toward all persons, including their worst enemies. No human being appears to have ever been highly moral. We approach morality asymptotically by becoming increasingly ethical and intelligent. See **Ethical** and **Morality**.

Moral Community   That group of persons who are primarily concerned with expanding creativity. The moral community includes artists, scientists, and technologists. A technologist is anyone concerned with producing goods and services which increase creativity. Physicians, farmers, teachers, laborers, and mechanics are all examples of technologists. The moral community represents the true workers of the world, who are exploited by the immoral community.

Morality   The ethical and intellectual development, apparently unique to *Homo Sapiens*, which leads to intelligence about our ethics, i.e., the ability to predict and control our own ethics, and to grow in ethics, even when our environment is not conducive to this growth. See **Ethics**.

Moral Sense   The genetically determined program, apparently unique to the human species, which makes humans value creativity above happiness. The moral sense is easily perverted into self-righteousness and intolerance by unethical persons who believe they have found ultimate, absolute truth, when in fact they have only found self-deception.

Moral Society   A system of autopoietic octets working together by unanimous consensus to maximize creativity for themselves and the universe without ever decreasing anyone's creativity. The next stage in the evolution of humanity after creating an Ethical State with critical mass. An angel is a metaphor for a moral society, i.e., a stage of evolution higher than humanity and closer to God.

Music   The purest art. It is devoid of conscious meaning and operates entirely at the unconscious level to communicate the creativity of a culture by patterns of abstract sounds which are perceived as beautiful.

Mystical Paradigm   A four-part system of related principles. First, there is at least one greater intelligence than humanity's collective intelligence somewhere in the universe. Second, the universe is neither random, chaotic, nor absurd, but has an ethical-moral structure to it, determined, at least in part, by a greater intelligence than ours. Third, it is possible for humanity to communicate with this greater intelligence of ethical-moral order. Fourth, the more ethically we behave the greater will be this communication.

Mysticism   Any systematic attempt to obtain truth through direct perception, independently of scientific evidence and processes. Mystical truth is always of subjective origin. When mystical insights are supported by scientific evidence, then mystical truth becomes objective. There is no conflict between mysticism and science, as long as mystical insights are not held to represent a higher reality than objective truth. It is in the nature of mysticism that its specialized adherents tend to substitute subjective truth for objective truth, and in the process become practitioners of psychofraud. All the major religions and traditional ethical and psychotherapeutic systems seem to have a mystical basis. Creative Transformation uses mysticism in conjunction with science. What all mystics have in common is a belief in a higher source of moral order and of greater knowledge than humanity's in the universe, and that humanity can communicate with this source through ethical behavior. This belief is the mystical paradigm.

Nature-Nurture Problem   The problem of determining whether differences between groups or individuals are due to heredity (nature) or environment (nurture). Both always seem to operate in all complex human behavior. Intelligence seems to be determined more by heredity than environment for most persons in modern, reasonably free societies. The more modern, and the more free, the society, the more both intelligence, and ethics will be determined primarily by heredity. At this time, ethics seem to be destroyed in most persons by the deleterious environments of family, school, work, and government. All children seem to be ethical when they are young.

Neuroses   Learned patterns of behavior which decrease a person's ability to predict and control his or her total environment. Uncontrollable emotionalism is not necessarily neurotic unless it has been caused by some learned experience. For example, persons who are filled with hate for some particular ethnic group are neurotic, because it is necessary to learn to hate a whole ethnic group, and this behavior decreases creative intelligence. Because neurotic behavior is learned behavior, it is susceptible to modification by all types of psychofraud, as well as by Creative Transformation and other learning experiences.

Noospace   The abstract space of mind where each dimension represents an orthogonal area of knowledge. For convenience, noospace may be seen in three dimensions—the physical, biological, and psychosocial. In reality, noospace probably has infinitely many orthogonal dimensions. Only by relating each dimension of noospace to all other dimensions can creativity be maximized. Knowledge can be specialized, up to a point, but creativity is holistic.

Noosphere   The envelope of collective human mind which surrounds the Earth. A word first used by Pierre Teilhard de Chardin to describe some aspects of the Moral Society. See **Biosphere**.

Nucleons   Protons and neutrons. All atoms have a nucleus of at least one proton and zero or more neutrons. Protons and electrons are complementary pairs in their charges, cross sections, masses and other atomic properties. A neutron represents a fusion of a single complementary pair of protons and electrons.

Optimal   The extremal (maximum or minimum) of an effect in a desired direction. Something is optimal when it is the best there is and there is nothing better. Optimality is not necessarily a unique property. In a game there may be many optimal strategies. When persons behave optimally, it means that they have done the best they could. It does not mean that someone else might not have done better.

Organization   A group of persons tied together by a set of commonly accepted objectives and rules. All organizations have the propensity for being turned into bureaucracies if they are deprived of feedback. All bureaucracies are organizations, but not all organizations are bureaucracies. A family is an organization tied together by mutual love. Organizations are turned into bureaucracies solely through fear and a lack of ethics.

Orthogonal   At right angles. When events or actions are orthogonal, then each can occur without necessarily affecting the other. However, orthogonal events are not necessarily independent.

Parasite   Any entity which produces pollution and consumes resources without in any way contributing to anyone's creativity. In general a parasite has higher entropy than its ancestors and can survive solely at the expense of an entity that has lower entropy. Humans can be parasites.

Perception   That property of mind which integrates sensed information into a meaningful whole resulting in knowledge.

Personal Morality   The deliberate desire to increase one's own personal creativity; true love of self. Personal morality must coexist with social morality or it will atrophy. Without social morality personal morality may become perverted into a desire solely for personal power. All ethical persons have both components of morality, but not necessarily in equal amounts. See **Social Morality**.

Personal Power   Control over the environment used solely as a means of producing personal security, without necessarily increasing creativity.

Personality   A subset of will which determines what will be predicted and controlled, and contains the resolve to do so.

Perverse   Having the quality of seeking to increase happiness in such a way that creativity is not increased. A pervert is any person who systematically seeks to increase his or her own happiness without increasing anyone's creativity, including his or her own.

Phenotype   The external appearance of an organism, its morphology and overt behavior. See **Genotype**.

Phylum   A group of life forms characterized by unique properties which make them distinct from all other life forms. For example, arthropods are characterized by jointed legs and a chitinous exoskeleton; chordates by the notochord; ethical beings, including humans, by intelligence about their own intelligence; and moral beings by intelligence about their own ethics.

Power   The ability to control the environment, not necessarily creatively.

Prediction   Imagining an event correctly before it is directly perceived. Prediction is essential to creativity. Without the ability to predict, an entity could not see the patterns which tie its perceptions together; it would have neither a past nor a future, but would exist solely in the present in a state of continuous destruction, as predicted by the second law of thermodynamics.

Prediction and Control   The essential property of intelligent organisms by which events are foreseen and made to comply with the organism's needs and desires. The ability to predict cannot exist independently of the ability to control and vice-versa. Humanity could predict astronomical events long before it could control them (as in the case of artificial satellites); it could not have predicted any astronomical events if it could not have controlled its observational procedures by controlling its own biological sensors (eyes, ears, etc.) and its created amplifiers of those sensors, such as clocks, calendars and telescopes. Any event which is controlled, is, by definition, predicted. Therefore, control is a higher property of intelligence than prediction, although each property is essential to the other.

Probability   The degree of confidence that a person has that a cause and effect relationship is true. Zero probability states that the person is certain that the relationship is false. A probability of one states that the person is certain that the relationship is true. Ethical persons always place a probability greater than zero but less than one on the validity of all cause-and-effect relationships in nature. We can be sure of our own thoughts and perceptions, but not of all their causes.

Programming   The encoding of information into a system. Human beings are totally programmed by their heredity, their environment, and their choices.

John David Garcia

Progress   The process of ever expanding creativity within the universe. The progress of the human race is indicated by humanity's increasing ability to predict and control the total environment. This progress is least evident in the psychosocial environment, but even here it occurs. Only immorality can stop human progress.

Psychofraud   An ideology about human behavior. Any model which purports to predict and control human behavior, and cannot be scientifically verified, is psychofraud. Examples of psychofraud are found in religions, political ideologies, the social sciences, and many forms of psychotherapy.

Psychosis   Compulsive destructive behavior. An extreme form of neurosis which involves organic factors. These predispose the psychotic to acquire information which grossly distorts reality. Unlike neuroses, psychoses cannot be cured unless basic organic factors have also been corrected. Some forms of psychotic behavior are, at least partially, corrected with vitamins and drugs.

Psychotherapy   A process for replacing false information, which decreases a person's ability to predict and control the total environment, with true information which increases the ability to predict and control the total environment. Psychotherapy is a special type of education; it does not necessarily include the use of drugs or surgery, although these techniques can also change behavior and possibly even increase creativity. The best criterion for the success of psychotherapy is an increase in the net creativity of the person. Most of the treatments called "psychotherapy" seem to consist mainly of psychofraud.

Quantum Field   An information-carrying field which permeates the universe and follows the patterns of Schroedinger's equation. The field modulates the transfer of information between our universe and the implicate order. The field is "nonlocal" and operates outside of our time and space. The receptivity of any object to the quantum field is proportional to its degree of evolution. The more generalized, intelligent, and ethical the object, the more information it will integrate through the quantum field. Evolution is a process for producing ever more intelligent quantum objects that increasingly derandomize the quantum field, in direct proportion to their ethics.

Quantum Object   An object whose mass is sufficiently small that it will be significantly affected by the quantum field. Larger objects can only be affected by the quantum field if a critical mass of the smaller objects constituting the larger objects have quantum coherence among themselves, as in lasers, superconductors, microchips, the human brain, and an autopoietic octet. The more evolved a massive quantum object with internal coherence, the more creatively it integrates from information from the quantum field.

Quantum Reality   A reality which exists outside of our time and space, and which is linked to it through our consciousness. Quantum reality has within it infinite, enfolded truth (the implicate order), which, through our consciousness and in other ways, affects the reality of our own time and space (the explicate order). See the work of David Bohm.

RNA (ribonucleic acid)   A constituent of all living cells and viruses. It has the capacity to store information. DNA can be built on templates of RNA. RNA can carry information between DNA molecules.

Racism   A belief that the future behavior of a person can be inferred from the *a priori* expected behavioral characteristics of the racial group to which the person belongs. Racism neglects to allow for widespread individual differences within races. Science indicates that there is a wide overlap in the behavior of all races; therefore, racism is a false, unethical belief.

Random   Lacking predictability with certainty. Any process of which we have incomplete information is random. Nature can only be exactly predicted when we possess all knowledge, i.e., when we are totally aware of everything. For this reason, nature will always seem random to any finite being. However, the accuracy, precision and extent of our predictions and control can increase asymptotically, albeit not smoothly, toward perfection, within quantum limits. The randomness is within ourselves, not necessarily within the external universe. The cosmic force will always seem to some degree random to any finite being, because entropy and evolution coexist in infinite extension, and we can never have complete knowledge of either process. The randomness of the quantum world is due to hidden variables, which are hidden because of our own fear and lack of ethics. Solely morality can surmount the uncertainty principle, by liberating our imagination and opening our mind to the infinite truth of the implicate order. The uncertainty principle is part of the cosmic quarantine.

Rational   Logically self-consistent; without internal contradictions. In the real world things are only relatively rational, since almost every system has some internal contradictions, although they may not be apparent. This results mainly from a lack of scientific knowledge, not necessarily poor logic. Newton's model of the universe was more rational than that of Aristotle but less rational than that of Einstein, although all these models were highly rational in relationship to the more popular models of their day. Solely moral, scientific mystics can be totally rational.

Real-Time   A term from process control technology, applied when information is obtained, processed, and acted upon almost as soon as it is available, i.e., almost simultaneously. As the delays in obtaining essential information lengthen, the process ceases to be "real-time."

Reality   That which we can predict and control or which we can know that we can neither predict nor control. Our thoughts and perceptions are always real but not the models we create about what causes our thoughts and perceptions. Solely models which enable us to predict and control are true. A belief in reality increases our creativity.

Relevant   Anything which expands creativity is relevant. That which best serves to integrate and expand the totality of knowledge is the most relevant. Relevance implies something that is both important and ethical.

Religion   Any ideology which (1) seeks to explain the basic causes and purposes of the universe and (2) stresses means for predicting and controlling our thoughts and perceptions beyond the limits of our lives. In religion, the most important truths are assumed to be known, and new truths are accepted solely insofar as they support the basic assumptions. Religions are an ethical attempt to create a coherent model of the universe and humanity's relationship to it. Religions become evil solely when they are closed systems which do not accept information contradicting the basic ideology. It is the moral sense which continuously causes us to seek the one true religion. It is the immoral sense (fear) which makes us believe we have found it.

Rightist   A person with the belief that human behavior is determined more by heredity than by environment. The characteristic exists on a continuum with the extreme rightist believing that all behavior is determined entirely by heredity, and that environment has no effect whatsoever on behavior. The extreme leftist believes that all different behavior is determined entirely by environment. See **Leftist**, **Liberal**, **Conservative**.

Robot   A machine which is self-directed and can predict and control its environment, but has no creativity or capacity for ethical choice.

Sanity   That property of mind which permits it to cope rationally with problems, and to see things as they objectively exist.

Science   A method for increasing truth which is based on the principle that all hypotheses and theories are to be held in doubt until proven tentatively true by controlled experimentation. Hypotheses and theories are held to be tentatively true solely so long as they make correct predictions. Those hypotheses and theories which make the most accurate and consistently correct predictions are the "truest." In science solely that which works is true. Truth is always tentative and incomplete. The main function of science is to help us distinguish between true and false ideas.

Scientific Generalist   See **Generalist**.

Scientific Illiterate   A person who has little or no scientific knowledge, i.e., knowledge obtained through the scientific method. In general, a person who has no systematic knowledge of mathematics, physical science, or biology is a scientific illiterate. In general, scientific illiterates are victims and practitioners of psychofraud. Specialized scientists tend to succumb to ideology in those parts of the environment about which they have little or no scientific knowledge. Since there is so little scientific knowledge of the psychosocial environment, this is the major area of ideology and psychofraud. All persons tend to create the illusion that they can predict and control their total environment. Therefore they fill their minds with psychofraud and ideology, when they are not scientific generalists. Scientifically illiterate mystics as well as scientists who do not apply scientific method to their mystical beliefs are filled with self-delusion.

Security   A state of mind in which persons believe they have, or can readily obtain, all they need, and have no fear of losing what they already have. External security, as well as external insecurity, are always illusions. The only true security comes from within, through creativity and the sole desire to expand creativity.

Selfless   Having the quality wherein personal security and happiness are seen as secondary to a higher purpose. The sole purpose which seems to have the potential for producing selflessness is the pursuit of creativity as an end in itself. We can become selfless, solely by taking our identity from our soul rather than our ego, solely by valuing our creative acts more than our happy experiences.

Sensors   That component of intelligence through which some of the events in the total environment are represented symbolically by information which is stored in the memory. In the body, sensors are visual, auditory, olfactory, kinesthetic, etc.

Sexism   An ideology analogous to racism, which ascribes behavioral characteristics to a person solely on the basis of gender. The scientific evidence implies that, although the genetic potential for various types of behavior may not be identically distributed in each sex, the full gamut of human behavior, other than the reproductive functions, probably exists within each sex. The best way to avoid both racism and sexism is to accept each person solely on the basis of individual merit and to avoid *a priori* judgments. Sexism is unethical.

Social Morality   The deliberate desire to help increase the creativity of others. Social morality must co-exist with personal morality, or it will become perverted into immoral decency, whereby a person seeks to increase solely the happiness of others. All moral persons have both components of morality, though not necessarily to the same degree. See **Personal Morality**.

Social Science   Any of the numerous attempts to develop scientific models of human behavior, e.g., economics, psychology, and sociology. In fact, most "social science" models are psychofrauds which have never been objectively shown to predict or control human be-havior, although some of these models, such as Marxism and fascism, are temporarily faddish in the academic community.

Socialism   A socio-political system in which every person is forc-ibly held responsible for the welfare of every other person. This is a *de jure*, theoretical concept of socialistic government. In all *de facto* socialist states up to the present, the main function of government has been to concentrate as much power as possible in the hands of the governing class, by claiming that it is fulfilling the theoretical goals of socialism.

The Ethical State may appear to be a voluntary socialistic system for each octet, but it does not have the goal of redistributing wealth, even at the theoretical level, as do most of the existing systems which call themselves "socialistic." Socialism through force is always un-ethical. In all current socialistic systems, "welfare" is considered syn-onymous with "happiness." In the Ethical State, "welfare" is synony-mous with "creativity."

It seems that socialism of any kind will not work practically or ethically for groups larger than an octet. Forced socialism, as occurs in democracies and Communist states, is unethical. Solely libertarian-ism is politically ethical. In democracies, socialism occurs when it is assumed by a majority of the voters that the main function of "good" government is to confiscate the fruits of the labor of the most creative minority of citizens, and then to redistribute them to the least cre-ative majority of citizens. It is almost universally believed that wealth should be redistributed on the basis of need. No person's need grants an ethical right to any part of another person's life, liberty, property, or privacy.

An ethical person may voluntarily invest equitably in another person's creativity, thereby helping that person help him or herself. But alms in any form are always unethical, since they lead to parasit-ism and the destruction of creativity for the recipient of these alms. Forced charity by government coercion, as occurs in all democratic and socialistic countries, is the most destructive form of giving alms. It eventually destroys all creativity, and even the vestiges of altruism.

Soul   That part of us which takes its identity from our creative ac-tions, and is driven solely by love and our desire to maximize creativity. The soul is our true self, which must merge and become one with our ego if we are to be creatively transformed. Unlike the ego, which dies with our body, the soul is immortal, and lives on in the creativity we engender in others. See **Ego**.

Specialist   A person who has developed depth of knowledge in one area at the cost of being ignorant in other areas. The specialist differs from the generalist not because of what he knows, but because of what he or she does not know. It is possible for a specialist to be more intelligent and have more knowledge in every area than a generalist. When a generalist and a specialist are of comparable intelligence, the generalist is always more creative. It is possible for a generalist to be more creative than a specialist in the specialist's own field, even when the latter is much more intelligent than the former. If a generalist is represented by a sphere and a specialist by an ellipsoid, then their total knowledge, which is a product of their intelligence, is represented by their surface area. Their creativity is a product of both their intelligence and their ethics and is represented by their volume. A sphere or hypersphere has maximum volume for a given surface area for any figure of fixed dimensionality.

Speciation   The process by which a new generalized phylum starting with a single species fans out into the biosphere by having suceeding generations adapt until they can fit into one, and only one, ecological niche. Each adaptation represents a new species which is forever separated from its former kin.

Spirituality   Belief in a reality beyond that knowable through the senses and their amplifiers. Spirituality is of two types: false and true. True spirituality is based on ethics and the mystical paradigm. False spirituality is based on superstition, and has little or no ethical basis.

Superstition   Other people's religious beliefs. False spirituality based on ritual and false beliefs. Beliefs are false when they in no way increase the believer's ability to predict and/or control anything in the objective world, and in fact decrease this ability.

Symbiosis   A process by which two different processes or life forms combine in such a way that their joint entropy is decreased or their collective intelligence is increased, so that the joint whole is greater than the sum of its parts.

Symbol   Something that stands for something else, and in the process encodes information. Letters in an alphabet are manufactured symbols of sounds. Sequences of RNA are non-manufactured, natural symbols that encode information for synthesizing proteins. Everything that exists encodes information within its structure. A machine is its own symbol, a specific manifestation of information for manufacturing more copies of itself.

Tachyons   Hypothesized subatomic particles which always travel at speeds in excess of the speed of light. Tachyons accelerate by losing energy until they are traveling at infinite speeds, when they have zero energy. Although the existence of tachyons seems theoretically feasible, they have not as yet been experimentally detected. Tachyons were originally postulated independently by Gerald Feinberg, Isaac Asimov, and Soviet scientists.

Technology   A scientific process for designing, building, and/or operating machines; the application of science to control of the environment.

Total Environment   All that can be perceived or conceived. The total environment may be divided for convenience into (1) the physical, which includes all of matter and energy; (2) the biological, which includes all life forms; and (3) the psychosocial, which includes all activities of the mind and the behavior of life forms. These divisions are only a convenience which should vanish with time. Ultimately, it should be shown that matter, life, and mind are all interrelated phenomena produced by a single cosmic force. In recent years, the apparent discontinuities between life and matter have been disappearing. Eventually all psychosocial phenomena should be understood in the same manner.

Trivial   Having the property of neither increasing or decreasing creativity. Trivial activity will increase entropy. In the long run, trivial activity may decrease creativity indirectly by increasing entropy to the point where creativity is no longer possible. Trivia is a set of measure zero. Almost all actions are either creative or destructive. See **Measure Zero**.

Truth   Information about a cause and effect relationship which increases one's ability to predict and control the environment when one believes it. All models of cause and effect relationships involve error. Therefore truth is a goal which is approached asymptotically as information grows. Whoever pursues truth will get ever closer to it. Only an entity who has infinite intelligence knows absolute truth. Even apparently tautological statements may involve semantic errors. See **Falsehood**.

Tunneling A quantum-mechanical process by which a quantum object can penetrate an energy barrier whose repulsive energy is greater than that carried by the quantum object. This is due to the probabilistic nature of quantum events, by which it is theoretically possible, i.e., has a probability greater than zero, for a quantum object to be on the other side of a barrier which it cannot, according to classical theory, penetrate.

Unconscious The source of unpredictable and uncontrollable thoughts and perceptions. The imagination seems to work primarily at the unconscious level. See **Conscious**.

Unethical (evil) Exhibiting behavior which decreases at least one persons's creativity. All unethical behavior is a strategy in the Game of Pleasure. A person is unethical when he or she plays the Game of Pleasure more often than he or she plays the Game of Life. Unethical behavior always increases entropy.

Unethical Society A society with most of its members unethical, and structured to decrease creativity. Every nation is an unethical society, or an incipient unethical society. Societies become unethical through bureaucracy, ideology, fear, and unethical government.

Uniformly Optimal Strategy A plan for minimizing our risks while simultaneously maximizing expected gains. Following the rules of the Game of Life is a uniformly optimal strategy in both the Game of Pleasure and the Game of Life. See **Minimax**.

Will That component of intelligence which directs the flow of information to the other components. Will is a vector quantity with a direction and a magnitude. The direction represents what type of information will be processed; the magnitude represents the means and resolve to process the information. The imagination and the effectors generate events which provide a critical mass of true information, at which point knowledge exists. Under the direction of the ethical will, all the components of intelligence operate to expand creativity continuously. Under direction of our animal (pre-ethical) will, all the components of intelligence operate to increase happiness, with no concern for creativity. Pre-ethical will in our bodies appears to be an effect of the three most primitive brains and may be unrelated to the neo-cortex. Our ethical will seems to be entirely a product of the neo-cortex, particularly the frontal lobes. The ethical will operates at the conscious and unconscious levels to program the will in the evolutionary direction of ever expanding generalized intelligence.

Also by John David Garcia
The Moral Society: A Rational Alternative To Death
Psychofraud and Ethical Therapy
Creative Transformation: A Practical Guide For
Maximizing Creativity
Available through www.see.org

ABOUT THE AUTHOR

JOHN DAVID GARCIA WAS BORN IN SAN FRANCISCO, CALIFORNIA IN 1935, BY PARENTS OF MEXICAN ORIGIN. EARLY ON IN HIS LIFE, HE REJECTED BOTH THE CATHOLIC CHURCH AND PARENTAL AUTHORITY, CHOOSING TO SURVIVE ON HIS OWN TERMS. BY HIS LATE TEENS, RECOGNIZING EDUCATION AS THE KEY TO HIS FUTURE, HE BEGAN STUDIES AT THE UNIVERSITIES OF CALIFORNIA, CHICAGO AND JOHNS HOPKINS. THESE COVERED BIOLOGY, CHEMISTRY, PSYCHOLOGY, PHYSICS AND MATHEMATICS, LEADING TO SEVERAL DEGREES, INCLUDING ONE IN ADVANCED MATHEMATICAL STATISTICS FROM BERKELEY.

GARCIA MARRIED BERNICE POSMAN IN THE 1950'S, FATHERED FOUR DAUGHTERS, EVENTUALLY WORKING IN RESEARCH AND DEVELOPMENT FOR GE, MELPAR, DOUGLAS FAIRBANKS AND IBM. IN 1968 HE FOUNDED HIS OWN R&D CORPORATION, TEKNEKRON, WHICH APPLIED ADVANCED METHODS OF SCIENCE AND TECHNOLOGY TO SOCIOECONOMIC AND BIOMEDICAL PROBLEMS. FOLLOWING THE COMPANY'S RAPID SUCCESS, GARCIA TOOK LEAVE TO FOCUS ON HIS REAL INTERESTS: EDUCATION AND POLITICS.

FOR THE NEXT THIRTY YEARS, HE WROTE ABOUT HIS IDEAS, TEACHING IN THE U.S. AND MEXICO, ULTIMATELY SETTING UP A VARIETY OF BUSINESSES AND NONPROFIT ORGANIZATIONS BASED ON HIS PHILOSOPHIES. NEVER DISSUADED FROM HIS VISION OF A MORE ETHICAL, MORE CREATIVE WORLD, GARCIA STROVE THROUGHOUT HIS LIFE TO LEARN, TEACH AND CREATE. EVER A SCIENTIST, HE WAS NOT DISCOURAGED BY FAILURE. HE SIMPLY LEARNED FROM EXPERIENCE, CONSTANTLY REFINING HIS IDEAS AND EXPERIMENTING WITH NEW ENTERPRISES, NEW INVENTIONS AND NEW TECHNIQUES FOR MAXIMIZING AWARENESS AND CREATIVITY.

IN ADDITION TO DOZENS OF ARTICLES AND TECHNICAL PAPERS, GARCIA PUBLISHED THREE PREVIOUS BOOKS *THE MORAL SOCIETY*, *PSYCHOFRAUD AND ETHICAL THERAPY*, AND *CREATIVE TRANSFORMATION*. THE BUSINESSES AND SCHOOLS HE DEVELOPED INCLUDED THE SCHOOL OF EXPERIMENTAL ECOLOGY, THE SOCIETY OF EVOLUTIONARY ETHICS, THE ELECTRONIC SIGNATURE LOCK CORPORATION AND MANY OTHERS.

JOHN DAVID GARCIA PASSED AWAY ON NOVEMBER 23, 2001 SHORTLY AFTER COMPLETING THIS MANUSCRIPT. HIS WORK ON *POLITICAL ETHICS* WAS THE DRIVING PASSION OF HIS FINAL DAYS. JOHN DAVID GARCIA'S STUDENTS, FRIENDS AND FAMILY INVITE YOU TO VISIT HIS WEB SITE AT WWW.SEE.ORG.

.

www.ingramcontent.com/pod-product-compliance
Lightning Source LLC
Chambersburg PA
CBHW022102280326
41933CB00007B/230